By the same author

Hope Deferred: girls' education in English history
How Different From Us: a biography of Miss Buss and Miss Beale
Rapiers and Battleaxes: the Women's Movement and its aftermath

INDICATIVE PAST

O = OPEN

X = CLOSED OR TRANSFERRED

CARLISLE X

NEWCASTLE O
X GATESHEAD

YORK
X

(LIVERPOOL)
BELVEDERE O
BIRKENHEAD O

SHEFFIELD
O

NOTTINGHAM
O

SHREWSBURY O

NORWICH
O

IPSWICH
O

SWANSEA X

OXFORD
O

LONDON ☐

BATH
O

TUNBRIDGE
WELLS
X

X DOVER

NEWTON
ABBOT X

WEYMOUTH
X

PORTSMOUTH X

BRIGHTON
& HOVE O

GREATER LONDON AREA

OPEN	CLOSED OR TRANSFERRED
BLACKHEATH	HACKNEY & CLAPTON
BROMLEY	HIGHBURY & ISLINGTON
CROYDON	PADDINGTON & MAIDA VALE
KENSINGTON	DULWICH
NOTTING HILL & EALING	CLAPHAM
PUTNEY	
SOUTH HAMPSTEAD	
STREATHAM HILL & CLAPHAM	
SUTTON	
SYDENHAM	
WIMBLEDON	

INDICATIVE PAST

A Hundred Years of
The Girls' Public Day School Trust

by Josephine Kamm

Foreword by Dame Kitty Anderson

London . George Allen & Unwin Ltd
Ruskin House   Museum Street

Printed in Great Britain
in 10/11 point Times Roman type
by Alden & Mowbray Ltd
at the Alden Press, Oxford

Foreword

Josephine Kamm's book is much more than a history of The Girls' Public Day School Trust; it is the story of the growth of educational opportunities for girls and is set against a fascinating background of changing social attitudes and ideas. It is mainly concerned with a group of schools which were among a small band of pioneers in girls' education in the nineteenth century; schools which have had the great satisfaction of seeing over the years the steady expansion of the nation's educational facilities and of becoming, themselves, members of the great concourse of British schools which, whether maintained, direct grant or independent, are all concerned to give the young people within their walls the best possible educational opportunities for development and fulfilment. Education is primarily concerned with people and this book is certainly about people.

It is a far cry, though it was not in fact so long ago, from when it was considered that learning in a woman 'was not only unnecessary but undesirable'. At the time of their foundation the schools of the Trust had many challenges to meet and exciting work to do in creating opportunities for girls. Times change, attitudes change but the challenge remains and the need does not diminish for the maximum use of the educational facilities available in every school, whatever its size. After a hundred years' service, the schools of The Girls' Public Day School Trust go forward eagerly and confidently to continue, in the years ahead, to make their contribution to education and to the education of girls.

Kitty Anderson.

Chairman of the G.P.D.S.T.

Contents

Illustrations

ILLUSTRATIONS

between pages 192–3

Acknowledgments

Except where otherwise stated all quotations are taken from original letters and other material in the possession of the Girls' Public Day School Trust and its schools. My grateful thanks are due to the Chairman of the Trust, Dame Kitty Anderson, and the Secretary, Mr W. L. Lister, to the immediate past Chairman of The Friends of the Girls' Public Day School Trust, the late Lilian E. Charlesworth, the Chairman, Miss M. M. Burke, and the Honorary Secretary, Miss P. R. Bodington, for much advice and help; and to the following for permission to use family papers: Mrs R. M. Balston, Miss Balston, Mr William Barnes, Mrs Campbell Ellis, Lady Alethea Eliot, Miss M. Jarrett, Frances, Countess Lloyd George of Dwyfor, Mrs Laurie Magnus and Sir Robert Mayer. I should like to express my gratitude to many other people who have given me information, among them Dr M. F. Adams, Miss G. Blackburn, Mrs J. H. Galbraith, Mrs V. H. Galbraith, Miss D. F. P. Hiley, Miss M. Leale, Miss K. D. B. Littlewood, Miss K. Lockley, Miss L. E. Neal, Miss M. L. Potter, Dame Mary Smieton, Mrs E. H. Sondheimer, Dame Lucy Sutherland, Miss E. M. Thorn, Miss P. N. Wilshere, Miss P. Winter, the late Elizabeth Wiskemann, Mrs S. Woodcock, Mrs Charles Wrinch, and particularly to the present and immediate past headmistresses who gave me so much of their time, to past and present members of staff, of governing bodies, and former pupils of Trust Schools. A special word of thanks is due to Miss G. H. Gill for much detailed information and to Miss M. D. Yardley for her patient and invaluable work in research; also to my publishers, Mr Peter Evans and Mr Philip Unwin, and to my agent, Miss Ursula Winant.

J. K.

Chapter 1
The Founders

'There is a pretty theory abroad, which is always brought forward when women's education is talked about, i.e. that they are educated to be wives and mothers. I do not know a more fallacious one. They are *not* educated to be wives but to get husbands.'[1]

So said Mrs William Grey in 1871. With the help of her sister Miss Emily Shirreff and of two other stalwarts, the Dowager Lady Stanley of Alderley and a much younger woman, Miss Mary Gurney, she was the architect of the Girls' Public Day School Company (later the Girls' Public Day School Trust) which over the next twenty-five years was to open thirty-eight first-rate girls' schools, twenty-three of which are still in existence today.

The older women had grown up in an age when, for the overwhelming majority of girls, education was woefully deficient and they themselves had had to rely mainly on their natural intelligence and intense desire for self-improvement.

Of the Shirreff sisters, Emily Anne, the elder, was born on November 3, 1814, a year before the Battle of Waterloo, and Maria Georgina on March 7, 1816. They were the daughters of Rear-Admiral William Shirreff and his wife Elizabeth Anne Murray, both of whom had French blood, the Admiral claiming, through his mother Margaret Bayard of New York, collateral descent from the famous Chevalier Bayard, 'sans peur et sans reproche'.

According to his daughter Maria, the Admiral was no scholar but a man of 'great natural abilities', determination and ingenuity. As a boy he had been spoilt by his mother, 'a woman', wrote his eldest daughter Emily, 'with more heart than judgment [who] exposed her son to his father's severity by her over indulgence'. The father, General Shirreff, had decided on an Army career for his son: the boy had other ideas. At the age of eleven he ran away from Westminster School and managed 'to get on board some craft in the river and so reach a naval port and slip on board a man-of-war on the point of sailing'. By an unlucky coincidence the Captain was a friend of the General's and he wrote to know what he should do with the boy. The General replied that the best punishment would be to allow him to stay on board and recommended that he 'should have his full share of hardship and be treated with the utmost severity' that the Captain 'might deem expedient'. Nothing loth, the Captain treated the boy as a rebel, 'and actually went the length on one occasion, of mastheading him for a whole week; but as he did not kill him neither could he kill the spirit within him'. The boy returned to England 'more determined than ever to be a sailor'. His father relented but refused to give him any help. There was no time for further schooling and William, wrote Maria, made do with 'such instruction as he could pick up in the course of most arduous naval service during war time'. He was still a boy when he came under the command of Sir Home Popham, the first reformer of naval education, who taught him 'the use of his instruments and laid the foundations' of a lifelong interest in science and astronomy, and encouraged him to read the English classics and books on practical science.

It was from the Admiral that the Shirreff girls inherited their pioneering spirit. Their mother, wrote Maria, 'was in many ways the exact opposite' of their father. She had plenty of common sense but, like most people of her day, she considered that learning in a woman was 'not only unnecessary, but undesirable'. She wished her daughters to acquire 'the modicum of general, historical and other information then considered sufficient for girls: more than this she did not wish them to know'.

Emily was a brilliant, precocious child. She learned to read very early but after a severe illness had to relearn the alphabet at the age of seven. From that time onwards Emily's health was a recurring topic in Maria's writings. The four Shirreff sisters – there were two younger girls – had lessons at home from a French-Swiss governess, who taught them to appreciate 'all great and beautiful things' but whose own knowledge was so scanty that 'she probably could not have formulated a single rule of education and would undoubtedly have failed in any examination'.

When Emily was fourteen and Maria twelve they were sent with one of their sisters to a boarding-school in Paris, where Emily was at once placed in a class with girls more than two years her senior. 'She kept it easily', wrote Maria, 'during the one term she was able to remain, but the living was so coarse and all the domestic arrangements so rough that her health . . . broke down under them, and she had to be taken away'.

This episode brought their formal education to a close. In 1830 Admiral Shirreff was appointed to Gibraltar and he did not think it necessary to engage another governess for his daughters. He had, however, built up 'a good collection of standard books, and there was an excellent Garrison Library in Gibraltar'. Although 'he was unable from his own want of reading, to direct ours, he gave us free leave to satisfy our eager appetite for knowledge, always saying that he did not care how blue a woman's stockings were if only her petticoats were long enough to hide them.'

When Maria was about seventeen one of her father's friends offered to teach the girls mathematics. The offer was 'eagerly accepted' even though it meant starting work at seven in the morning, but the lessons were soon 'broken off by illness' – Emily's presumably – and 'the point reached did not go beyond the mere elements of geometry and algebra'. 'Regarded as knowledge', Maria commented, 'the result was nil, and circumstances have always prevented me carrying it any further; but regarded as *training*, as cultivation of the reasoning powers, it was invaluable.'

The studious girls redoubled their efforts at self-improvement. During a summer spent not far from Cadiz, at a spot 'famous for its mineral waters, which had been strongly recommended for Emily', they learned, 'under pressure of necessity', to speak Spanish, since 'there was not a soul in the place who understood anything else, except two old ladies who could manage a little French.' Emily, intellectually ahead of her sisters, learnt to write Spanish as well as to speak it fluently, and for some years afterwards corresponded 'with a most agreeable elderly gentleman at the head of the Observatory in Cadiz'.

Emily and Maria remained sharply aware of the deficiencies of their education for the rest of their lives. In 1850, in their first serious book, *Thoughts on Self-Culture*, they looked back on the days when they 'stood as young girls on the threshold of life', their childhood, 'with its so-called education behind them, the untried future before'. They recalled 'the painful sense of inconsistency between life as it appeared in reality and the religious theory of life', the confusion of their ideas, 'the want of some comprehensive principle by which to regulate thought and action, of some real aim for exertion; and the vain seeking for some guiding thread to lead [them] out of this perplexing labyrinth, into light and a straight path'.[2]

There was ample time in the Shirreff household for serious discussion as Mrs Shirreff discouraged frivolity; and in her description of life in Gibraltar Maria does not mention any meetings with other young people and there is no hint of flirtations. In 1834 Mrs Shirreff brought her four daughters home to England. There Maria, a slender, pleasant-looking girl, met her first cousin William Grey, a nephew of Lord Grey under whose premiership the Reform Bill of 1832 was passed. William Grey, who lived with his widowed mother and aunt, was a wine merchant but his chief interests were Greek and mathematics. He gave 'our minds', wrote Maria, 'the bent towards philosophical speculation and study' by introducing them to the works of Locke and Bacon, of the philosopher Dugald Stewart 'and others which remained with us through life and to which I trace back our early study of education, the natural sequel to study of the human mind'.

The bond between Emily and Maria was exceptionally close and, as Maria wrote, her marriage to her cousin William in 1841 was 'a crushing blow to Emily'. Owing to William Grey's affection for Emily, however, 'it did not separate us as she had feared it would'. The Greys, who had no children, were a devoted couple, but Maria was clearly the dominant partner. In the *Memoir*, which she wrote many years later as a tribute to her sister Emily, she was very reticent about her husband but, as she said elsewhere, 'true happiness is only to be found in marriage'.[3]

She was less reticent about their circle of friends, to whom they owed their 'chiefest pleasure'. Through friends they met 'in turn almost every man of note as a leader in thought and science', among them the future Master of Balliol, Benjamin Jowett, Thomas Huxley, Herbert Spencer, the physicist John Tyndall, the historian George Grote and his wife, the aged novelist Maria Edgeworth and the Reverend Frederick Denison Maurice, Professor of English Literature at King's College, London, and a leading figure in the fight for girls' education.

The two youngest Shirreff girls married and had children of their own, and two brothers died very young but Emily remained single. She was her father's favourite child and he wanted her constantly with him. He even went as far as rejecting an appointment in South America because the delicate Emily suffered so dreadfully from sea-sickness that it would have been impossible to take her with him. The relationship between father and daughter may well have prevented Emily from marrying. It was not until after his death, when she was nearly forty, that she came under the influence of another man. He was the historian Henry Thomas Buckle, a delicate young man seven years her junior, author of the monumental *History of Civilization*. Buckle and Emily were close friends – indeed, Emily is reputed to have told one of the first students at Girton College, Cambridge, that they were engaged to be married: if they were Maria did not mention it. She admired Buckle immensely but considered that his influence on Emily 'was that of a strong and fruitful stimulus to independent exertion rather than in changing the direction of her efforts or her views of life'. He certainly encouraged Emily to study. She learned enough Latin and Greek to read the classics in the original, added Italian to French and Spanish, and was persuaded by him to learn enough Dutch to read Grotius. Much later in life, Maria recorded, she taught herself to read German, 'for a language to her was a key to open up a literature. . . . But she threw study to the winds if her help was wanted in sickness or sorrow by those she loved.'

Buckle died in 1862, at a moment of family crisis. Emily, wrote Maria dramatically, had recently been 'struck down by a carbuncle of the worst kind at the back of her neck, and . . . while the surgeon was telling me of her extreme danger from the nearness of the wound to one of the great arteries of the neck, my husband fell down in a fit, the forerunner of the paralytic stroke which came ten days later'. Buckle's death was 'a blow very heavily felt by Emily in her still weak state'. For the next two years Maria acted as nurse to her husband. In 1864 he died, and Maria was 'left to build up my life without him'.

Three years later the Dowager Lady Stanley of Alderley, the third of the founders of the Girls' Public Day School Company, also became a widow. The fourth, Mary Gurney, was unmarried and still a young woman.

There can scarcely have been a greater contrast between Maria Grey and Emily Shirreff on the one hand and Henrietta Stanley on the other. The sisters, high principled, dignified and devoted to self-improvement, were typically Victorian. Henrietta Stanley, though only seven years older than Emily, belonged to an earlier age. 'She was always downright, free from prudery, and eighteenth-century rather than Victorian in her conversation,' wrote her grandson Bertrand Russell.[4] Born in 1807 Henrietta Maria Dillon, she spent most of her girlhood in Florence where her father, Lord Dillon, was British Minister. The seventh Viscount Dillon had followed James II into exile and the family was staunchly Jacobite. Henrietta, an exceptionally pretty girl with long golden curls, attended the weekly receptions held by the widow of the Young Pretender, but in later life 'she used to say that the only thing she regarded as stupid about her ancestors was their having been Jacobites'.[5] She spoke fluent Italian and French and developed a romantic interest in the Young Italy movement. She was very popular with the Italians, who admired her for refusing to dance with the Austrian officers even though, as she said, they danced much better than the Italians.

19

At nineteen Henrietta married the Whig politician Edward Stanley, later the second Lord Stanley of Alderley. Edward Stanley, who served with no particular distinction in Palmerston's cabinets, was a man of great charm (when he chose to exercise it); he was also extremely able though too lazy to use his abilities to the full. Famous for his mordant wit, he was known among his friends as Ben, after Sir Benjamin Backbite, but he became more tolerant as he grew older and his wit was less malicious. Henrietta doted on him, despite his frequent escapes from domesticity and the numerous infidelities with which she taxed him. She seldom accompanied him to London or the country houses of his friends, and his visits home were generally followed by the birth of yet another child. Henrietta Stanley had twelve children, of whom a turbulent brood of nine survived, four boys and five girls. She loved them all, some more than others, but found them a continual source of anxiety.

Henrietta's mother-in-law, the first Lady Stanley of Alderley, was a dominating, fearsomely outspoken woman, who wrote almost daily to 'Hen', as she called her daughter-in-law. 'You might be glad of the Children being longer in the country than you would like yourself sometimes', she wrote in 1841, a few months before the birth of Kate, the future Lady Amberley and Bertrand Russell's mother, 'but the truth is, & an unpleasant truth it is, that Edward has no taste for the company of Wife & Children by themselves and that you are afraid of being . . . left . . . when he is amusing himself in Town.'[6]

Hen bore these home truths meekly but continued to fuss and worry. When the children went to stay with their grandmother she was terrified that they would misbehave. 'I am not at all afraid of the little boys being troublesome particularly,' wrote her mother-in-law tartly in 1844. 'It is a very large family altogether & especially feeding time that is oppressive. . . . I wish I could explain to your clear understanding, that I am more annoyed sometimes by your own anxiety to keep the boys quiet & your unceasing attention to them, than by anything they can do – & I would like girls, & all, to be more *natural* than they are with me and that they should not be lectured too much into pretty behaviour & that if I find a trifling fault & say don't do or do do such a thing that you should neither be offended nor yet say anything to *back* me, as if it was necessary.'[7]

Occasionally Henrietta rebelled. 'I do not know why we were asked here it is so evident our presence gives no pleasure,' she wrote to her husband in 1845 while visiting his mother. 'It is impossible to make things go smooth where every action or expression must be moulded to suit the imperious pleasure of one nothing can please. The poor girls are quite subdued & it gives one an indigestion.'[8]

The children's health, her husband's and her own formed an absorbing topic of correspondence. 'Edward has set up a nervous headache in half his head at a fixed hour every day,' she informed his mother in 1843, 'I am attacking his stomach.'[9] Some years later she was complaining to her husband that her heart was so weak that she dreaded any shock but found walking for five hours a day efficacious. For headaches she took a lethal mixture of arsenic, bark, ether and camphor, supplemented by a full diet of meat three times a day and a supper of soup and wine. If she thought that these complaints would bring her 'dearest Love' home or persuade him to remonstrate with his mother she was very much mistaken.

Soon after her marriage she had started to prepare for a family by studying the educational theories of Locke and Rousseau. She took more than a passing interest in the local school, entertaining parties of schoolchildren to tea and making sure that the villagers sent their children to school and had them vaccinated during a smallpox epidemic.

Her own daughters were taught by a succession of governesses, most of them incompetent. 'It does seem wonderful that good or even tolerable governesses shd. be so scarce', wrote her mother-in-law in 1843, '& that their expectations should be so exorbitant in times when one might suppose many would wish for a governess who cannot afford to pay them high, & that very many well educated persons must be wanting bread. I am much afraid you will not get *all* you require under £100.' Hen ought to be content with 'a sensible woman ... who will improve their minds & be able to converse with them on what they read hear or see. ... I quite agree with you that the *manners* of a gentlewoman are essential especially as they generally though not always prove the *mind* of one besides.'[10]

Henrietta was more ambitious for her daughters, eliciting the inevitable rebuke: 'I am going to affront you – you half kill them with your novelty education mania.' She had been told by a friend about the drawing class 'that poor, unfortunate, delicate, ailing Blanche* attends. She said the room was so crowded & hot she wd. not on any account allow her girls to go there ...'[11]

It was only natural that Henrietta should worry about the girls'

---

* Blanche, Henrietta's second daughter, later the Countess of Airlie, died at the age of ninety-two.

education. 'I rejoice in my children & thank God I am placed so as to have all my energies called forth in such a heart filling work,' she wrote to her husband in 1848. 'Your mother said I ought to have done greater things considering the time & thought I have spent on education but it is not given to us to judge of what good is done at so early a time & I do not think each in their general capacities are improving.'[12]

Eventually she discovered a satisfactory governess who stayed until all the girls were grown up and superintended the education of Rosalind, the youngest daughter, who was born in 1845.* Rosalind started lessons at the age of five and was soon able to write in French as well as English. At nine she began Italian, at ten German, and she learned to speak the three languages fluently and to read them extensively. At fifteen, in a single year, she read the whole of the *Iliad* in translation, most of the *Aeneid* and some Herodotus. Between the ages of fourteen and eighteen she read and summarized Mill's *Representative Government* together with histories of the French Revolution, the Great Rebellion in England and other weighty subjects. She was not taught mathematics or science except for botany and astronomy, but she studied music and singing and learned a great deal of poetry by heart. It was not possible for Rosalind Stanley to go to a university, for she was a married woman with several children before Girton College was founded. She did attend some classes and lectures in London, probably at Queen's College, in which her mother had an interest.

Like all the Stanleys, Rosalind was strongly individualistic. 'It is difficult with so many children not to have trials with them', Henrietta wrote to her mother-in-law in 1858, 'and I dread praising any for fear the next day they should do something to vex me.'[13] Although her published letters give the impression of a weak, subservient woman, there is evidence that within the family circle she was a considerable power and that her children derived from her much of their intellectual vigour and originality. A niece of Edward Stanley's, Constance Adeane,† born the same year as Rosalind, had heard alarming reports about the young Stanleys before she paid her first visit to Alderley. 'I was exceedingly alarmed at entering that terrifying circle by myself,' she wrote. 'I do not recollect, however, that my terror of them lasted long. . . . Most of

* Rosalind married George Howard, afterwards the Earl of Carlisle, and became a redoubtable matriarch. A later Countess of Carlisle was a member of the Council of the Trust.

† Later Mrs Hugh Smith and the mother of Countess Buxton G.B.E., who was a pupil at Kensington High School.

them were always kind, though very outspoken. . . . They had been brought up from earliest childhood to be used to take keen interest in all sorts of subjects: all political points to them were daily bread: at every meal, everyone discussed every kind of topic with the utmost freedom. Reverence was an element completely ignored in that family. . . . Aunt Stanley used to lead the conversation but in liveliness of retort I don't think one of the family much excelled the other. . . . Uncle Stanley sat at the end of the table in saturnine silence. If he did make any observation, it was a bitterly sarcastic one. . . . He liked to hear his children's lively talk and, if he ever expressed an appreciation of them, the favoured one was highly pleased.'

Throughout her husband's life Henrietta Stanley remained very much in the background, emerging into public life only after his death in 1869. At that time she had not met Maria Grey and Emily Shirreff, or Mary Gurney, the fourth member of the 'quartette'.

Very much less is known about Mary Gurney than about the other three. Born in 1836, she was nearly thirty years younger than Henrietta Stanley but, like the others, she lived to a great age. Her family was an offshoot of the famous Gurney tribe and according to one report she was 'the daughter of the shorthand writer to the House of Commons'.[14] She lived with her father and stepmother in South London and for many years in Wimbledon. She was a striking-looking young woman but far from beautiful, with a prominent nose and large protruding eyes. She was an excellent horsewoman, and even in old age drove a dog-cart through the streets of London. She was an admirable linguist and published her own translations from French, German, Italian and Spanish literature. She was also extremely musical and loved foreign travel, often starting her travels at a continental music festival, and sharing with Henrietta Stanley a special devotion to Italy.

At home Mary Gurney gave lessons to her young step-sisters. She was a natural teacher, with a brilliant, lively imagination and in later life one of her sisters remembered weeping miserably when these lessons were brought to an end.

Mary Gurney's interest in the wider aspect of girls' education probably grew spontaneously from her teaching experience. Henrietta Stanley was drawn to it by Frederick Denison Maurice, incumbent of the church she attended in London. Maurice was also a friend of the Greys and undoubtedly helped to focus Maria's and Emily's attention on a subject which was very much in his own mind during the 1840s.

At that time there was a wide discrepancy between educational

23

facilities for boys and girls, especially between those of the middle and upper classes. For boys there were, of course, the great public schools and many excellent grammar schools; for the children of the poor, girls as well as boys, there were a certain number of national and charity schools; but for the vast majority of girls above the poorest level there was very little education at all, even in the domestic lore in which eighteenth-century women had been so well versed. There were schools of a kind in which, at considerable expense, girls were given a little superficial information and taught a number of accomplishments. There were private governesses, some of them able and intelligent, but many with little more knowledge than the pupils they professed to teach. It was an age when most girls were expected to marry. If a girl remained single and could not live in semi-idleness at home the only occupations open to her were those of paid companion or governess. As a governess her salary might well be as low as £25 a year – the £100 a year mentioned by the first Lady Stanley to her daughter-in-law was very far from average.

Sick-pay and pensions had not been invented and many teachers and governesses were half-starved if they were not destitute. In 1843 the Governesses' Benevolent Institution was founded in a house in Harley Street, London, with the object of providing annuities for the aged and financial help to those temporarily in need. The appeals which came pouring in showed how desperate was this need. Maurice, a Christian Socialist and a leading member of the committee which launched the Institution, decided that charity was not enough: what was required was education and a training to enable teachers to hold a respected position and command an adequate salary. He therefore arranged an examination for a teaching diploma, only to find that the candidates fell short of the most modest intellectual standards. He next arranged a series of lectures for women given by himself and his friends, among them Charles Kingsley and Dean Trench, a future Archbishop of Dublin.

The series, first given in 1847, became the prototype for a regular course of lectures which were delivered in the house next door to the Governesses' Benevolent Institution. Within a year the house had become known as Queen's College for Women. Although designed primarily for the education of governesses it admitted girls of twelve and over and was soon offering a training comparable to a latter-day secondary education. Six months later a second college – Bedford – was opened, evolving from a set of classes held in the house of Mrs Reid of Bedford Square.

The students were chaperoned at lectures by lady visitors –

women with a good social background and literary interests. One of the first lady visitors – brought in by Denison Maurice – was Henrietta Stanley. Among the earliest students were the two pioneer headmistresses, Frances Mary Buss, who founded the North London Collegiate School in 1850 and in 1871 the Camden, a school with a more limited form of education, and Dorothea Beale, who became Principal of Cheltenham Ladies' College in 1858. Miss Buss, who began teaching at the age of fourteen, cut right across the rigid social distinctions of the day and offered an excellent all-round education for girls from rich and poor homes alike. Under Miss Beale Cheltenham became both a school and a college, with its own teacher-training department. These two women made the first real educational break-through. The numbers their schools could accommodate were extremely limited: it was left to the quartette to find room for the others.

Chapter 2
Early Writings

Some two years before the Governesses' Benevolent Institution was established Emily Shirreff and Maria Grey published their first book. This was not an educational treatise but a novel with the intriguing title *Passion and Principle*. Originally published anonymously, it was reissued a few years later under their own names in a revised and abbreviated edition. Surprisingly, in women of such impeccable dignity, the *Passion* is no misnomer, but the sisters did find it necessary to kill off the beautiful secondary heroine who had tarnished her reputation by paying an innocent visit to a man in his rooms. The novel, like so many of its kind, rests on a series of misunderstandings, with the real heroine winning the hero's love in the end. It is instructive to compare the sisters' half-fledged ideas on education in 1841 with those they evolved during the next few years. The motherless heroine had been educated by her father, who, 'with a woman's tenderness watched over and trained that young and tender mind. He gave, with a father's wisdom, the guidance and instruction needed by his child, and fostered, with a mother's brooding love, each good and noble quality of her soul. . . . When [she] reached the age when girls generally go out, her father took her abroad.' Such a training was no preparation for a career but, left destitute on her father's death, the girl managed to support herself (it must have been easier then than it is now) by selling her own paintings and contributing articles to 'a review of high literary character'.

With the publication of *Thoughts on Self-Culture* in 1850 the sisters' intellectual pattern was fixed: the book embodied educational principles which they never changed, nor had need to change. It derived directly from their consciousness of what they themselves had missed. 'The authors,' they wrote, 'at the cost of many years of struggle and trial, of failure and consequent suffering . . . bought at last the experience they would so gladly have derived from other sources, and their aim is now to save such as may stand in the same position, from this struggle which consumes the best years of youth, and absorbs, in seeking the path of duty, the energies which should be employed in following it. . . . Their highest hope has been to do good in their own generation; to add their mite to the great treasury of human knowledge and improvement.'[1]

The chief stumbling block was woman's '*external* position . . . still one of entire subjection. To judge from the rights conceded to her in law . . . she seems scarcely to have been considered worthy to attract the attention of the legislator.' On issues of any importance 'her opinions are passed over in silence; in questions that most nearly concern herself, her claims are unheard in the national councils; whenever her interests clash with those of men, they must at once give way'. Woman, however, was 'armed with a power which man can neither cast off nor abridge', a power which 'lies deep in the passions and affections of men',[2] which had often throughout history been abused by the intrigues of designing women and was hampered in its finer manifestations by 'a defective education, and an inactive existence'. The former prejudice against educated women, the sisters insisted – over-optimistically as it was to prove – had largely disappeared, and yet it was not just in particular branches of knowledge but in 'the whole scope and purpose of education' that learning remained defective. Responsibility for this state of affairs 'only marks the heavier blame due to those who have the opportunities and do not use them. . . . It is always . . . as a moral power that the influence of woman is needed. . . . [That] power now to accomplish its purpose, must be strengthened by mental vigour – and it is in this that modern education so signally fails, and it is for this that we call it no less defective in its purpose, than superficial in its results.'[3]

The remedy both for inactivity and for the defects in learning was the evolution of a sound system of education and of an improvement in the status of women. Women must learn to become self-reliant but 'the self-dependence we advocate we desire to rest . . . on a basis no human laws or caprice can interfere with: namely, on the *spiritual* equality of all human beings endowed (though in various degrees) with the same faculties, born under one moral law, under one condition of trial here, to one hope of a higher existence hereafter'. Woman's inalienable 'rights and privileges are distinct from, and in no wise interfere with, her due observance of the duties arising from the subordinate station she occupies on earth, in relation to men'.[4]

This 'subordinate station' involved her in the 'household cares' from which she could not expect to be entirely absolved. But 'it is not uncommon to hear ladies talk of household affairs with a degree of pompous mystery that would be laughable in a secretary of state; [yet] when we come to look into the matter we find few things more simple than the management of an English household.' The sisters were, of course, thinking in terms of domestic servants and even of a housekeeper to relieve 'the mistress of all but superintendence in the widest sense'.5 While they did not wish an intelligent woman to spend too much of her time in the kitchen she should, at least, have some practical knowledge of cooking. 'Little delicacies are often required in the sick-room, which are more relished if prepared by a beloved hand', they added with true Victorian sentimentality. 'Would the skin be less white, the fingers less taper, or more unfit for the harp or the pencil, if they could make a custard pudding, or mix a cup of gruel?' Far from it: 'The really best educated woman will always prove herself, when circumstances demand it, the most fit for the humblest, or most irksome duties, and will display in them the vigour and activity of mind which she has cultivated in higher pursuits.'6

The sisters were most forward-looking in their attitude towards study. Method, self-discipline, and 'steady application' were required, with special concentration on such subjects as arithmetic and geometry which forced 'the mind to act, instead of leaving it to follow passively the narrative and reasonings of others'.7 Equally necessary was the study of English and of foreign languages, of history, elementary science and politics, which prejudice 'with regard to women . . . has put . . . under a ban'. A girl's education should not automatically cease 'after the early period when female education is supposed to be finished. . . . If . . . at the close of what is usually termed education, we have learnt *how to learn* . . . we shall have gained an advantage as great as it is rare.'8

Thoughts on Self-Culture was well received. 'To our surprise and gratification', wrote Maria, 'it sold well enough to cover expenses and to give a fair profit at the end of the year!' By the time it appeared Emily was working on her first independent venture, *The Intellectual Education of Women*, encouraged by her historian friend Buckle from whom, Maria thought, she gained much 'in breadth of knowledge and in width of view'.

Intellectual Education, published in 1858, covers the same ground as the earlier book. Emily excused herself for the repetition by explaining that the first book was written for young girls: the new one for mothers willing to educate their daughters. The excuse is naive: the full title of the first book, though seldom used, is *Thoughts on Self-Culture addressed to Women*.

In *Intellectual Education*, however, she laid down in rather more detail the course she would like to introduce. There should be no compulsory lessons before the age of seven, but by the time she was twelve a girl should be able 'to read and spell English perfectly, write a neat hand and be able to write a clear and simple letter'. She should have some knowledge of Bible history and the spread of Christianity and 'be well acquainted' with the Gospels. 'She might also know something of the leading events of ancient and modern history . . . aided by reading the lives of great men.' She should be 'familiar with the four first rules of arithmetic', have a nodding acquaintance with geography and music, have a memory 'well stored with such poetry as she is able to take pleasure in' and be proficient in sewing. Mothers of young children were advised to engage 'a Swiss *bonne* . . . to be in constant attendance'[9] and, later, a German governess who could teach French as well as German.

Above the age of twelve the curriculum would comprise elementary mathematics and the principles of mechanics, physical science, physiology, economics (or political economy as it was then called), English language and literature, foreign languages, history and, if possible, Greek and Latin. Music and art should not be neglected but they should be taught seriously and not simply used as vehicles for display.

With the exception of the North London Collegiate School, the Cheltenham Ladies' College and one or two other proprietary schools there were no schools in which such a wide curriculum was even envisaged; and in 1858 there seemed no likelihood that it could ever be put into practice on anything but a severely limited scale. Even at that date, however, Emily Shirreff and her sister were thinking ahead.

Maria Grey, soon to be absorbed in nursing her dying husband, was not actively working on an educational book. Instead, after William Grey's death, she produced another novel, *Love's Sacrifice* in which, as in *Passion and Principle*, the secondary heroine dies of a tarnished reputation. *Love's Sacrifice* opens in a Paris boarding-school obviously modelled on the spartan school which the Shirreff girls had themselves attended so many years before. It has an additional strain of autobiography, probably unrecognized by the author, for the heroine sacrifices herself to marry a tiresome invalid who becomes mentally deranged: during the last years of his life William Grey's illness affected his mind. The novel ends happily with the death of the invalid husband and the remarriage of the heroine. For Maria Grey there was no remarriage. It is improbable that she would have ever considered it. Now nearing fifty, she had long since lost the delicacy of her early good looks and was turning

29

into the dumpy, strong-featured woman of her later life. But if writing *Love's Sacrifice* was an emotional release, she was soon to follow it with work of an entirely different kind.

For several years Emily Davies, the demure-looking but iron-willed champion of women's rights had been doing her best to prove the revolutionary theory that girls were just as capable of learning as boys. In 1863, after a great deal of preliminary skirmishing, she was at last able to get permission for a number of girls to take, privately and unofficially, the Cambridge University Local Examinations, for juniors under sixteen and seniors under eighteen. Frances Mary Buss provided twenty-five candidates out of the total of ninety-one and the results were good enough for Emily Davies to organize a memorial to the University authorities begging them to open the examinations to girls on a regular footing. By good generalship she collected over a thousand signatures. Among them were those of Frances Mary Buss, the social reformer Octavia Hill, who was running a girls' school at the time, Anne Jemima Clough, the future Principal of Newnham, also at the time a headmistress, and Henrietta Stanley, who was making her first public appearance as an educationalist. After due deliberation the Cambridge authorities decided to allow girls to compete on equal terms with boys on condition that neither their names nor their places in order of merit should be published. The concession was only temporary at first, but after further argument it was put on a permanent basis and led to the opening of other public examinations to girls.

Initially there were very few schools capable of supplying suitable candidates. The scarcity was dramatically underlined by the results of the Schools' Inquiry Commission, 1864–7, which was aptly named by Maria Grey the Doomsday Book of women's education. An earlier Royal Commission, the Clarendon, had dealt with the boys' public schools; the Newcastle Commission had examined conditions in elementary schools. The scope of the new Commission – named the Taunton Commission after its Chairman, Lord Taunton – lay roughly between these two extremes. Girls' schools were not included in its terms of reference but because they had not been definitely excluded Emily Davies was able to edge them in.

The reports issued by the Commission were a damning indictment of inadequacy. 'The general deficiency in girls' education', the Commissioners declared, 'is stated with the utmost confidence, and with entire agreement, with whatever difference of words, by many witnesses of authority. Want of thoroughness and foundation; want of system; slovenliness and showy superficiality; inattention to rudiments; undue time given to accomplishments, and those not taught intelligently or in any scientific manner; want of organization – these may sufficiently indicate the character of the complaints we have received, in their most general aspect . . .'10

Maria Grey never forgot these strictures, nor the recommendation of Professor T. H. Green, the philosopher and Assistant Commissioner for Birmingham, that a girls' school was needed on the outskirts of every considerable town which would give girls an education similar to that provided in the best boys' grammar schools.

This recommendation also pleased Emily Davies and her friends. So, too, did the blessing given by the Assistant Commissioners to the admission of girls to public examinations, the suggestion that institutions were needed for the higher education of women, and the strong recommendation that endowments should be provided for girls' schools, a recommendation which was embodied in the Endowed Schools' Act of 1869.

After 1869, the year she became a widow, Henrietta Stanley emerged completely from her husband's shadow to become a power in her own right. Her name had already been of use to Emily Davies. Now she was to be involved – as was Emily Shirreff – in Emily Davies's great creation, Hitchin (later Girton) College.

Emily Davies would have no dealings with the special advanced examinations for women over eighteen which were opened the same year by the Universities of London and Cambridge. In her college women would be expected to work for the Cambridge Tripos examinations, taking only the same time as the men, three years and one term.*

Henrietta Stanley and Emily Davies first met through their common interest in the women's suffrage movement. 'Do you think it worth while to cultivate high society?' wrote Emily Davies to her friend Adelaide Manning† in 1866. 'Lady Amberley has asked me to one of her parties, and Lady Stanley was very kind the other day and asked me to go any Wednesday. They have tea at five, and people go in and out . . .' Adelaide Manning advised her to accept and, with an eye to the main chance, she went. She was disappointed that there was no talk of women's education, nothing, in fact, but gossip about people she did not know; she was also slightly resentful of the elegant setting. 'I felt directly,' she told Miss Manning, 'that if I went to Lady Stanley's again, I must get a new bonnet. And is

* Anne Clough at Newnham allowed her students to use the advanced examination and did not insist on the time limit for the Tripos.

† The first Secretary of the Froebel Society which began work in England in 1874.

it well to spend one's money in bonnets and flys instead of on instructive books? But on the whole, I think the advantages preponderate.'[11]

The following year Emily Davies asked Henrietta Stanley to join a working party to help launch her college. Edward Stanley was still alive at the time and Henrietta refused on the grounds that while in full sympathy with the scheme 'it is not liked to see my name before the public'. Emily Davies was disgruntled: she had felt that the presence of Lady Stanley, who had six grown-up daughters and many grandchildren, would have been a guarantee of respectability. In 1872, however, she repeated the invitation and this time Henrietta Stanley accepted.

Hitchin had already been in existence for almost three years. It was near enough to Cambridge for lecturers from the University to attend, but work for the Tripos examinations was putting a severe strain on the students, who were not nearly as well grounded as the men and so had an immense amount of leeway to make up. Though constantly in evidence, urging on the students to greater endeavours, Emily Davies refused to take the post of Mistress of the College (she did so once in an emergency) because she did not want to jeopardize her freedom to treat with the University authorities.

Mrs Manning, the first Mistress, step-mother of Adelaide, soon resigned through ill health and Emily Shirreff was invited to succeed her. Emily hesitated, then accepted although, as she said, 'a proposition to go as missionary to Fiji would at that time have caused less amazement' among her friends.[12]

'Do you know anything of a Miss Emily Shirreff who wrote a book a long time ago on the Intellectual Education of Women?' Emily Davies asked a friend and supporter, Anna Richardson. 'She is to succeed Mrs Manning, as a volunteer. In some respects, I like her better than any one else that has been thought of. She has a stoical way of talking which attracts me. Her view of coming here is simply that if she is wanted, and can do it, she ought. She takes a modest view of her duties, and undertakes them simply, without any grand air of self-sacrifice. It is a spirited thing to do, from mere interest in the idea at her age. She is I believe fifty-five, ladylike and gentle in manner, and I fancy a good deal of a student.' By this time Emily Davies had bowed to the unpalatable necessity of cultivating people outside her own circle. 'Evidently there is still a great deal to do in making the College known,' she wrote in a second letter to her friend. 'I am hoping that Miss Shirreff will bring in friends of a new set. She . . . moves in such high circles that scarcely anybody I know has ever seen her . . .'

Emily Shirreff, who took up her duties as Mistress in February 1870, soon lapsed into one of her numerous bouts of illness, but recovered and returned to work. She was remembered by one of the students as 'elderly, beautiful, and beautifully dressed, of the fine-lady type, a contrast to the plain-speaking and downright manners of Miss Davies and Lady Stanley of Alderley', a frequent visitor. 'She was full of reminiscences and talked in an interesting way about the distinguished people she had known – Buckle, for instance, to whom she had been engaged.'

Emily Davies noted with approval that the new Mistress seemed charmed with the students. 'Miss Shirreff is as much struck as Mrs Manning was by the elevation of their talk,' she wrote complacently to Adelaide Manning.[13]

Relations between Emily Shirreff and the students remained friendly despite the frequent occurrence of unexpected problems. The students were only just beginning to discover the meaning of hard and sustained work: this was their first taste of institutional life and they grumbled at the discipline and the food, which was decidedly institutional. The college gates, like college gates elsewhere, were locked at a certain hour each evening but the students resented this restriction on their freedom. Emily Shirreff rescinded some of the minor rules, such as having to ask permission to be absent from Sunday church, and the need for a chaperon at lectures.

It was inevitable in a pioneer venture that some mistakes should be made. The duties of Mistress had not been properly formulated and, while Emily Shirreff was nominally in charge, the real power was vested in Emily Davies. 'In spirit she was continually with us', wrote an early student, 'and her will was felt to be the driving force.' It was indeed, and Emily Shirreff was little more than a glorified house-mistress. Mrs Manning had been content with this arrangement and had not wanted to interfere in any way with the organization of the studies. Emily Shirreff, with educational theories of her own, was far from satisfied. 'No doubt she would prefer to have the whole internal management, including the direction of studies, in her hands', wrote Emily Davies to Mrs Manning, 'but . . . nothing was said to justify her expecting it.'[14]

Another point at issue between the two women concerned the Governing Body of the College, the Executive Committee. 'Neither the Mistress nor the lecturers were permitted to sit on this Committee', wrote the historian of Girton, 'except the first Mistress, Mrs Manning, who had been there as of right.'[15] Emily Shirreff (and also her successors) felt that she, too, should have a seat on the Executive, and when this was denied her she offered to resign.

'Miss Shirreff is certainly an amiable, affectionate person, and warmly interested in the College', Emily Davies admitted, 'and I feel inclined to persuade her to stay on, if she is willing, considering how difficult it is to find any one exactly made for the post. . . . She evidently thinks that the power of active helping depends much more than it does on being on the Committee . . .'[16]

Emily Davies was accustomed to persuade or bully people into doing what she wanted but she had reckoned without the intellectual honesty and strength of the quiet and gentle Emily Shirreff, who had no intention of allowing herself to remain a cipher. She resigned, wrote Maria Grey, 'on finding a persistent opposition to her influence and views of the government of the College, which made her feel that the sacrifice of her own time and freedom of action was useless for the objects she cared for'. She never lost her interest in the progress of the College and was especially concerned about the lack of a good library.

This lack was made good by Henrietta Stanley after the College had moved to Girton on the outskirts of Cambridge in 1874. She not only gave £1,000 for the library but also provided a laboratory and a gate lodge.* Once during an emergency she acted as Mistress. 'Lady Stanley was great fun,' wrote one of the students. 'We all liked her notwithstanding her sharp tongue. She was very lively and amusing, entered into the situation, and seemed to enjoy it with no formality of any kind.'[17]

She would have nothing to do with the much-canvassed idea of building a chapel because she herself insisted on freedom of religious belief and also because she felt that any available funds should be devoted to education. 'So long as I live', her grandson Bertrand Russell heard her say, 'there shall be no chapel at Girton.'[18] The chapel was built, he added, immediately after she died.

As a boy, this brilliant grandson was terrified of her 'for she had a caustic tongue, and spared neither age nor sex'.[19] On one occasion when, in response to persistent questioning, he told her that he had read none of the popular books on science which she herself admired she turned with a sigh to the visitors present, saying, 'I have no intelligent grandchildren'. She was, he considered, a woman 'of vigorous but not subtle intelligence, with a great contempt for "nonsense" ', which included 'every form of feminine silliness . . . and every kind of enthusiasm, except for science, enlightenment,

* Mary Gurney, who in 1894 was appointed a member of the Executive Committee (later the Council) of Girton College, was also a generous benefactor. Her gifts included £1,000 for the chemical laboratory and a substantial legacy in her will.

34

women's education, and Italy. . . . Her dislike of humbug went so far that she never concealed her good opinion of herself. "I have left my brain to the Royal College of Surgeons", she used to say, "because it will be so interesting for them to have a clever woman's brain to cut up".'

At the time her grandson remembered her, Henrietta Stanley spent most of her afternoons receiving visitors, 'mostly either relations or eminent persons. I have known her when an eminent person had just gone, turn wearily to the others and say: "Fools are so fatiguin".' He was aware, however, that in her earlier years 'she had been full of kindness . . . a wisely beneficent mother, attending to her children's needs without fuss or sentimentality or interference'.[20]

It was some time during the 1860s that Henrietta Stanley, an inveterate attender of lectures at the Royal Institution, asked the woman sitting in the next seat if she might know her name. 'Why', she exclaimed on hearing it, 'you must be one of the authors of *Self-Culture*, which I give my daughters as they grow up.'[21] The woman was Maria Grey.

Chapter 3
The National Union

In 1871 when their joint work began to take shape Henrietta Stanley, at sixty-four, had long since grown stout and matronly but her face had not lost all signs of her early beauty. Maria Grey was fifty-five and the only existing portait shows her strong-featured face hardened into severity by ugly, steel-rimmed spectacles. The writer Augustus Hare, meeting her a few years later, described her as 'a little lady ... with glistening silver hair ... very pleasant – a bright, active, simple mind, which finds its vent in excitement for the superior education of women'.[1] Emily Shirreff, two years older than her sister, wore the same ugly spectacles: even so her face had a gentle, serene expression, with a glimmer of humour which Maria's lacked. Mary Gurney, the baby of the quartette, was only thirty-five, making up in intelligence what she lacked in beauty. 'Miss Mary Gurney, of few words, but these straight to the point',[2] was an apt description of her.

Maria Grey had made her first appearance as a speaker the previous year. In 1870 women had become eligible to serve on the school boards created under the new Education Act which laid the foundations of a national system of public education. It was very unusual at the time for women to speak in public and, wrote Maria, 'Emily and I were startled by a request that one or other of us should become a candidate for the Borough of Chelsea at the approaching election for the first School Board of London. The position was such an entirely novel and unheard-of one for a woman to assume that the proposal revolutionized all one's ideas. Emily refused at once. I took a few days to consider, and then refused also.' The following Sunday she listened to a sermon 'which made me feel ashamed of my cowardice and see that it was my duty as a woman, free from absorbing home duties, with independent means and some brains, to do unpaid work for the people's education and help to give it the right direction. The following six weeks were spent in all the turmoil of a hotly-contested election, which I lost at last by a few votes – I think mainly because my supporters were too confident of my success.'* But despite her failure she felt that she had gained much, in particular 'a knowledge of the *bona fide* working men . . . who had grasped the idea that their social superiors seem so slow to understand, that they had girls as well as boys to send to school, and, therefore, that women were wanted on the School Board to look after the girls; and who, having grasped it, gave me (I might almost call it) chivalrous support and help throughout my canvass.' She also gained friends 'who proved invaluable helpers and colleagues to Emily and me in all our later work'. Among them were J. B. Stansfeld M.P., who was to be largely responsible for the admission of women students to the wards of the Royal Free Hospital, Sir Henry Cole, Director of the South Kensington Museum, and his son-in-law G. C. T. (later Sir George) Bartley M.P., who, with Stansfeld, was to be extremely active in the work.

'I should not have dwelt on the story of the School Board election', Mrs Grey continued, 'but that it became a turning point in Emily's life and mine, by leading to our work for the higher – I always preferred calling it the better – education of women which was to be the work for the remainder of our active lives.' Before its dissolution her election committee had asked her if she would be prepared to form another committee 'for the purpose of promoting the education of girls of all classes. I was very willing to accept the task, only asking for time to consider what form it should take.' She was also asked to deliver a lecture on education at the Chelsea Vestry Hall, which she gave early in 1871. Emily, suffering from some unspecified illness, 'was too unwell to attend'.

Maria Grey had several other tasks in hand. She had, for example, just published a pamphlet *Is the Exercise of the Suffrage Unfeminine?* Like so many of the educationists, Maria and Emily were convinced suffragists, and Maria demanded for girls an education which would prepare them to accept their civic responsibilities. Let men, she argued, be compelled to educate women 'not as graceful playthings or useful drudges, but as the possessors of a power which society must, at its peril, teach them to use for its benefit'.[3]

At the same time she was taking up the question of endowments. Despite the Endowed Schools Act of 1869, girls' schools were still not getting their fair share, and Maria Grey was especially interested in the needs of Miss Buss's schools, the North London Collegiate and the Camden. She had learned 'with painful astonishment, not unmingled with bitter feelings', she wrote to *The Times* on March

---

* Among the successful women candidates were Emily Davies, Elizabeth Garrett and the suffragist, Lydia Becker.

28, 1871, that money collected specifically for a girls' school had been diverted to an already well-endowed boys' school. 'Will you, sir', she added, 'not raise in the name of the nation, a protest which cannot easily be set aside? Will you not at least make it clear to the public that this is not a woman's question but a man's question, a national question; and that to leave uneducated one-half of the people – and that the half which moulds the associations, habits, and life of the other half – is a course so suicidal that of the nation which deliberately follows it we are tempted to exclaim in bitterness of soul, "Quem deus vult perdere prius dementat"?"*

Maria Grey was busily formulating her own answer. What she envisaged was the creation of a national movement which would combine the efforts of organizations and individuals working, often in isolation, to promote women's education. She went for help to the Society of Arts and was invited to embody her plan in a paper which she read before the Society on June 30, 1871.

The paper emphasized 'the equal right of women to share in the existing educational endowments of the country, and to be considered, not less than boys, in the creation of any new endowments'. The Education Act of 1870 gave equal – if inadequate – opportunities in the elementary schools to the sons and daughters of the poor, and so she confined herself to the needs of those above that level, the girls, as she said, who were not being educated to be wives and mothers but simply to get husbands.

The paper concluded with a reasoned plea for the creation of an 'Educational League' or Union to carry into effect 'what might be characterized as the Educational Charter of Women – first, the equal right of women to the education considered best for human beings'; secondly, their equal right with boys to share in the creation of any new endowments; and thirdly, 'the registration of teachers, with such other measures as may raise teaching to a profession no less honourable and honoured for women than it is for men'.

Maria Grey was an admirable speaker, clear, incisive and very persuasive. The audience was appreciative and sympathetic. Had Emily been present she would have been proud of her sister: needless to say, she was abroad convalescing after yet another of her mysterious illnesses. In fact, Emily had not been in favour of her

* Miss Buss obtained her endowments eventually from the Brewers' and Clothworkers' Companies. 'It seems like something in a fairy tale', Maria Grey wrote to her on July 20, 1879. 'It does one's heart good, and makes one think better of life, to see such a brave, life-long fight as yours crowned at last— crowned, too, while your head can still wear the crown . . . I have often feared that you would break down under the strain [and] final success come too late. Thank God it is not so.'

sister undertaking any administrative work fearing, so Maria wrote, 'that my strength would be unequal to such new and arduous labours at my time of life'. But once Maria had become the driving force of the scheme Emily was to give her entire 'devoted help in committee work which she detested, with her pen which she loved and which was her real and powerful weapon, and even at times on the platform, by the public speaking she dreaded, forgetful of self, following and serving me as her leader, as if she had been one of the common rank and file'.

The principal aims of the scheme were embodied in a circular issued by the Council of the Society of Arts inviting influential people to join a general committee. They were: '(a) to bring into communication and co-operation all individuals and associations engaged in promoting the education of women and girls, so as to strengthen and combine their efforts; to collect and register for the use of members information on all points connected with such education; (b) to promote the establishment of good and cheap day schools for all classes above those attending the public elementary schools; (c) to raise the social status of female teachers by encouraging women to make teaching a profession, and to qualify themselves for it by a sound and liberal education; and (d) to create a sounder public opinion with regard to education itself and the national importance of the education of women, by means of meetings, of lectures, and of the press, and thus to remove the great hindrance to its improvement, the indifference with which it is regarded by parents and by the public.'

To create this union and make of it 'a practical working organization', wrote Maria, 'formed the work of my life and Emily's during the following years'.

The response to the circular was sufficiently enthusiastic to encourage Mrs Grey to proceed. She introduced her scheme to a public audience in Liverpool a few weeks later at a meeting of the North of England Council for Promoting the Higher Education of Women. The Council had been founded by Anne Clough with the help of George Butler, Principal of Liverpool College, and his wife Josephine. Maria Grey had been invited to speak by Josephine Butler, well known – so Maria put it – 'as the apostle of a cause bearing even more vitally on the interests of women than education'.

The 'cause' was, of course, Josephine Butler's courageous crusade against the state regulation of prostitution and her championship of these unfortunate women and of others wrongly classed as prostitutes. The crusade produced a deep and agonizing rift in the ranks of the women's movement: the educationists were divided on the issue, but it was generally agreed in the interests of their own campaign that they should not intervene.

Aware that Maria Grey's views were opposed to her own, Josephine Butler was surprised when her invitation was accepted. 'I will confess', she wrote shortly before the meeting, 'that I have thought it would probably militate against your own endeavours in the direction of the educational work you have at heart for you to have the smallest connection with me, or with any organization with wh. my name is connected, for I am abhorred by every one above the middle class who happens to know anything about it.* . . . Some of my best friends have frankly told me that they must get rid of my name in their schemes or committees for good objects, although *they* heartily follow me in my special work, wh. you, I grieve to know, do not . . .'

Whatever her feelings on the subject, Maria Grey was not the sort of woman to refuse to meet the social pariah. From this meeting grew a lifelong friendship which, she said, 'I have held to be one of the greatest honours of my life'. She may well have been a little annoyed, though, at her friend's frankly expressed disapproval of her policy of enlisting the help of the great. 'My own private feeling about great names', wrote Josephine Butler, 'is that they do harm to a good cause – not only that they do it no good . . .'

It was at the meeting of the North of England Council that Maria Grey first met Dorothea Beale of Cheltenham, whose competent summary of the reports of the Schools' Inquiry Commission 'was the armoury from which I drew my strongest weapons of attack against the existing state of things'. She also met, among others who were to help her, Henry Sidgwick, Fellow of Trinity College, Cambridge and Professor James Stuart, also a Fellow of Trinity, whose special course of lectures for women had provided the impetus for the formation of the North of England Council.

In October 1871 the Social Science Association held its congress at Leeds, attended by members of Maria Grey's general committee. Among them was Mary Gurney, who had written a paper on *Middle-Class Schools for Girls*: it was based on Frances Mary Buss's work at the North London Collegiate School, which had become a public school in 1870, and on her second school the Camden (or Lower) School, which she founded the same year. At that time Mary Gurney was nervous about speaking in public and

---

* She was not exaggerating. To take only one example: J. B. Stansfeld risked his whole political future when a few years later he joined the ranks of her supporters.

her paper was read for her. In it she referred especially to the sound system of education at the Camden, at fees ranging from £4 4s to £6 6s a year, and with scholarships to enable the most promising girls to complete their education at the North London, where the normal fees ranged from £9 9s to £15 15s a year. 'It may seem surprising that a good education can be offered at so low a price', she said, 'because in England no public or national efforts have hitherto been made to educate the mass of girls between the "young ladies" whose parents pay £80 to £100, or even £200 or £300 per annum for instruction principally in so-called accomplishments, and girls trained in elementary schools on payment of 1d or 2d weekly.' The type of education she had in mind 'must be the same as in boys' schools', with good teachers, 'able to supply a thorough literary education, such as to call out the powers, and produce thoughtful women, ready for every emergency in life'.

Maria Grey had also prepared a paper, *On the Special Requirements for Improving the Education of Girls* and, as before, she read it herself. It was confined to girls belonging to the 'classes above those attending the Public Elementary Schools . . . because there is abundant evidence to prove that their education is actually worse, and is far less adequately provided for them than that of the lower class'. Schools were urgently needed, she said, 'at such a reduction of expense as shall induce parents, too ignorant themselves to know what is good, to prefer the sound teaching which is also cheap, to bad teaching which is expensive'. She was in favour of extending to intellectual girls the benefits of higher education, since 'no organization of education . . . can be complete without the College, to supply the higher knowledge which the school-training has prepared the mind to desire and receive'. But, 'let it not be supposed that I think every young woman should go to College, or that . . . I undervalue all other forms and the efforts made in other directions to attain the same end . . .' She was thankful, she concluded, that men and women were coming forward to help in the cause: but they must not rest until they had won 'for women the right and the means to the highest culture of which their nature is capable'.*

The papers of Maria Grey and Mary Gurney, made an excellent impression but, according to *The Echo* of October 10th, much time 'was wasted . . . by two factious men. They spoiled the discussion . . .

* Maria Grey's paper *On the Special Requirements for Improving the Education of Girls* was No. 1 in a series published by the Women's Education Union. No. 2 was Mary Gurney's *Are We To Have Education for our Middle-Class Girls?* and No. 3 was *The Work of the National Union* by Emily Shirreff.

by two childish speeches, the one in disparagement, the other in eulogy of women'. One of the two, the Reverend Hugh Smyth, felt that women 'had more influence now than they would have if called upon to jostle with the rougher sex in the daily pursuits of life' and he feared 'that by transferring the education of girls to large schools, and then drafting them off to the Universities, instead of their character being elevated it would be deteriorated, and they would lose the charms which men engaged in the strife and battles of life most admired'. *The Echo* did not report the remarks of the second 'factious' man, merely commenting that the Chairman 'had the greatest difficulty in shutting them [both] up'.

A provisional committee was formed at the Social Science Congress and the union proposed by Mrs Grey was christened the 'National Union for the Education of Girls of all Classes above the Elementary', a title soon shortened to the 'Women's Education Union', or the 'National Union'. Mrs Grey and her friends then proceeded to recruit a number of influential Vice-Presidents. Henrietta Stanley was perfectly willing to serve and used her influence to bring into the movement, among others, her son-in-law Lord Airlie. Lord Lyttelton, member of the Endowed Schools' Commission and keenly interested in the education of girls, also joined and promised to take the chair at an inaugural meeting to be held at the Society of Arts on November 17, 1871. An early and most constant helper was his daughter Lady Frederick Cavendish, whose husband was to be a victim of the Phoenix Park murderers in 1882. Among the other Vice-Presidents were the Bishop of Exeter and the Dean of Westminster. An offer to find recruits among the clergy came from Canon J. W. Blakesley of Norfolk to whom Mrs Grey had sent a copy of her paper. It failed to arrive and she sent another. 'I am not surprised at the fate attending its precursor,' wrote the Canon. 'I had some artificial teeth come down by the Post, and the box containing them was smashed to atoms and its contents dispersed throughout the postbag.' He believed, he added, 'that among the officials there are a number of misanthropes who . . . find a fiendish delight in disorganizing packets and missending letters'.

There were a number of refusals, several from Roman Catholics who were deeply suspicious of predominantly secular education. 'No difference can exist between us as to the raising of the intellectual cultivation of women', wrote Henry Manning, Archbishop of Westminster, '[but] I believe the culture of men and women should not be the same but analogous. I believe men and women to have functions which cannot be interchanged without departure from their respective highest perfection.' He wished the scheme success, however, if it could promote 'the intellectual culture of women without lessening the gravity and grace of our country and of the feminine perfection'.

Cardinal Cullen of Dublin, the first Irish Cardinal, was more forthright. 'Every one knows that new theories on education are proposed every day,' he wrote. 'Time and experience will probably prove that many of them are dangerous to society and religion. However if any thing of real intrinsic value be proposed I wish it success', but he was convinced 'that nothing good will be done . . . unless instruction in wordly matters be sanctified by religion. . . . I dread that a bad or non-religious education will produce the worst results.'

A thoroughly intemperate refusal came from the Duchess of Northumberland. 'The object of all female education', she wrote, *'ought* to be to enable a woman to fill her position in after-life— wife, mother, mistress or servant.' All that girls – except those of the highest social class – really needed to know was 'something practically of cooking, washing and ironing, nursing both of the Sick and of Infants, and of . . . plain needlework in all its branches, and of cutting out. You may', she conceded, 'add to these any amount of instruction which does not indispose the mind for these prior objects. . . . Schools for women are in themselves, in their very nature, bad, and to be avoided as much as possible – of course some girls go to them, but the smaller they are, the less public . . . the better. If Industrial Schools can be established . . . I will gladly give my name; but to help to make girls' education like that of boys, *public*': and to encourage girls to think of a university career 'will never have assistance from me, for I believe such a system would be an unmixed evil . . .'

As Louisa Drummond, the Duchess had been a girlhood friend of the Shirreff sisters. In later years the friendship was revived, wrote Maria Grey, 'notwithstanding her total want of sympathy for our educational objects. She once wrote me word that she would rather see her daughters, if she had any, standing at the wash-tub than pupils in a High School.'

Fortunately the sisters' educational ideas received more than enough support to encourage them to hold an inaugural meeting. Among the Vice-Presidents elected – some at the meeting, others soon afterwards – there were in addition to Lord Lyttelton and Lady Stanley an assortment of peers and peeresses, including Lord Lawrence, the former Viceroy and Governor-General of India. Among the Members of Parliament were J. B. Stansfeld and H.

43

Austin Bruce (afterwards Lord Aberdare). The Church was represented, in addition to the Dean of Westminster, by the Bishops of London, Manchester and Exeter. The Bishop of Manchester had hesitated before finally accepting. 'I dare say that our girls, as well as our boys, would be the better for a more thorough and real intellectual culture,' he wrote to Mrs Grey; but he felt 'that the result of our competitive Examinations ... has been to encourage "cram" and superficiality rather than reality and thoroughness' in boys and girls alike.

The list of Vice-Presidents was a long one and naturally included a number of educationists. Chief among them was Sir James Kay-Shuttleworth Bt., the pioneer worker for the welfare and education of the children of the poor. Sir James was also a powerful advocate of teacher training and a supporter of the Teachers' Training and Registration Society which the National Union started in 1876, and he himself opened a training college in Battersea which served as the prototype for many others.

At the inaugural meeting of the National Union a central working committee was set up. Maria Grey, who had been offered but refused the post of Chairman, was appointed Honorary Organizing Secretary, with Miss Shirreff and Mrs Henry Kingsley as joint Honorary Secretaries. Among the members of this Committee were Lady Stanley and Miss Gurney, Sir James Kay-Shuttleworth, James (afterwards Viscount) Bryce, one of the Assistant Commissioners of the Schools' Inquiry Commission, Joseph Payne, the first Professor of the Science and Art of Education at the College of Preceptors, and Miss Buss.

Lord Lyttelton's support of the scheme, wrote Maria Grey, 'was simply invaluable' and it was through Lord Lyttelton that the Union acquired a Royal President, Queen Victoria's sixth child, the twenty-three-year-old Princess Louise, who had recently married the Marquess of Lorne (afterwards Duke of Argyll).

As a girl the Princess had been known in the family as 'poor Louise' because she was thought to be lacking in the intelligence shown by her sisters. 'Today is poor Louise's fifteenth birthday,' the Queen informed her eldest daughter, the Crown Princess of Prussia, on March 18, 1864; but a year later she had revised her estimate. Louise, she wrote, 'is so handsome (she is very much admired) and is so graceful and her manners so perfect in society, so quiet and lady-like, and then she has such great taste for art'.[4]

In fact, the Princess was a vivacious, talented young woman, an amateur sculptor who indulged her 'taste for art' in a statue of her mother. 'She is (and who would some years ago have thought it?)'

wrote the Queen on her daughter's twentieth birthday, 'a clever, dear girl. . . .'[5]

The Princess was certainly an acquisition to the National Union. From the outset she took her presidential duties very seriously. She was not only prepared, when required, to preside over meetings and attend functions: she insisted on her right to be consulted on all major questions. 'Nothing shd. be regarded "as final" without the President's sanction,' wrote Lord Lorne to Mrs Grey on April 23, 1872. A week later he modified this sweeping demand. Instead, he asked for information about the Committee. For this purpose he wished for the minutes of all meetings to be sent to her and stipulated that if 'any new and striking change were proposed in the plans of the Union it shd. be in her power to ask you to call a special meeting of the Committee for the reconsideration of any resolution to which they might have come . . . of which the Princess might not be able to approve. If at such a special Meeting (at which the P'cess shd. also be able to vote) the majority shd. still adhere to their previous determination the resolution shd. then be valid and not before.' Lord Lorne added that he did not anticipate that such a contingency would ever arise (there is no record that it ever did), but he thought the arrangement should in fairness be made 'as it gives the P'cess an opportunity of stating an objection if at any time it might be necessary for her to do so'.

The Women's Education Union spread its gospel by every means within the power of its members, carrying on its work, wrote Maria Grey, 'with unwearied energy and no little success'.[6] It gave a fillip to advanced education by offering scholarships to successful candidates in the University Local Examinations, to be held at 'some place of higher education',* an example 'largely followed afterwards by other bodies'.[7]

The Union also set up branches in a number of provincial cities. As soon as the internal organization had been satisfactorily settled the Central Committee turned to its most urgent task, the establishment of schools open to all those girls whose educational needs were not covered by the Education Act of 1870. According to a statement in its first Annual Report, the Central Committee 'determined on the formation of a Limited Liability Company, for the purpose of establishing Public Day Schools for Girls, which

* In 1878 London University opened all its degrees to women with the exception of medicine. By that time Cambridge had two women's colleges – Girton and Newnham; and in 1879 two were opened in Oxford – Lady Margaret Hall and Somerville. In none of these, however, were women who passed their final examinations admitted to degrees.

should give a first-class education at fees placed as low as was compatible with the Schools being self-supporting and paying a fair interest on the capital invested'.

It was, wrote Maria Grey, 'Miss Buss's original creation, the North London Collegiate School, that the Women's Education took as their model, but warned by the difficulties she had encountered . . . and feeling, moreover, that the secondary education of girls in England could not, and . . . ought not, to be provided out of charitable endowments',[8] the Central Committee decided that the schools must be self-supporting. It therefore put forward a plan to open a day school in south-west London, the funds to be raised in shares of £5 each, the Limited Liability Company to be capable of extending its operations to other localities where similar schools were wanted.

While this plan was being formulated Maria Grey went, in January 1872, to spread the gospel in Ireland. She had introductions to a number of influential people in Dublin and Belfast, among them the Archbishop of Dublin, formerly Dean Trench, one of the founders of Queen's College. 'I have written to the Archbishop', wrote her indefatigable friend Canon Blakesley, 'and told him of your crusade. I have also endeavoured to neutralize any fears he may have entertained – but I cannot in conscience go so far as to describe you as "quiet and elderly".' He hoped, he added, 'to prevail upon the Archbishop to take the shilling (or rather pay the five shillings)' but he was obviously worried about what the Archbishop would think of her acquaintanceship with a woman like Josephine Butler who was 'much before the eyes of public men . .'.

He need not have worried: the Archbishop agreed to become a Vice-President of the Union. So, among others, did Dr Lloyd, the Provost of Trinity College, Dublin, Lord and Lady Dufferin, and Jane, Countess of Antrim. Maria Grey had worked extremely hard. Indeed, 'the arduous labour . . . [of] public speaking, visiting educational establishments, and social engagements I could not refuse, sent me home so utterly exhausted that I had to take to my bed, and to that I trace back the beginning of the nervous breakdown which prostrated me completely a few months later.' There is no record that Emily accompanied Maria to Ireland: presumably she was either suffering from one of her numerous ailments or nursing a sick relation, a task she was often called on to undertake.

Fortunately Maria recovered in time to play her part at a momentous meeting which took place at the Albert Hall in June 1872, with Lord Lyttelton presiding – the meeting which launched the new Girls' Public Day School Company. It was hoped, said

Maria in her address, that the schools which the Company planned to open would 'be places not only of instruction, but of education in the true sense of the word, and a training of the individual girl by the development of her mental and moral faculties, to understand the relation in which she stands to the physical world around her: to her fellow-beings, whether as members of her family, her country or her race; to her God, the Father and supreme Lord; and to know and perform the duties which arise out of these relations'.

Although there was to be a strong religious element in the teaching at the schools it was to be undenominational. This was an entirely new idea: even in Miss Buss's schools, where parents might withdraw their daughters from any part of the religious instruction to which they objected, the teaching was on Church of England lines. In another important way, however, the Company's schools were to resemble hers: there were to be no class distinctions.

In some quarters both these ideas were considered pernicious. 'When we were organizing our first school', wrote Maria Grey later, 'I was asked again and again whether I was mad enough to suppose that any gentleman would send his daughter to a public school.' And the impact of her speech at the Albert Hall was nearly ruined by the Bishop of Manchester, who had been specially invited to speak with the object of showing that in making the schools both classless and undenominational 'we did not mean them to be godless'. The Bishop, as requested, moved that the scheme be adopted but, according to a press report, while 'urging that the schools should be opened to as many as could be got to enter . . . [he] warned the meeting that it would be an illusion to suppose that the children of fashionable people would be found sitting down with the daughters of their grocers and bakers'.

Dr Barry, Principal of King's College, London, hastened to pour oil on the troubled waters. 'One part of the scheme, which to some appears a weak point', he said, was to him 'one of its great advantages – there was to be no social exclusiveness.'

The absence of denominational teaching and, even more, of class distinctions continued to arouse suspicion and opposition but 'there is little fear', wrote Emily Shirreff reprovingly in *The Work of the National Union*, 'that the gentleman's daughter will lose her home refinement because she follows a teacher's demonstration on the same board which is gazed at also by the children of the small shopkeeper . . . and I believe that neither levelling up, nor levelling down will in this matter result from the fusion of classes at school'. The vital point was that in the schools the teaching 'must be first-rate for all'.

The question of whether or not the girls should mix out of school was for the parents to decide. And although, as Maria Grey wrote of the Company's first school in Chelsea, 'every class was represented . . . from an earl's daughters to a very small tradesman's in the neighbourhood', it is unlikely that they ever met out of school hours.

It was inevitable that the Union should encounter prejudice against the idea of giving girls an academic education similar to that of boys: indeed, the question has been debated ever since. The opposition came to a head in 1872 when women made a poor showing in the Cambridge Higher Local Examinations. Emily Shirreff, who read a paper on *The Higher Education of Women* at a meeting of the British Association at Brighton, was accused of trying to force girls into a training beyond their capacity and also of sowing class dissension. One speaker maintained that girls should be taught only such subjects 'as would be compatible with the position they looked to fill' and prophesied that 'demands for education were such that the future generation would not know what a housemaid or cook was, for these would become "helps" only'.

Members of the Union had, therefore, to demonstrate first, that girls should be educated and, secondly, in the face of what Emily Shirreff called the 'shirt-button and slipper' argument, that a man's home would not be made uncomfortable by the presence of an educated wife. One man, however, when asked to support the campaign, 'bluntly expressed what many more implied, that women were getting out of hand and wanted instead of help, "to be taken down a peg" '[9] and when the idea was mooted of starting some classes for women in a London suburb it was urged that cooking and needlework should be the main subjects. Emily Shirreff, normally so mild mannered, was sometimes goaded into uncharacteristic sarcasm. On one occasion, her sister recalled, her neighbour at a dinner party, well aware of the work she was doing, 'took advantage of a pause in the conversation to ask her: "What do you think, Miss Shirreff, of strong-minded women?" "I think", she quietly but distinctly replied, looking him full in the face, "that they are very unfortunate when they find themselves in the company of weak-minded men." '

Despite continuing opposition to their objectives members of the Union went ahead with their plans. A prospectus announcing the formation of the Girls' Public Day School Company was sent out accompanied by a letter signed by Princess Louise. The Company aimed at raising a capital sum of £12,000 in 2,400 £5 shares, the capital to be used for the purchase, hire or erection and the furnishing of school buildings, a proportion being left to form the nucleus of a Reserve Fund. Any profit which might arise after the establishment of a school would be applied to the payment of a 5 per cent dividend on the shares.* Eight hundred of the shares were immediately taken up. Among the first shareholders were Maria Grey who took twenty, Henrietta Stanley and James Kay-Shuttleworth, with ten each, Emily Shirreff with five, Joseph Payne with two and Mary Gurney with one. Others included Lord Lorne, Lord Airlie, Samuel Morley M.P., J. G. (later Sir Joshua) Fitch, an Assistant Commissioner on the Schools' Inquiry Commission, Anne Clough, Dorothea Beale and Frances Mary Buss, together with members of her family.

The Central Committee of the Union was now transformed into an executive council with power to appoint its own committees: chief among these were the Education, Finance, and Sites and Buildings Committees, which have remained the principal committees to this day. The Royal President became Patroness of the Company's schools but the Vice-Presidents remained in office. The vacant post of President went to the Earl of Airlie, Lady Stanley's son-in-law, who held it until his death in 1881 when he was succeeded by Lord Aberdare. Sir James Kay-Shuttleworth was asked to become Chairman of the Council: he refused owing to pressure of work but remained an active member. The chair was therefore taken in rotation until December 1872 when Charles S. Roundell M.P., was elected. Ten years later the Women's Education Union, its work completed, was dissolved.

* The capital was increased from time to time: by 1880 it had been decided to increase it to £100,000 in 20,000 £5 shares.

Chapter 4
The First Schools

Each of the Company's schools was to have three departments, Preparatory, Junior and Senior, under a headmistress with the same powers and duties as the headmaster of a boys' grammar school and, as far as possible, with a staff of trained teachers. A class of student teachers was to be attached to every school, with special arrangements for training in the theory and practice of education.

The need for the schools to become self-supporting at the earliest possible moment and to provide some return on the capital expended meant that the strictest economy had to be practised. The schools, as Emily Shirreff explained in her pamphlet, 'must evidently not be expected to vie, either in external appearance or in costly fittings, with establishments on which thousands have been lavished in free gifts'. There should, however, be no false economy in the salaries of the headmistresses and their assistants.

In order to maintain a high standard, the schools were to be tested by regular inspection and examination by suitably qualified men. Pupils were to be prepared for the Oxford and Cambridge Local Examinations and for those of the College of Preceptors which demanded a slightly lower standard of attainment. The course would include non-sectarian religious instruction, reading, writing, arithmetic, book-keeping, English grammar and literature, history, geography, French and German, the elements of physical science, drawing, class singing and harmony, and calisthenic exercises. In the senior department there would be more advanced classes in ancient and modern languages, history, mathematics, the elements of moral science and logic, physiology as applied to the laws of health, and elementary economics.

The plan to open the first of the Company's schools in south-west London was submitted to the Endowed Schools Commissioners who thought that educationally it was 'perfectly sound. . . . The locality selected appears to be a very suitable one, well fitted to supply Pupils of a class requiring the education which it is intended to provide.'

The search for suitable premises now began. An excellent house was found in Brompton Road but the tenants of the neighbouring houses objected to its being used as a school. Negotiations for several other houses fell through, and the Council reluctantly decided on Durham House in Smith Street, Chelsea, which was owned by Lord Cadogan. It was recorded in the Council Minutes that 'the neighbourhood ... was considered so objectionable, as entirely to counterbalance whatever advantages as to size and the arrangement of rooms could be urged in its favour' but after one of the principal objections – unspecified – had been removed 'both Mrs Grey and Lady Stanley were in favour of renting it'. It was also agreed, after one member had expressed his fear that 'there would be a risk of dividing the Council', to open a second school in Bayswater as soon as possible.

Durham House, once the home of Sir Isaac Newton, stood in its own grounds and, apart from the kitchen quarters, had eighteen rooms, some of them very large and lofty. When arrangements had been made to rent the house, which has long since been demolished, the Council turned its attention to the appointment of a headmistress. It was decided 'that the attainments of the candidate selected for the position ... should be tested by Examination before the final Election took place; and directions were given to invite Miss Buss and Mr Bruce* to undertake the Examination'.

Since there were few teachers with any experience of teaching in large schools and fewer still with any knowledge of administration, it is hardly surprising that the preliminary sifting produced no qualified candidates. Eventually a suitable teacher was found in Miss Mary Porter, who had been teaching since 1860 and had been among those called to give evidence before the Schools' Inquiry Commission. Miss Porter was duly appointed at a salary of £250 a year, plus a capitation fee of 10s a year on every pupil above a minimum of one hundred. She was expected to pay for her own accommodation on the school premises at a charge which varied between £30 and £50 a year and was forbidden to accept gratuities from parents.† It was also agreed that the post of second mistress should carry a salary of £140, and Miss Porter was invited to nominate assistant teachers for the Council's consideration. She

* Later Lord Aberdare.

† This rule persisted, no teacher being allowed to receive a present from a girl or her parents. In 1923, for example, a request from the girls of Sutton High School to give a wedding present to a teacher who was leaving to get married was refused on the grounds that 'there is no way of safe-guarding against the evil of canvassing on such occasions'. Today, however, girls may make a small voluntary collection for a leaving teacher of ten years' standing.

was to have the right of nomination and dismissal but in the event of a dismissal was expected to report her reasons to the Council within a week, the Council reserving a similar right to dismiss any teacher whose removal was considered desirable or necessary. Miss Porter's first choice was unfortunate: her second mistress resigned within a month of appointment and several months before the school was opened.

A scale of fees was fixed, ranging from £4 4s a term for pupils entering between the ages of nine and twelve, a sum which was never to be raised throughout their school life (an arrangement which led to a great deal of trouble) to £8 8s a term for girls entering above the age of fifteen. The fees were modest enough, yet the Council was soon receiving angry letters from shareholders complaining, as one of them wrote, that the scale was 'so high as to amount to a breach of faith on the part of the Company which was formed to provide "cheap" schools'. There was a small but most unpopular extra charge for stationery; and more than once parents had to be threatened with legal proceedings before they consented to pay it.

Hours of attendance were the same as those at the North London Collegiate School, from 9.15 a.m. to 1.30 p.m., but there was in addition a voluntary afternoon class for preparation. There was a break in the morning for 'recreation' and 'light refreshments' of coffee and buns, and a midday dinner was provided for girls who could not go home.*

It was as a result of Emily Shirreff's special interest in the training of young children that the Council agreed that wherever possible a kindergarten should be included in the Preparatory Department.

The Council next considered the question of publicity. It was decided to insert discreet advertisements in the local press and to invite editors 'to draw public attention to the advertisements, by inserting paragraphs or otherwise'. There was to be no advertising in the national press, but some unscrupulous rival body tried to sabotage the Company's plans by advertising the opening of a West London Public Day School for Girls in *The Times*. This, the Council agreed, 'so nearly resembled that by which the Company is registered, as to be calculated to deceive the Public'. The acting Secretary, the Rev. Dr Hiron, was instructed to write to the editor and to the company's solicitor to caution the advertisers 'against

* In 1877 the charge for coffee and buns was fixed at 6d and the midday dinner at a shilling. In another of the Company's schools, the Clapham Middle School, where the fees were lower the price of dinner was fixed at 10d, or 9d without pudding.

the infringement of the Company's title'. This had no effect, a similar advertisement appearing the following month. Mrs Grey then suggested that the schools might be given the distinctive title of 'Louise' schools. Fortunately for posterity she was persuaded to withdraw this idea and other names put forward later – 'Royal', 'Imperial', and 'Queen Victoria' – were also withdrawn. In due course the Company's schools became known as High Schools for Girls, but the Company could not prevent similar schools which were opened during the next decade from using the same title.

Since there was so little available capital, and that little was shortly to be stretched to provide a second school, the Council were making what Miss Porter considered to be the most outrageous economies. 'I feel sure we cannot begin the work of the school in a satisfactory manner with less than two teachers beside myself,' she protested. 'The pupils . . . must be arranged in different classes as girls of varying ages and attainments cannot be properly taught in the same class. The Head Mistress cannot take the *sole* charge of a class as she must sometimes watch the teachers in other classes and take those classes in the presence of their teachers.' The Council had offered her only one assistant and some part-time help in languages and music, but now agreed to the appointment of a second assistant at the princely starting salary of £50 a year.

Miss Porter had expected the Council to appoint a housekeeper to superintend the domestic staff. This consisted of a cook-general and a housemaid who, at seventeen, was considered by several members of the Council to be far too young for the job. When no housekeeper was appointed Miss Porter complained, but was told that 'in asking her to supervise the servants . . . for the present' the Council 'did not wish her to undertake any duties not consistent with the due performance of her duties as Head Mistress'.

Estimates for the supply of furniture had been invited from several firms. The Council eagerly 'commenced to go through one of the estimates, item by item, but eventually abandoned the attempt, and ultimately ordered the Secretary to expend a sum not exceeding £60, in the purchase of such articles of furniture as were indispensable'. Special desks had been ordered from Sweden but as it seemed unlikely that they would arrive in time for the opening the Secretary had to hurry round to the South Kensington Department of Science and Art to borrow tables and chairs. When he had completed this negotiation and dealt with Miss Porter's further complaints about smoking chimneys and icy classrooms, he was instructed to call on the ministers of the various denominations in the district to solicit their support for the school.

On January 20, 1873, a public meeting was held in the Chelsea Vestry Hall, presided over by Samuel Morley M.P., a substantial shareholder. Next day the Chelsea School opened, with 'seventeen pupils whose fees had been paid in advance', three whose fees had not yet been paid, and the promise of five more. To mark the occasion the Council met at Durham House instead of at its offices in Sloane Street. Joseph Payne took the Chair, and among those present were Maria Grey, Emily Shirreff, Henrietta Stanley and Mary Gurney. At the end of March the School was visited by Princess Louise who 'expressed to Mrs Grey her satisfaction with the arrangements'.

Two problems in particular were worrying the Council at the time: the first was the student-teacher scheme, the second the provision of boarding houses. As early as February 1873 'a long and animated discussion' took place 'during which opinions were expressed that it was premature to arrange a scheme for student teachers while the Company had but one school, and in that school so few pupils'. On the other hand, it was argued that the scheme had been mentioned in the prospectus and enquiries were already coming in. Spurred on by Maria Grey and Mary Gurney the Council agreed that a start should be made: three months later Mary Porter appointed her first student teacher.

The boarding-house question was more complicated. By February applications from parents were being received and also from 'one or two ladies' who were anxious to receive boarders. The applications were duly noted but the question was not settled immediately. In fact, it kept reappearing as one school after another was established, and although a certain number of licensed boarding-houses were opened the Council as a whole looked on boarders as a necessary evil. 'The Schools of the Company being Day Schools, the existence of Boarders is intended to be recognized rather than encouraged,' ran the Regulations for Boarders issued in 1875. The following year the Education Committee recommended that the question should be settled once and for all 'on the principle of an absolute disclaimer by the Council of all responsibility for the subject'. This advice was not accepted. For many years a number of the schools had boarding-houses attached: some were licensed by the Trust, some were run by Trust headmistresses or a member of the staff. Only three now remain – at Bath, Brighton and Hove, and Oxford.

As pioneer headmistress Miss Porter had much to contend with. There was, for example, the ever-present problem of money. The Council voted her only £15 for the purchase of school materials including reference books, maps and drawing materials. When she asked for petty cash she was given £20, and her request for an additional sum for bookshelves was met with a stony demand for estimates, which she failed to produce.

She was also instructed to get an estimate 'for fixing painted or galvanized wire outside four windows . . . looking out into Durham Street; great inconvenience having arisen from stones thrown at the windows and into the kitchen'. At the same time the Secretary was instructed to do his best to make 'the schoolhouse secure against . . . housebreakers'. Council members who had objected to Chelsea as a bad neighbourhood now seemed vindicated; but the Council as a whole 'thought that the best plan to abate the nuisance would be to set a man to watch for offenders and inflict summary punishment upon them'. Luckily for Mr Hiron, the Secretary, he was not ordered to do this himself, only 'to arrange for a watch to be kept'. He wrote to the police but received no satisfaction beyond an official acknowledgment; he wrote again, still without effect. The nuisance continued until the windows were suitably shrouded in galvanized wire. No one seems to have considered the possibility that the offenders had merely been throwing stones to attract the attention of the seventeen-year-old housemaid.

Since Durham House was old and in a poor state of repair the Council was continually having to advance small sums of money to deal with the defects and to cope with complaints about the house and the neighbourhood. A particularly ominous letter came from a doctor who stated that he was 'attending a pupil at the Chelsea School, for low fever and suggesting that this may have arisen from the drinking water'. The Secretary was instructed to communicate with the Water Board and at the same time to order the builder 'to examine the drains . . . and clear away the rubbish from the cellar under the dressing-room'.

In other ways the school was doing well enough although the numbers were still very small. This was in some measure due to the fact that the Company held faithfully to its principles – for some parents hesitated to send their daughters to a school where there was no Church of England teaching and no class distinctions. It also worked the other way, by making it possible, for example, for Jewish girls whose parents did not wish them to receive any religious instruction to attend. In 1873, the year the first Jewish pupil was admitted to Chelsea, the National Union offered the first of its scholarships to enable a girl from an elementary school to continue her education at one of the Company's schools or at the North London Collegiate School. It was quite true, as Maria

Grey claimed two years later, that no social distinctions were recognized in any of the Company's schools.

As far as the education was concerned, the ambitious curriculum was being faithfully followed. Sir James Kay-Shuttleworth who visited the Chelsea School in 1873 and was present at a lesson on economics, 'spoke with warm approval of the skill with which [it] was given, and the general intelligence of the Class'. This 'favourable opinion . . . was received by the Council with much gratification', and led to the introduction of experimental courses on physiology and mathematics. During the summer an examination was held 'identical with that set for University College School'. There were eighteen candidates, two of whom obtained 70 per cent of the possible marks. The examiner appointed to correct the papers found that most of the girls gave an able answer to the question: 'Which does more for the promotion of industry and commerce, he who expends a given amount of wealth on his own direct personal enjoyments, or he who profitably invests the same, and why?' Even the girl at the bottom of the list who only got 10 per cent was presumably able to give some sort of answer to this one.

Among the top two was a girl named Edith Mullet, who was the cause of serious trouble the following year. Her father wrote to the Council to complain of her 'dismissal . . . by Miss Porter', and was invited to appear at the next Council meeting. Before his arrival Miss Porter, who had also been asked to attend, 'made a statement . . . of the circumstances of the case'. At the request of the Council Miss Porter, who was in no position to make conditions, declared her 'willingness to accept from Miss Mullet an apology in writing for certain language of an insolent character addressed by her to Miss Porter in private, and her readiness in that case to receive back Miss Mullet as a pupil'.

It must have been galling for the unfortunate Miss Porter to be forced to eat humble pie: nor was Edith Mullet the only girl to get her into trouble with the Council. On another occasion Miss Porter was instructed to mollify an irate father who had complained that she had given his daughter an adverse leaving report. She also had staff troubles, in particular with her second-in-command who had been appointed after some delay and who, according to Miss Porter, was guilty of 'insubordinate conduct'. This affair died down because the second mistress had already applied for a post in another school. Miss Porter herself did not last very long. She resigned in January 1875, to become headmistress of Bradford Grammar School for Girls, with a testimonial from the Council commending her 'skill and earnestness in teaching'.

Miss Porter was not a great headmistress but, as a pioneer, she had to endure tribulations such as public prejudice against girls' education and the lingering disapproval of women appearing in public. She herself was well aware of her difficulties. Nearly thirty years later she wrote a letter to the *Daily Chronicle* in reply to an article which stated that the high school movement 'was hailed with joy in its beginning'. As one of the pioneers in the movement, declared Miss Porter, 'I beg to differ... We had to strive for years against continual opposition.... I have grounds for thinking that the work of the present Head Mistresses is of a higher character than that of the former generation, for we, alas! did not enjoy the advantages which they have had in preparation for their work.'

Miss Porter's successor at Chelsea stayed only a year before she too left to take another post. A third headmistress, Miss M. E. Bishop, proved more durable. Educated at Queen's College, Miss Bishop had had only three years' teaching experience before she became headmistress of Chelsea, family claims having kept her at home. After three years at Chelsea she was appointed headmistress of another of the Company's schools, Oxford High School which had been founded in 1875 and at which she had originally taught.* The Chelsea School did not really begin to settle down and flourish until after 1879 when it was moved, under the direction of Miss Hitchcock, from the dubious neighbourhood of Chelsea to the respectable atmosphere of Kensington, where it took on a new lease of life as the Kensington High School for Girls.

Among Miss Hitchcock's first pupils were a pair of close friends, both distinguished public servants – the future Dame Meriel Talbot and the future Countess Buxton. They were blissfully happy at school, although Mildred Smith (Countess Buxton) who in later years became a Vice-President of the Company and a highly efficient and sympathetic Chairman of the Governors of Brighton and Hove High School, complained bitterly because her mother made her wear a long skirt at school, 'while everyone else wore a short one, lace instead of a collar, and a spotted muslin apron'. She was critical of the school building, 'a hideous and monstrous house', and of the lack of scientific equipment. 'But in spite of the drawbacks the impression left in my mind is that my school life was a time of intense enjoyment.'

Her friend, grand-daughter of the Company's supporter Lord Lyttelton and a niece of Council member Lady Frederick Cavendish, was especially pleased to meet in school 'every kind of girl from

* She resigned from Oxford to become Principal of the Royal Holloway College.

every kind of home and very mixed backgrounds. Some were not of the upper class but were splendid people. I liked them all and my time at school left me with a facility for enjoyment of people of very different types,' something which proved of great value to Dame Meriel in her career of public service.

It seems unlikely that at this period there was much mingling outside school of girls from different types of home. Before very long tentative friendships were being formed, and certainly by the second decade of the twentieth century these were taken as a matter of course. Dr Elizabeth Wiskemann, the historian of modern Europe, a former pupil of the Company's second school – Notting Hill and Bayswater – remembered that one of her closest friends was the daughter of the local postman, a gifted scholarship girl. The two remained friends throughout their school life, and the friendship only waned when the latter, after taking her degree, accepted an academic post in a Canadian university. Friendships such as this were mutually enriching, and the complete integration of scholarship girls into the life of the community was to prove one of the Company's great strengths.

The opening of Notting Hill and Bayswater High School, in September 1873, had been greeted with some apprehension. Kay-Shuttleworth, ever cautious, considered that the founders had acted unwisely. George Bartley, a Council member and joint editor with Emily Shirreff of the National Union's journal, was extremely worried. 'I hear', he wrote to the Chairman, 'that a Head Mistress was appointed at the last Council Meeting, also that an additional Mistress was appointed at Chelsea School [for mathematics]. As neither of these very important steps were announced on the Agenda paper I shall be glad to be informed whether there is not some mistake. . . . The mode of adding to the Staff at Chelsea is most unsatisfactory and if done in this chance and offhand way will not fail to land the Company in Ruin.'

Chelsea had many teething troubles but Notting Hill High School, although it opened in a house in Norland Square with only ten pupils, was soon forging ahead. The school was exceptionally fortunate in its first headmistress, Miss Harriet Morant Jones, an outstandingly able woman. Harriet Jones who came from Guernsey where she had had some teaching experience, was forty at the time of her appointment to Notting Hill and she remained there until her retirement in 1900. She was recalled quite recently as 'a rather awe-inspiring personality, a combination of dignity and kindliness; [with] superb vitality, erect and stately carriage, keen glance, a coronet of plaits', much addicted to wearing 'regal purple with trailing skirts'. Initially, however, she was doubtful if a public school for girls could possibly succeed. The premises in Norland Square, which had been bought by Emily Shirreff and leased to the Company on very favourable terms, had once been a boys' school: they were dark, dismal and draughty and without a proper playground, and much had to be done to make them habitable. Then, too, the educational standard of some of the pupils was abysmally low. Several of the girls, Miss Jones told the Council, were so backward that they were 'fit only for a preparatory department'. It was suggested that for the time being she might arrange for special help for the younger girls, and Mrs Grey was quick to move that the existing preparatory department 'be formed into a kindergarten and a teacher appointed'. The low standard of entry of girls coming from private schools or home schoolrooms proved to be a recurring problem. Some girls were intelligent enough and soon took their rightful places; others were incurably backward and had either to be taught in a separate class or judiciously mixed with other girls of their own age.

Miss Jones was at first expected to teach both French and German, and she was authorized to appoint only one assistant teacher at a salary of £100 a year and a capitation fee of 5s on every pupil above the first seventy. This figure was very soon reached: by the end of the first year the school numbered 124, at the end of the second, 200, and before long the figure was nearly 400. Large girls' schools were still so rare that they gave rise to all sorts of misconceptions. On one occasion, Miss Jones remembered, she was called downstairs 'to see a respectably dressed woman, who asked me for a ticket for the Eye Infirmary. I said that I had none to give. "But I have been told that this is an Eye School," she said. "No", I replied, "a High School, where a good education is given." "Oh!" she said, "I see, College like." and she went away disappointed.'

In the first two years of its existence there were many indications of Notting Hill's rapid progress. In 1875, for example, it was noted at a Council meeting that 'for the first time a grant of £10 5s 9d has been made for scientific apparatus'. In 1876, of eight pupils sent in for the Cambridge Higher Local Examination six passed, five with honours. This progress, which seems to have continued without interruption, was very largely due to a headmistress who was a brilliant teacher and administrator, able to get the very best out of her staff and pupils. Miss Jones was never daunted by prejudice or submerged by domestic difficulties or the problems of discipline which had baffled Miss Porter and were to prove too much for several headmistresses: instead she proceeded serenely and confidently on her way.

Notting Hill High School had not even come into existence when the Council began to debate the question of opening a school outside London, at Croydon in Surrey. The over-cautious Kay-Shuttleworth, whose opinion was asked, sounded a warning note. At first he 'declined to express an opinion, as he took a different view from that which appeared to prevail with regard to the establishment of further schools. Ultimately, however, [he] gave it as his opinion that the Council would be unwise in committing itself to the imprudence of starting a second school so soon after its first experiment, and while the success of the Chelsea School was still problematical.'

Kay-Shuttleworth was overruled. Maria Grey and Emily Shirreff, who had moved and seconded the proposal triumphed, as they usually did, but the Croydon High School, with eighty-eight pupils, was not opened until September 1874, a year later than Notting Hill. It was started, wrote Mrs Grey, 'on the conditions then laid down by the Council and never departed from since, of going only where a school was asked for, and where the locality proved the bona fides of the demand by forming a Local Committee and taking up a certain number of shares [usually 400], enough to cover the initial expenses of the school'.

The headmistress of Croydon High School, Miss Dorinda Neligan, was also an excellent choice, although she had no previous teaching experience. The daughter of an Army officer who had served in the Peninsular War, Miss Neligan had herself served with the Red Cross in France during the Franco-Prussian War of 1870-1 and had been left in sole charge at Metz during the siege. Keen-faced and blue-eyed, Miss Neligan like Miss Jones showed a distinctive taste in dress: she always wore a lace mantilla over her head and shoulders in school and almost always a black silk dress. Personality and natural intelligence, practical ability and a sense of humour combined with a beautiful and effective speaking voice were Dorinda Neligan's chief assets. She also had a highly developed sense of justice and plenty of moral and physical courage. These qualities carried her successfully through twenty-seven years as headmistress of Croydon and on into old age when, incensed at the long delay in giving women the vote, she became a militant suffragette. On one occasion she protested by refusing to pay her rates: her silver teapot was distrained but redeemed and returned to her by the grateful parent of one of her former pupils. On another occasion she assaulted a policeman but was not sent to prison, presumably because of her age.

Miss Neligan, who was just over forty when she took up her appointment, was dubious of her own powers. 'I remember as if it were yesterday', she wrote to Mrs Grey many years later, 'you coming to the opening [of the school] . . . and your speaking to the children in the large room in the basement and how badly I spoke myself – doubtless because [in] those days I was too *self-conscious* – too burdened with my own personality – a fault I hope I have somewhat overcome now.'

Less confident than Miss Jones, Miss Neligan early ran into difficulties. Since the Council had to consider every penny, a house in very poor condition had been taken, with defective ventilation, an inadequate playground and a singular shortage of earth closets. The pupils also left something to be desired. In 1876 the case was considered 'of two pupils . . . whom for want of cleanliness it was desirable to remove from the School'. The pupils in question were duly removed and a term's fees refunded to the parents. Two years later the ruling of the Council was asked by the Finance Committee 'in a case where they had ordered legal proceedings to be taken for a term's fee in lieu of notice, and where they have since learned that it is intended to be pleaded that the pupil was improperly taught Physiology at the Croydon School'. There is no record of any action taken: but physiology remained on the syllabus.

Miss Neligan herself was not immune to criticism. In 1875 two members of the local committee of shareholders brought serious charges against the management of the school and against the character of its headmistress. The Education Committee, having examined the charges and Miss Neligan's defence, advised the Council that the complaints against the management showed 'at worst, defects of system due in great measure to the difficulties incidental to the starting of a large new school in inadequate premises', and that the defects had to a considerable extent already been remedied. The complaints against Miss Neligan involved 'charges of untruthfulness, false reports to members of the Council, evasions of the printed regulations . . . refusal to support Assistants in the maintenance of discipline, and partiality in treatment of teachers and pupils'. Miss Neligan certainly had her ill-wishers but the evidence, declared the Education Committee, 'absolutely fails to establish any of these charges: and Miss Neligan's character for honour and justice has been fully vindicated'. The Council stood by her – as well they might – as they were to stand by other headmistresses in times of stress and trouble.

It had become clear, however, that the school premises were hopelessly inadequate. The Council decided to spend money on new buildings and the Archbishop of Canterbury, Dr Tait, was invited to lay the foundation stone. The Archbishop had already brought his influence to bear on the Council in an endeavour to get them to agree to provide 'definite religious instruction for children of Church of England parents'. The Council refused: it remained 'a cardinal principle', that the religious instruction should be undenominational. The Archbishop relented: he had performed the opening ceremony of the first school premises and now consented to lay the foundation stone of the new buildings, which were completed in 1880. By that time the school was growing very rapidly.

Similar religious difficulties occurred elsewhere, notably in Shrewsbury where a group of local people asked for a high school to be opened in 1884. The clergy, anxious that religious instruction should follow Church of England lines, were in favour of a school opened under the auspices of the newly-founded Church Schools Company; the lay people preferred the experience of the Girls' Public Day School Company and were ready to find a suitable house and raise the necessary number of shares. 'Religious teaching was the bank on which we have grounded for a time', wrote a leading layman to the Chairman of the Council, 'as many, but no means all, of the Church of England clergy . . . appear to think that in the Girls' Public Day School Company's prospectus, this branch of instruction is passed over too lightly and left indefinite'. A committee was appointed to obtain further information from both companies and ruled in favour of the older established body. Opposition to the Girls' Public Day School Company gradually subsided and Shrewsbury High School was opened in 1885. There was a different situation at Bromley where, in 1882, three Church of England vicars, a Methodist minister and an Independent minister signed with other local people a letter to the Company asking for a high school to be opened. As a result of this petition Bromley High School was established the following year.

Chapter 5

Internal Affairs

With Chelsea, Notting Hill and Croydon High Schools in being the Company turned further afield. A request for a school had been received from a committee of local people in Norwich and Maria Grey and her sister went to Norfolk to make a preliminary investigation. It is, perhaps, superfluous to add that 'Emily was very unwell during the whole of our stay'.

Norwich High School opened in 1875 with sixty-one pupils. During the same year five more schools were founded – Bath, Hackney and Clapton, Nottingham, and Oxford; and at Clapham a Middle School, with lower fees and a more modest curriculum. Emily was too ill to accompany her sister to Oxford, where the Master of University College remarked that the establishment of a high school 'was an historical event, being the first on record of town and gown uniting to carry a common object'. By 1876 when the ninth school, St John's Wood High School (afterwards South Hampstead) was founded, there were just over one thousand pupils compared with 349 in three schools in 1874. 'In every instance', said the Chairman of the Council, the Company 'have adhered to their plan of requiring a local subscription of 400 shares as a condition precedent to the establishment of a school'. Two other high schools – Brighton and Hove, and Gateshead – were opened in 1876, Paddington and Maida Vale in 1877, and four more in 1878 – Dulwich, Highbury and Islington, Ipswich, and Sheffield. The movement spread until at its zenith the Company (later the Trust) was controlling thirty-eight schools in London, the suburbs and the provinces,* from Carlisle and Newcastle in the north to Brighton and Portsmouth in the south, from Norwich in the east to Bath in the west, with a total of 7,209 pupils. The expansion owed much to the foresight and persistence of Mary Gurney who saw the schools as an integral part of a country-wide movement.

As a prominent member of the Council and of its various committees, she supported the Council's policy of rigid control over the

* See Appendix II.

schools and their headmistresses. On appointment a head signed an undertaking binding her to discharge her duties to the best of her ability and agreeing that if she were removed by the Council she would 'acquiesce in such removal'. Since several headmistresses left to take up appointments in schools which were not under the Company's jurisdiction a clause was added to the existing regulations in 1892 to the effect that for a period of five years after she left a headmistress must not teach or have an interest in any school 'within a distance of five miles from the School of the Company where she had been Head Mistress'. As head, she could appoint and dismiss her staff but she had to give an annual report to the Council on each of her teachers* and in the case of a dismissal had to account for her action within a week. The Council also reserved the right to dismiss an assistant teacher 'with or without notice for neglect of duty or any other misconduct as in their judgment shall justify such dismissal' in which case 'no salary shall be payable after the date of dismissal'.†

No headmistress could be certain of staying at a school for any length of time. Miss Ada Benson, the first headmistress of Norwich High School, which was opened in 1875, is a case in point. At the opening ceremony at which her brother, the future Archbishop of Canterbury, officiated she solemnly handed him her Bible, which he as solemnly handed back as an indication that it was her privilege to read the appropriate passage. Miss Benson, who had equipped herself for her post by spending ten days at the North London Collegiate School, was influenced by conditions at Rugby School where her brother had taught and she took his advice in matters great and small. At Norwich she was remembered chiefly for her grey dresses and the jingling chatelaine which warned pupils

---

* This practice was kept up until 1939.

† These regulations have, of course, been modified over the years but they were still being rigorously applied in the early years of the present century. In 1906, for example, the Education Committee recommended that 'no Teachers be exempted from signing' a new form of agreement which had just come into force. Miss Gavin of Notting Hill High School reported, however, that five of her staff had protested vigorously against the regulation which forbade any one who had taught in a Trust school to carry on a school in the neighbourhood without the permission of the Council; and also against the provision which had been imported from the earlier form 'enabling removal of a Teacher without assigning cause . . .' As late as September 1923, the *Times Educational Supplement* printed an anonymous letter complaining vociferously about the clause preventing teachers from opening schools in the neighbourhood of a Trust school. As the schools were in receipt of state aid, he thought it was high time 'that the general public was made acquainted with the agreements in force between the assistants and the Council in all state-aided schools'.

of her approach; but she had no time to impose her personality on the school before she was whisked away to become headmistress of Oxford High School.* There, still influenced by her brother, she introduced the prefect system and the writing of impositions. She was admired and respected but she cannot have been an easy colleague. She sought to imbue her staff with something of the fierce energy which caused Miss Beale of Cheltenham to remark that she might well have been called 'Zelotes'. The results were remarkably successful, for eight members of a staff of thirteen and eight of her pupils became headmistresses. Miss Benson thus set a precedent which has been followed ever since in Trust schools. By 1923 – the year of the Golden Jubilee – over a hundred and fifty headmistresses had been supplied to schools outside the Trust, the greater number of them to the maintained schools which came into being after 1902.

Another head who was moved by the Council from one part of the country to another was Miss Mary Alger, the first headmistress of Clapham Middle School. After three years at Clapham Miss Alger was moved to Sheffield High School, and within a year she was transferred from Sheffield to Dulwich. The Council's policy was, of course, aimed at the welfare and progress of the schools concerned, but it must have borne hard on an individual who, having built up one school from scratch, had to start all over again at another. If numbers showed signs of dwindling the headmistress was taken to task, the Council intimating that unless 'they should be better satisfied with the position of the School in regard to numbers, they may feel it necessary to consider the desirability of effecting a change in the Head Mistress-ship'.

During the first few years a headmistress might expel a refractory pupil although, as in the case of Miss Porter and the insubordinate Edith Mullet, if the Council thought she had acted improperly she had to take the girl back. After 1879, however, the Council and the Chairman had absolute power 'and without assignment of cause' to refuse to accept a girl in a school and to expel an unsatisfactory pupil. A headmistress might suspend a girl, in which case she had 'forthwith to report to the Chairman the grounds for such suspension' but she could not expel. In 1879, for example, Miss A. A. O'Connor, who had succeeded Miss Alger as headmistress of Clapham Middle School, and was remembered for the 'placid demeanour [which] exerted an ennobling if somewhat frigid influence throughout the School', had to explain to the Council her reasons

---

* This was apparently no hardship for she suffered badly from chilblains in the cold Norfolk winters.

for the suspension of a certain Miss Ada Powell and, these not being considered adequate, she was directed to readmit the girl and to apologize to her mother. Ada Powell, however, 'having been in the opinion of the Council guilty of insubordination to the Head Mistress' was required 'as a preliminary condition, to apologize therefor'. The heinous crime for which the girl had been suspended – and of which the Council decided she had not been guilty – was 'misconduct in injuring and interfering with the book of Miss Jane Cooper'.

In other ways, too, headmistresses were kept in check. The Council authorized the payment of small grants for school libraries, generally £10 per school: but a headmistress not only had to account for every penny she spent but also to submit for the approval of the Education Committee the title of every book she proposed to buy. She could appoint one of her staff as librarian, but her annual report to the Council had to affirm that 'the Library books are in good order and correct' since the books belonged not to the school but were the property of the Council. The books in a special section of the library were set aside for Sunday reading and these, wrote a pupil at Kensington High School, 'though of a more serious character, are by no means less interesting than the books which are more suitable for every-day amusement'. The girls were charged 1s a term for the ordinary books and 6d for the Sunday books.

Quite early in the history of the schools the girls were encouraged to form guilds of service, but not before the Council had scrutinized and approved their objects. 'Latitude is allowed the Head Mistresses in the recommendation of objects suitable for their schools, bearing in mind the undenominational religious character of the latter, but new objects thus recommended must be reported at once to the Chairman of the Council.' Making clothes for waifs and strays was considered unexceptionable, guild members being instructed that 'all the garments should be such as are suitable for the poor, i.e. of strong, lasting material and workmanship and of simple and serviceable form'. They must have been spurred on to greater efforts by the news that the flannel petticoats supplied the previous year 'were especially appreciated'. Nevertheless, the idea of service to the community inculcated in the early days has persisted.

Political activity was severely frowned on. On one occasion the Council considered a letter published in the *Newcastle Chronicle* 'complaining that at the recent Parliamentary election teachers and pupils had been asked in the School to canvass'. It was resolved that the headmistress in question 'be informed that politics must be kept entirely out of the Schools', and a circular to this effect was sent to all headmistresses. In fact, undue publicity was to be avoided at all costs. The Council laid down, for instance, that any headmistress who permitted the performance of a play must 'disallow scenery; disallow any Teacher taking part; disallow male dress [and] allow none but ordinary dress, i.e. not costume, on any public occasion'.

Headmistresses had to deal with questions arising from the examination and inspection of their schools. In an endeavour to set academic standards for the schools, the Council arranged for the Oxford and Cambridge Schools Examination Board to carry out written examinations for all senior forms in a number of subjects and to report on the results. In 1878 the Council authorized the appointment of the Rev. W. Jowitt as Schools' Inspector. 'Should he notice any case in which the rules of the Council do not appear to be properly observed', each headmistress was informed, 'it will be his duty to call your attention to the point; and you can make any explanation either to him or directly to the [Education] Committee'. The heads may well have quailed: the Rev. W. Jowitt was exceedingly thorough. He was also, however, perfectly just, and when occasion demanded it generous with praise. There could have been no better vindication of Miss Neligan's character – if one were still needed – than Mr Jowitt's description of the 'great consideration and insight into character and any special fitness' which she showed 'in the assignment of work and classes to her assistants'. Teachers were not overburdened with work and he commended Miss Neligan's practice of spreading 'the best teaching power . . . over the School' instead of confining it 'to the two or three higher forms'. He found the tone and the discipline of the school excellent. 'Under its brave and conscientious Head Mistress law is supreme, but it is the law of love and liberty.' This relationship between the headmistress and her staff so highly commended by the Inspector was reflected in the attitude of the Council towards the headmistresses, which became increasingly flexible and generous despite the seeming rigidity of the *Regulations*.

In addition to their administrative and teaching duties headmistresses had to deal with domestic problems ranging from leaking roofs and faulty drains to epidemics. All complaints were submitted to the Council for action. In 1876, for instance, the Company's builder was ordered to 'take down the skirting in the upper room' at St John's Wood (later South Hampstead) High School, 'and do what is necessary to extirpate the insects'. The problem may well have continued until 1883 when the school was moved to purpose-built premises in Hampstead. Similarly, the headmistress of

67

Nottingham High School was moved with a fine disregard for spelling to complain most bitterly of appalling 'sanatory' conditions and to implore the Council to take heed of the local doctor's opinions on the subject since, 'in the event of any mother's asking him whether all is quite safe, his answer would . . . do sad mischief in so very gossipy a town as this'. Headmistresses' reports to the Council are full of well-justified complaints, about the poor conditions of buildings and playgrounds, outbreaks of infectious disease, and other trials and difficulties.

The superabundance of problems and anxieties coupled with inexperience in controlling large numbers or an inability to delegate responsibility led several of the early headmistresses to overtax their health. Two or three resigned: others needed short periods of sick leave, even the vigorous Mrs Woodhouse of Sheffield who was able to return to work after a term's absence. Born in 1850, Mrs Woodhouse was left a widow at the age of twenty-three. She prepared herself for a teaching career by studying at the North London Collegiate School under Miss Buss and was then appointed to the staff of Clapham Middle School under Miss Alger. When Miss Alger left to become the first headmistress of Sheffield High School Mrs Woodhouse went with her, succeeding her as headmistress in 1878 and, during a reign of twenty years, building up the school from thirty-nine to more than 350 pupils. In 1898, after making a reputation as a teacher, administrator and a pioneer in the development of physical education and medical inspection, Mrs Woodhouse was transferred to Clapham High School and presided over its merger with the Middle School.

Another casualty was Miss Benson who was forced to resign from Oxford High School after a long period of illness. She recovered and in her late thirties contracted a romantic marriage with Andrew McDowall, the first permanent Secretary of the Company. McDowall owed his appointment to the influence of Sir James Kay-Shuttleworth who thought highly of him. He had looked forward to the post which he thought would be 'pleasant though badly paid'. Initially, he found it 'not altogether agreeable. . . . There are some ladies connected with the Company who are rather crotchety and a little difficult to keep in order, they are so unpractical.' He settled down, however, and remained in his post for thirty-five years. His wife had had one child and was expecting another when she applied for the headship of Bedford High School, which was not one of the Company's schools. Surprisingly in the circumstances she was appointed, but she died in childbirth, leaving her husband disconsolate.

The Council were always generous in the matter of sick leave realizing, sometimes too late, that a conscientious headmistress would drive herself too far. This was inevitable at a time when Council and heads had so few precedents to guide them, but long before the end of the century – in 1885 – the Council introduced a contributory pension scheme which relieved headmistresses of some of their anxieties. The retiring age was fixed at fifty-five, the Council reserving the power 'to defer retirement to sixty when they think it desirable'.

The standard of teaching in the schools was generally good but it varied from school to school according to the ability of the head-mistress and her staff. Every incentive was given to the girls to work. From 1873 onwards scholarships and prizes were offered to the schools and received by a grateful Council. The first was the Reid Scholarship – named after Mrs Reid in whose house the infant Bedford College was born – which provided free education at Bedford for two years.* In 1878 Lady Stanley offered a three-year scholarship of £50 a year at Girton, to be awarded to the pupil from any of the Company's schools to take the highest place in the College entrance examination, 'provided she passes the Examination to the satisfaction of the Committee of the College'. Scholarships to Notting Hill and Oxford High Schools had already been awarded by local residents, and in 1878 the great philologist and linguist Professor Max Muller offered Oxford High School a special scholar-ship – the 'Ada Scholarship' – in memory of a daughter who had died, to be awarded, after a special examination in German, for 'general proficiency and good conduct'. Then, too, there were the Company's scholarships, open to girls between fifteen and seven-teen who had been in a Company school for at least a year, and awarded on the recommendation of the Education Committee, a report from the headmistress and the results of the University or other annual examination, provided 'that no girl be elected without a certificate of previous good conduct and steady industry'. These scholarships – the highest academic award in a school – became the Trust Sixth Form Scholarships: several are awarded in each school for girls hoping to proceed to the university.

Each of the schools had its own individuality, a quality shown from the earliest days in the reports of the examiners and the Inspector and in articles in various school magazines.

From the outset Notting Hill under Miss Jones had enjoyed an exceptionally high reputation and was described in 1879 by the examiner of the Oxford and Cambridge Schools Board as 'excellent in all respects'.

Oxford High School, with pupils drawn in the main from

* Since discontinued.

University families, also had a good scholastic record. In other respects it was less satisfactory, at any rate in 1879 when complaints were received from local residents that 'the High School . . . does not teach manners [but] makes the girls rough and boyish. The behaviour of some of our girls in the street often justifies this complaint.' Since 1879 was the year in which the dynamic Miss Benson finally succumbed, it is possible that the lapse in school manners was due in some measure to her breakdown in health. Oxford's academic standard was maintained by Miss Bishop, who succeeded Miss Benson and who left in 1887 to become Principal of the Royal Holloway College, and also under her successor Miss Lucy Soulsby. Miss Soulsby, when asked before her appointment to state her educational qualifications, had replied 'None, but a clever mother'. After home teaching she had taught for two years at Cheltenham under Miss Beale. At Oxford she was remembered as competent if not great, 'a very Victorian figure both in the strength of her convictions and in her slightly over-strained emotional earnestness'. In later years the clever mother, who lived with her and attended daily prayers and all school functions, became something of an incubus. A member of the Council had to be deputed to tell the Headmistress that she must no longer allow her mother to be present at interviews with parents.

After 1879 Kensington (formerly Chelsea) High School also got into its academic stride. 'The School is an exceedingly good one,' reported the Oxford and Cambridge Schools Board Examiner in 1881. 'Particular Forms are sometimes checked for a time by the rapid influx of new girls; but the intellectual tone is very high.' The first move, from Chelsea to Cromwell Road, had not proved satisfactory: 'I cannot refrain from saying how unsuitable the present building is, from its great height, and the perpetual noise of passing wheels,' the Examiner declared two years later. He was most relieved when in 1887 the school was again moved, to quiet St Alban's Grove, for 'the excessive noise of trains and carts must have been a really terrible trial'.

The examiner found the same difficulty at Hackney and Clapton High School (later transformed into Clapton Middle – or Modern – School), 'where the noise of passing tramcars is a most decided element of evil'. Hackney must have been noisy within as well as without, for in 1880 the Council presented the school with a printing press. The Company's Inspector visiting it the following year, however, found the girls 'full of a laudable spirit of diligence'.

In Norwich, too, the girls worked under difficulties. The school moved in 1878 to the beautiful Assembly Rooms which, wrote the

Examiner, had been 'very successfully adapted'. It was a pity, he added, that 'the class-rooms upstairs are somewhat low in proportion to their size, and liable to an influx of heated air from below'. Nevertheless 'the girls gave their best attention, appeared interested in their work, and eager to do their utmost.' There were 'not many brilliant pupils', he admitted a few years later, 'but there is no reason to be discouraged'.

It was only natural that some reports should be more encouraging than others. In 1884 Sutton and Carlisle High Schools, both recently opened, were marked as extremely promising; so too, in 1887, was newly opened Sydenham, 'even though some girls are not as quick as those in the older schools'.

Wimbledon High School, the special protégé of Mary Gurney who lived in the district for many years, was 'one of the best I ever saw'. The school had come a long way since the opening day in 1880 when, according to one of the first pupils, twelve girls assembled, ranging in age from seven to sixteen. The older girls wore long dresses and one, a fourteen-year-old, sported 'a greeny-brown garb of skirt and Norfolk jacket – later she was known as "Froggie" '. Among the younger girls was one who 'had some delicacy and was allowed a foot muff for her feet'. The pupils' attainments varied, as the second mistress discovered when she gave the first lesson on an apple. 'At the end of the lesson notes were dictated, and it was found that four were unable to cope with anything so difficult, so four others wrote their own and those of the incapable.' To commemorate the occasion the school adopted an apple as its emblem.

Brighton and Hove, an older school, stood 'forward prominently for the general excellence of its work'. And at Bromley, another new school, if the Examiner could not praise the work he was 'much pleased with the happy look of the girls, and their great interest in amusements'. Bromley was soon forging ahead to become a hive of 'wonderful mental activity . . . and good teaching'. Ipswich was an example of 'good administration, diligence, and a sense of honour and responsibility'. At Portsmouth High School, which moved in 1885 to the purpose-built premises which it occupies to this day, he found it 'pleasant to see the well-ordered, ladylike and yet untrammelled way' in which the pupils behaved. Nottingham, one of the older schools, was 'well worthy of its high reputation'. Dulwich was full of 'thought, life, public spirit and brightness'. Bath showed 'signs of vigorous corporate feeling'. At Shrewsbury, only just getting into its stride in 1885, 'the order and discipline [were] exceptionally excellent'. The teaching of mathematics at Weymouth came in for 'special commendation'. At Tunbridge Wells, still a very small school, 'much interest seemed to be taken in games, and the drilling in the lower part of the School was admirable'. York High School was 'good in everything but numbers'.

There were always some black spots, and York High School presented a peculiar problem. In 1885 Mr Jowitt, the Inspector, reported that he had heard 'a good deal of the objection caused by social feeling in York to the older girls walking to School unprotected, and of the dreadful risk of their passing daily the same boys on *their* way to St Peter's School'. Many of the older girls had been removed from the school and of those who remained few returned for the afternoon preparation sessions. He could, he added, see 'no reason *within* the School' to account for the falling-off in numbers, but thought that if the headmistress, who had already been given a term's sick leave, 'had health and energy [she] might perhaps affect public opinions, in these matters'. The headmistress in question, who had already complained that she felt too languid to meet the parents of her pupils, roused herself to retaliate. 'I should like to have more time to go out and about. But this I am afraid is not to be hoped for. . . . In estimating the School I should like the Council to understand that no undertaking is ever pecuniarily successful in York. . . . No one who knows the town well ever dreamt a High School could be a great success here, and as for its being profitable, if it were it would be the only public undertaking in York which was, or ever had been, which was not likely.' York, she concluded, was a place 'with very little money and very little collective zeal for education or improvement'. In this she was proved wrong. After her resignation four years later York High School prospered for many years, one of its most successful features being the kindergarten opened in 1891 which gave some of the older girls their first year's training as kindergarten teachers.

Liverpool High School* (founded in 1880) also appeared something of a black spot, for Mr Jowitt reported in 1882 that it was 'in an exceedingly unsatisfactory condition as to tone, discipline and unity. Some of the Mistresses are evidently ill at ease, and the Staff is divided by jealousy and etiquette.' The headmistress blamed the trouble on the parents who bombarded her with requests, interfered on every possible occasion and treated her in a most high-handed way. Their daughters, she complained, were 'sharp

---

* Situated in Belvidere Road, the school was renamed the *Belvedere* School, Liverpool, in 1912. A request from the headmistress that the name of the road should be changed to Belvedere met with no response.

and cunning and indescribably turbulent'; they disregarded the rules and some of them had even taken to petty pilfering. The Inspector told the Council that 'unless an improvement is secured, the Liverpool High School will not long add to the reputation of the Girls' Public Day School Company'. His fears proved groundless. Two years later the unsatisfactory headmistress was replaced by her second-in-command Miss Huckwell who, according to one who knew her, looked 'lovely with her fair hair and green frock'. In order to get to know the girls Miss Huckwell taught every form in the school. She noted that the rules had been disregarded during her predecessor's rule and informed the girls that 'God would not love them and they would never go to Heaven if they did not obey the rules'. This warning was evidently taken to heart; and Miss Huckwell appears to have been a popular and stimulating teacher. By 1887 Mr Jowitt was able to report that the school was 'in a better and stronger intellectual condition than I have ever seen it before'.

This improvement was cemented by the arrival of Miss Rhys in 1903. Miss Rhys possessed great powers of leadership and organization, and during the nineteen years of her reign the school's traditions were upheld and successive problems were tackled and overcome.

In the meantime Miss Huckwell, Miss Rhys's predecessor, had been sent (in 1893) to take charge of the newly opened East Putney High School. There she surprised her pupils one morning by taking prayers clad in a bicycling outfit, an Eton jacket and a leather-bound skirt with straps protruding from the hem which she fastened under her shoes when riding. 'We were real Victorians', wrote one of her pupils, 'and rather prudish and I was deputed by the Form to ask if she considered it ladylike. She smiled and offered us lifts on her bicycle, and soon we were all clamouring for them.'

Miss Huckwell's successor at East Putney, Miss E. H. Major, was also a distinctive character. Vivacious, witty and informal, she was later to gain one of the prizes of the educational world – the Mistress-ship of Girton. Her appointment was celebrated at a dinner and she sat impassively through the complimentary speeches. Afterwards the headmistress of the school at the time, the brilliant, charming Miss M. G. Beard, asked her if she had felt embarrassed. 'I never listen on such occasions,' replied Miss Major. 'I always repeat *The Lay of the Last Minstrel* to myself instead.'

In the course of his school inspections Mr Jowitt had found a distinctive problem at Paddington and Maida Vale High School:*

* Originally called Maida Vale High School, it was renamed Paddington and Maida Vale in 1900.

this was the prevalence of Jewish pupils whose parents did not wish them to take any part in the religious instruction. Some Jewish families had lived in the district for many years and their daughters were 'remarkable for excellent behaviour'. Others must have been recent immigrants from the ghettos of Eastern Europe. These, said Mr Jowitt, came to school 'in an offensive condition both as to their persons and garments'. He was pleased to find in 1882 that when the senior pupils were told to learn by heart a speech from *Richard II* containing words 'repugnant to Jewish feeling' a request 'that another piece might be selected instead came from senior girls who were not Jewesses'. He did not consider that the headmistress was prejudiced but thought she was tactless in arranging for prize day to be held on the Jewish sabbath. Paddington had been ruled by the same head since its opening in 1877. By 1887 Mr Jowitt felt that she was beginning to lose her grip. The school had recently moved to new buildings and 'was not so clean as one would wish. I was repelled by seeing the front door opened by a very drab of a girl [a domestic servant] who had not even dispensed with the dishcloth she carried.' Two years later the headmistress gave the Council a chance to ask for her resignation. She was, she maintained, in good health and would be happy to continue in office but would resign if requested. She was: and she did!

When the girls in a particular school acquitted themselves well during inspections and examinations the headmistress concerned was congratulated: if not she was censured. Congratulations to the heads of Sydenham, Brighton and Hove, and Oxford High Schools in 1898, for example, were offset by a sinister note to the effect that the Education Committee were 'in communication' with the headmistress of Gateshead 'as to the bad results of the recent *viva voce* examination'.

The order and discipline so often singled out for praise was clearly exceedingly strict. Headmistresses, nervous at the prospect of having to control large numbers of girls and fearful of arousing local antagonism, were probably far more repressive than they need have been. They were especially insistent on the silence rule which prohibited talking in the cloakrooms, in the hall and on the stairs: any girl who disobeyed it without being caught was expected to report herself. So rigidly was the rule enforced at Gateshead that new girls who occasionally got lost in the building remained lost because they dared not break the rule by asking the way and no other pupil would break it by giving directions. Yet despite the strictness of the regime Miss Cooper, an earlier headmistress,

1879 to 1891 – was loved and respected by a succession of high-spirited girls.

The social position in the Company's schools was based on compromise. In some, children from poor homes were made welcome and settled down well; in others, a rule which forbade a girl to walk to or from school without the written consent of both parents was probably introduced to forestall complaints from middle-class parents. At Weymouth High School, however, Mr Jowitt had found in 1885 that 'the old evil custom of isolating each pupil from her fellows through a fear of social difficulties had disappeared', and he believed that the barrier had been 'broken down without any appearance of threatened ills'.

The strictness of the discipline was offset by the growing awareness that the girls needed an outlet for their energies in physical education. At a time when the Council were considering the provision of gymnastic apparatus most schools were excelling in 'musical drill', successor of the original calisthenics. By the mid-eighties the girls of Norwich High School were being drilled by an Army sergeant-major: his stentorian tones brought a nervous request from the headmistress to modulate his voice, which he took to mean that he might shout louder than ever. The gymnasium which, together with a studio and a laboratory, was built for Sheffield High School in 1884, was one of the first of its kind and was used as a prototype for gymnasia in many other schools.*

Athletic sports seem to have made their first appearance at Shrewsbury High School in 1888. A games club was founded at the school with a subscription of 1d a head. This soon had to be raised to 2d owing to the poor condition of the hockey sticks, which had to be replaced.

Physical education was especially dear to the heart of Miss Soulsby, the third headmistress of Oxford High School. In 1889 she invited parents and others to hear a lecture on the subject – 'one of great interest and importance' – given to the Teachers' Guild by the eminent medical pioneer and gynaecologist, Dr (later Dame) Mary Scharlieb, who claimed that girls were 'delicate in consequence of the neglect of their physical education' and strongly recommended 'all drill and gymnasium exercises, as well as plenty of fresh air, early hours and good food'. In 1891 Miss Soulsby was pressing for a gymnasium, and by 1897 a complete set of gymnastic apparatus had been installed in the school hall. In the meantime a games club

* The gymnasium is still in use. It is often visited by students from Physical Education colleges so that they can see one of the earliest examples of girls' school gymnasia in the country.

had been founded on the initiative of the parents and a ground was secured where the girls played cricket, lawn tennis, fives, and bat, trap and ball in summer, hockey, rounders, and prisoners' base in winter. The games were supervised by a parent 'or other suitable chaperon', and the management of the club was in the hands of a committee of parents and sixth-form girls. The club was a great success; and three years later the committee could proudly report that organized games, 'while they supply the interest and distraction that are needed to counterbalance the strain of mental work, do not make girls unladylike and . . . their association in the playground is no less natural and no less conducive to health of mind and body than association in the schoolroom'.

As early as 1874 the Council had accepted an offer made by a gymnastics instructor to teach one member of the staff in every school, and in the early 1880s the teachers at Croydon and Wimbledon High Schools shared a course of instruction, finding it extremely useful.

Initially opportunities were hampered by convention. A pupil who attended Clapham Middle School and found the teaching admirable remembered that there was 'no studio for the artless schoolgirl, no hockey, no netball, no "sport" (she might break a limb!), no swimming (she might get drowned!), no gymnasium'. Instead they had a drilling class 'without apparatus, no rope to climb, no wooden horse to vault over. Clad in a warm navy serge smock reaching to the knees and covering another garment called bloomers, we did simple exercises on the Swedish model, to strengthen the various parts of the anatomy. . . . Sometimes too we executed a kind of jugglery, casting an india-rubber ball from the right shoulder to the left and back again.'

Before the end of the century conditions had greatly improved and most schools were holding annual drill displays. In the summer of 1898, for example, thirty Kensington High School girls clad in loose blue and white blouses, blue serge skirts and red sashes 'went through a series of exercises', acquitting themselves well, 'handling dumb bells, poles, balls and clubs with surprising energy' despite the heat of the day, and winning 'deserved applause' for their dancing of the hornpipe.

The following year Mrs Woodhouse, the former headmistress of Sheffield who had recently been appointed head of Clapham High School, spoke of the need for medical inspection. 'It is essential that a pupil's sight, hearing and breathing be medically examined', she said, 'and that the conditions of throat, lungs, heart, spine and muscles be known, if we are rightly to estimate her capabilities for intellectual effort.' The examination should not be a once-and-for-all: the physical condition of a girl first examined at the age of eleven might be very different if she were to be re-examined at fourteen.

While the Council considered the physical needs of the children they were also giving thought to the need for such intellectual adjuncts as science laboratories. One of Miss Jones' pupils at Notting Hill, the expert on nutrition, Dame Harriette Chick, remembers that 'we had no laboratories at all and girls like myself who wanted to do Science had nothing. We learned Science almost theoretically but it was exceptionally well done', and her teacher, Miss Adamson, 'was the very first [woman] to take a B.Sc. in the London University'. Gateshead High School was equipped with a chemistry laboratory as early as 1886; in 1899 a new and improved laboratory was Kensington's reward for good work. Proposals were made at the same time to introduce a secretarial course in several schools. One such course, comprising book-keeping, shorthand and typing, which was started in the senior school of Streatham Hill (founded in 1887 as Brixton High School) developed into a successful secretarial sixth form which still exists today.

By the end of the century the majority of the schools were achieving considerable academic successes. In 1899 the Education Committee reported 'that of six Girton Scholarships Numbers 2, 3 and 5 had been taken by pupils at the Blackheath, Clapham and Nottingham Schools' while open scholarships to Somerville had been won by girls from Putney and Oxford High Schools. Until the end of her long life Lady Stanley eagerly welcomed successive winners of her Girton scholarship to her band of 'most choice children'.

The choice child of 1889 was a pupil at Notting Hill High School, Georgina Walrond (Mrs Buckler), an outstandingly able girl who 'with characteristic initiative and zest' convinced the headmistress of the necessity of forming a cricket eleven. Mrs Buckler served on the Council of the Trust for twenty-five years and for most of the time was Chairman of the Education Committee. She was a woman of immense vitality, a scholar of distinction, and a good administrator. Her benefactions to her old school were legion, among them an annual prize for Greek. When the school was moved in 1931 to larger premises in Ealing and renamed the Notting Hill and Ealing High School she arranged for the panelling in the hall of the old building (it is not a thing of beauty!) to be transferred to the new and also provided a covered way linking the hall with the dining-hut. During the autumn term of 1939 her house in Oxford was

77

handed over for the use of Kensington High School and Mrs Buckler, then aged seventy, made a gallant attempt to move the furniture out of the drawing-room herself.

Notting Hill High School had always been in the academic fore-front. By the time the indomitable Miss Jones retired in 1900 the school numbered over four hundred and a total of sixty-five open scholarships had been won to the Universities of Oxford, Cambridge and London. Miss Jones had earned the reputation of making her pupils work extremely hard but, as a Council member had pointed out a few years earlier, 'they do not seem any the worse for it . . . and every teacher of competence is only too glad, if she can, to obtain a post at Notting Hill School'.

In 1892 when Mr W. H. Stone (Chairman of the Council from 1877–96) presented Miss Jones with a diamond star and her portrait by Shannon he rightly praised her great contribution to education and looked back 'with respectful admiration' to all the other pioneer teachers who had overcome ignorance and prejudice to make their schools real centres of learning.

School prize days had long since become legion. There were also monster prize-givings attended by girls from all the Company's schools, several of them taking place in the presence of Princess Louise. In 1883 she brought off a coup, securing her brother the Prince of Wales (King Edward VII), who made a suitably platitudinous speech, and his wife (Queen Alexandra) who handed out the prizes. For this all-important occasion the girls sported different coloured rosettes, each school having its own distinctive colour* They wore their own dresses with the addition of white muslin fichus edged with lace, each a yard square, folded corner-wise, with the two points gathered into the waist. At the end of the formal proceedings there were refreshments for all, the Council having sanctioned the expenditure of 6d per head.

Princess Louise also attended prize-givings at a number of schools. In 1880, for example, she presided over the prize-giving and the official opening of Blackheath High School, the first of the Company's schools to be purpose built. The Princess's visit, according to the local paper, 'was evidently regarded with the liveliest satisfaction and interest by [the] inhabitants, who had taken

---

* In 1969 the Headmistress of Notting Hill and Ealing High School received through the post a dark red badge and a letter from a former pupil now living in California, who wrote: 'You might possibly be interested in this ring back to the days of Long Ago. My sister wore it at Notting Hill round about 1881 and I followed her some ten years later, still under "Jonah" at the end of her long reign . . .'

pains by means of a plentiful display of flags and other decorations to make the thoroughfares . . . look as attractive and inviting as possible. The streets were lined on either side . . . with an orderly and well-dressed crowd of people.' The Princess, who was met at the school gates by a detachment of the First Kensington Rifle Volunteers, was tastefully dressed in dark brown cashmere 'with a dolman of the same material trimmed with rich fur'. Her bonnet was made of bronze straw 'with puffings of cardinal silk, and ornamented on the left side with a flamingo's wing'. She was escorted over the building by Mr Stone, who indicated its principal features, chief among them a lofty central hall with access to all eight classrooms and balustraded staircases leading to the upper floor. We do not know if she was also shown the cloakrooms 'and heated chambers for drying wet clothing and umbrellas'. Nor do we know if the plaster cast of the Venus de Milo presented by the architect was yet in place.* Copies of the statue were also presented to other high schools and came in for some heavy criticism on the grounds of indecency. The great event at Blackheath was described with enthusiasm in the *Englishwoman's Review*. 'Upon entering the hall, the Princess was presented by (sic) a handsome bouquet by Miss Robertson, the first pupil in the Scool (sic), after which she took her place upon the platform, and formally declared the schoool (sic) open, by saying, "I have much pleasure in declaring this School open, and in wishing it every prosperity. May it be as successful as the last." '

In 1896, among her annual duties as President, the Princess with her husband attended the prize-giving at Norwich High School. 'The sight which met [their] gaze was exceedingly pretty,' wrote a reporter from the *Eastern Daily Press*. 'The children, dressed uniformly in white, with tan shoes and brown stockings, were ranged on either side of the room, in rows rising one above the other. The universe might safely be challenged to show a more refreshing vision of budding womanhood.' The Marquis of Lorne, congratulating the headmistress, Miss L. Gadesden, 'upon the excellent appearance of her pupils, said, "They have exhibited a grace of demeanour and a prudence of mind which fill the hearts of the Members of Parliament who are present with envy." '

* In 1916 the Finance Committee reported with regret that 'the life-size statue of the Venus of Milo in the Assembly Hall was broken by the Clock-winder in circumstances induced by his negligence'. As a result 'of his encounter with Venus of Milo the Clockwinder in question . . . had been in Hospital with a broken arm, and blamed the arrangements at the School for the accident'. The Committee, while repudiating the charge, recommended that the cost of repairs should not be laid at the Clockwinder's door.

In 1955 a former pupil at Birkenhead High School remembered that, at nine years of age, 'I disgraced myself, my family, and worst of all my school on the great day' of the prize-giving. She had made her curtsey and was waiting for her book prize when the Princess handed her a rolled-up certificate. 'As I hesitated to take it I heard a hoarse whisper from [the Headmistress], "the prizes got mixed up, take this now, you will get your book later on".' The child took the roll 'and marched away quite forgetting to walk backwards as I had been taught. There was an awful gasp of horror and I realized my enormity. So I turned and walked back to the Princess. Sad to relate the girl following me was just beginning her curtsey. I pushed her away, curtsied myself for the second time and walked away successfully backwards.'

The stage managing of these royal events must have put a great strain on local committees, headmistresses and girls: nevertheless they were a source of pride to all concerned.

1. *Above*: Admiral Shirreff's Daughters, left to right: Maria (later Mrs William Grey); Emily, Caroline (later Mrs Bowyer); Katherine (later Mrs Hilton). *Below*: Maria Shirreff.

2. Henrietta Maria, Lady Stanley of Alderley, at the time of her work for the foundation of the schools.

bove left: Mrs William Grey. *Right*: Miss Emily Shirreff. *Below left*: Lady ley of Alderley. *Right*: Miss Mary Gurney.

4. H.R.H. Princess Louise, President of the Women's Education Union and Patron of the schools until her death in 1939.

5. H.R.H. The Duchess of Gloucester, Patron of the Trust since 1940.

6. Miss Harriet Morant Jones, Headmistress of Notting Hill & Bayswater High School, 1873–1900.

Miss Dorinda Neligan, Headmistress of Croydon High School, 1874–1901.

7. Miss Ada Benson (later Mrs McDowall), Headmistress of Norwich High School, 1875, Headmistress of Oxford High School, 1875–9.

s Woodhouse, Headmisss of Sheffield High School, 79–98, Headmistress of ipham High School, 1898– 3.

8. *Above*: Ipswich High School; playground - the Giant Stride - about 1890.
Below: Streatham Hill & Clapham High School, Judo, 1971.

Chapter 6
Alarms

A sound academic standard was set in all the Company's schools. The standard was higher in some schools than in others, but the Council were insistent that in no circumstances should it be achieved by over-pressure. As early as 1875 the Chairman had pointed out that while the majority of the pupils would automatically enter for the University local examinations there must be no 'cramming' of a few girls at the top of the school to the detriment of the rest. Furthermore, as the schools were open to girls of all types the special needs of the backward girls must be taken into account.

It was easy to formulate principles, more difficult to ensure that they were put into practice. In 1880 a warning note was sounded by one of the Examiners of the Oxford and Cambridge Schools Board. 'May I be pardoned for expressing a fear lest these good Schools should suffer from over-examination?' he said. 'Some of the forms come to me exhausted, having passed the Oxford Local Examination in June, and since done paper work for the Board before encountering this serious ordeal of a *viva voce* Examination. Some even contemplate the Cambridge Local in December. Much examining stimulates bad Schools, but cripples good ones.' At about the same time it was clear from the Inspector's reports that in several schools the girls in the lower forms were being neglected in order that the girls at the top could be specially coached. In one school – Kensington – there was no such trouble. 'The Head Mistress', wrote Mr Jowitt, 'is of opinion that in her School there is very little danger of girls suffering through over-much brain work, and remarks that if the four hours' morning teaching is too long children offer a passive resistance to further instruction by getting into a sleepy condition, which preserves their brains from any ill results.' The Council took the problem of cramming and overwork very much to heart: headmistresses were instructed to issue time-sheets to be filled in by pupils and signed by their parents, and were told to ensure that the work allotted and the time allowed were 'properly apportioned'.

No headmistress, however vigilant, could be sure that an

F

ambitious or over-conscientious girl would not exceed the time limit or get her parents' signature under false pretences. Inevitably, if this happened and a girl became over-tired there were complaints. In 1881 the Council received a memorial signed by thirty-four doctors who stated that in their knowledge cases had occurred 'of permanent injury to pupils from overwork and suggesting a re-arrangement of the hours of study'. One of the doctors attended a meeting of the Education Committee by invitation. After questioning him the Chairman came to the conclusion that he had produced 'no substantial proofs' in support of the allegation; and further that the memorial had been drawn up several years earlier and kept in reserve for a suitable occasion.

The problem recurred from time to time during the next twenty years. In 1907, for example, the intellectual and highly respected Miss Haig Brown, headmistress of Oxford High School for thirty years, rightly complained that in their enthusiasm for the maximum percentage of marks children sometimes came to school when for reasons of health they should have stayed at home. This, she remarked, 'showed a grave defect in home discipline'. Miss Haig Brown achieved academic triumphs for her girls as a matter of routine and without subjecting them to any pressure. Following her advice, the Council instructed all headmistresses to be 'on their guard against overpressure from eagerness'. Two years later another respected headmistress, Miss Bell of Sutton, complained not so much of overwork but of 'the danger of overstrain and excitement in school life'. She thought that the existence of a variety of school societies and the emphasis on games and physical edu-cation were too absorbing: she hoped, she said, to see 'fewer societies and more dullness generally in school life'.

An accusation often brought against the Council was that it kept too much power in its own hands. In 1877 the committee of share-holders which had been formed in connection with the establish-ment of Clapham Middle School in 1875 made a strong bid for representation on the Council. In a middle – or modern – school the fees were lower than those in a high school, ranging at Clapham from £6 to £10 a year. The curriculum, though more limited than a high school's, comprised English language and literature, French, geography, arithmetic, book-keeping, English history, physiology, class singing and elementary drawing; with Latin, German, music, algebra, elementary mathematics and physical science as extra subjects. The Company had offered to open a high school in the district in addition to the Middle School but had been informed by the local committee that it was not wanted.

82

When Samuel Morley M.P., took the chair at the Company's Annual General Meeting on February 28, 1877, he was aware that a number of carefully selected shareholders had received a circular soliciting their support for a proposal that local committees should be represented on the Council. In moving the adoption of the report he said that as a member of the middle classes he was glad to see that so many parents were anxious for their daughters as well as their sons to be well educated; but added a warning that since the education of 'the lower classes was decidedly and rapidly improving' the education of the middle classes must be 'attended to' or the lower classes would 'soon be treading on the heels of those professing to be socially above them'.

The Chairman of the Council, Charles Roundell*, who seconded the adoption of the report, said that he 'hoped to mature' a scheme to bring local committees of shareholders into closer touch with the Council, possibly by inviting a particular member to be present at a meeting at which matters concerning the school in which he was interested were to be discussed.

This suggestion was not nearly radical enough for one of the Clapham school's three trustees, Mr Bidder Q.C., who weighed in with a caustic attack on the failure of the Company to provide any schools – apart from Clapham – for the 'lower middle class'. He congratulated the Council on the success of the high schools but, he said, 'they gave plum cake to those who asked for bread'. He was convinced that the Council were planning to open a high school in the district and to close the Middle School despite the heavy demand for places; and this fact alone demonstrated the need for co-operation between the Council and the local committees. He therefore moved that the committees should be represented on the Council, and his resolution was supported by another trustee, General (later Sir Richard) Strachey, the father of, among other famous children, Lytton Strachey.

Charles Roundell replied that the Council 'felt obliged to meet the resolution with determined opposition'. Mr Bidder had not seen fit to send his circular to members of the Council, and they had learned only by accident of his suggestion to secure the election of Mrs Strachey as a Council member in place of Miss Mary Gurney who, according to the circular, 'lived at Wimbledon, had no local interest in the schools, and whose whole interest in the Company was confined to two shares'. It was perfectly correct, he said, that the Council wished to open a high school in Clapham but

* He resigned later in that year after seeing the Company through five difficult years and was succeeded by Mr W. H. Stone.

they had no intention of closing the Middle School: all they wished to do was to move it from an old and inconvenient house (Clarence House, once the home of Captain Cook) to better premises. He was especially concerned about the quite unwarranted attack on Miss Gurney. It was true, he said, that she lived in Wimbledon where there was as yet no high school,* but her attendance at Council and committee meetings was exceedingly regular, and she took the greatest interest in the welfare of the existing schools. Mary Gurney, one of four retiring members of the Council eligible for re-election, was re-elected with acclamation. She was to serve the interests of the schools for another forty years.

Mr Roundell then put forward an amendment to Mr Bidder's resolution to the effect that the Company should 'take steps with a view to placing the Council in communication with local representatives'.[1] General Strachey seconded the amendment, which was endorsed by the meeting, and Mr Bidder withdrew his resolution. The trustees did not withdraw their support of the Company. General Strachey remained a shareholder, as did his wife and, later, his children Lytton and Philippa.

Nevertheless, the main point at issue remained: the local committees continued to question Council decisions and to clamour for representation. Charles Roundell may well have hoped 'to mature' a scheme for closer co-operation but he never achieved it. In fact, as the Secretary of the Company wrote to the Board of Education in 1900, the committees of shareholders were only kept in being because 'we find it useful at times to have bodies to consult when a question arises on which local opinion is valuable'.[2]

In the meantime the demand for a high school to be opened in Clapham had been growing. The trustees of the Middle School were persuaded to withdraw their opposition to the scheme, and Clapham High School came into being in 1882. Initially the High School creamed the Middle School of its brightest pupils, but the balance was soon redressed and the Middle School remained in existence until 1898 when it was merged with the High School. By that time the Council had come to the conclusion that it would be wiser always to open a high school in advance of a middle school. In the future a middle school would be opened only if it appeared likely to fill a need not already met by the high school.

During the 1880s the Company was involved in one other dispute which received an airing in public. This concerned the conditions and pay of assistant teachers, whose salaries ranged from £70–£90 a year for an untrained assistant to £135–£200 for a senior assistant.

* Wimbledon High School was opened in 1880.

In December 1888, the Chairman of the Council drew attention to a letter published in the *Pall Mall Gazette* under the unfortunate heading: 'Are the Girls' Public Day School Company Sweaters?' The letter (it was signed 'Emily R. King', a name unknown to members of the Council) alleged that assistant teachers were being exploited under a sweating system 'as bad as any at the East-end [of London] which has evoked the sympathies of the public'; that they were obliged to work long hours for pitifully low salaries, and that the Company was deliberately reducing the number and salaries of the teachers in order to provide shareholders with a 9 per cent dividend.

These charges were patently untrue, wrote Maria Grey, in a letter to the *Gazette* which showed her concern for the teachers and also her sense of responsibility towards the shareholders. The salaries paid by the Company compared favourably with those paid in similar schools, 'as proved by the fact that the Girls' Public Day School Company's schools always command the pick of the profession, and that for every vacant post there are tens [even] scores of applicants. I am not saying', she continued, 'that I think the salaries satisfactory, and with all my heart I wish they could be raised; but they stand high in market price. . . .' The suggestion of overwork was ridiculous. Teachers had breaks during the day amounting to nearly two hours and their weekends were completely free. 'This', she wrote, 'does not look much like sweating.' Finally, at no time had the shareholders received a dividend higher than 5 per cent and during difficult years they had been content to receive no dividend at all. Nevertheless, as she explained to another correspondent who suggested that salaries might be increased if the dividend were to be reduced and fees in the schools were raised, the low scale of fees was part of the Company's 'contract with the public. . . . I for one should consider it a breach of faith to raise them, unless we at the same time started a Middle School . . . near each High School, with a narrower curriculum and much lower fees.' Indeed, 'the fees you think so low are felt to be very heavy by parents in the classes who most want such an education as our High Schools give their daughters.'

This was no exaggeration: the records of Council meetings are punctuated by parental complaints about fees. Several times during the 1880s the question of raising fees to meet ever rising expenses was debated, but the Council was most reluctant to act and on each occasion a decision was postponed.

In the face of rising costs, however, the Council with its Finance and Education Committees was obliged to insist on the observance of the strictest economy in the schools. They must have been heartened in 1893 to receive from a teacher at Dulwich High School an unprecedented request for her salary to be reduced by £50 a year, 'her work being less than it was, and the Head Mistress supporting her request'.

The financial problems persisted, but in other ways the Company's work prospered. By the end of the century most of the outstanding problems had been overcome, and the schools had a magnificent record of achievements to their credit. In spite of attitudes which today may seem snobbish and uncompromising, the schools had begun to produce, within their own communities, a genuine social mixture and were breaking down the old barriers of class and status. Their impact on the education of girls was powerful. As Sir Joshua Fitch wrote in 1890, the formation of the Company 'has perhaps had a larger influence on the improvement of feminine education than any single measure . . . [familiarizing] parents with institutions of a comparatively new type. . . . There is hardly an important town in England which has not its Public Day School for Girls. . . . The whole system has greatly helped to raise the standard of instruction, and to encourage the due training and preparation of highly qualified teachers.' And, as an additional point in its favour, the Company had 'induced many middle-class parents to quit the seminaries',[3] which offered only the most superficial education, and to allow their daughters to mix freely with girls from other social classes.

Chapter 7

The End of an Era

It will be remembered that from the very beginning Maria Grey and Emily Shirreff had been concerned with the need to provide a supply of adequately trained teachers and that it was partly on their initiative that the Froebel Society was able to form a branch in England in 1874. Emily Shirreff was the second President of the Society: her generosity with money she had inherited from family friends helped it through its early difficulties, and her papers on the theory and practice of kindergarten teaching impressed a largely indifferent public with the necessity of training teachers of young children.

By 1875 – thanks mainly to the work of Sir James Kay-Shuttleworth – the need for trained teachers in elementary schools had been universally recognized, but the same need in secondary schools had not been generally acknowledged, and as yet there was no more than a tiny nucleus of university women willing and able to teach.

A start had been made in 1873 when, at the suggestion of Miss Doreck and Miss Buss, a training course was founded at the College of Preceptors under Joseph Payne. The National Union hoped to provide facilities for training students in the theory and practice of teaching in all the Company's schools but in many cases this did not prove practicable although most of them found room for a few student-teachers. The Teachers' Training and Registration Society founded by the National Union in 1876 with Lady Stanley as President then took on the task. 'Teachers of both sexes were contemplated', wrote Maria Grey, 'but the Council felt that the first claim upon them was that of women . . . and in May 1878, their first Training College for Teachers in Middle and Higher Schools for Girls'[1] was opened in Bishopsgate in London with four students. Bishopsgate had been chosen because there was a large girls' school in the district which the students could use as a practising school. The infant college soon outgrew its premises and in 1885, with fifty-three students, it was moved to Fitzroy Square.

In that year it was christened the Maria Grey Training College, a name which it bears to this day.*

The title was conferred on the college in 1892, and the news was conveyed to Mrs Grey by Miss Buss, a member of the council. 'I am very glad to tell you', she wrote, 'that "our" Training College is to retain its name, the one by which it has always been known and the one you bear. Women who worked in the early days of the movement for the improvement of Women's Education know the deep debt they owe you both for the splendid work you did in *the* cause and the untiring energy and goodness with which you fought in what was then almost a forlorn hope. I wish I could express a small part of my admiration and respect in proper terms. But I really mean what I have said.'

It was indeed true, as Sir Joshua Fitch had remarked, that the Girls' Public Day School Company had fostered 'the due training and preparation of highly qualified teachers'. By 1890 the schools were also in a position to recruit university women. As early as 1886 Miss F. Gadesden, headmistress of Blackheath High School and sister of the headmistress of Norwich, claimed that the supply of teachers from Girton and Newnham was becoming plentiful. So, too, were the girls, many of whom, with the object of teaching, went on from school to the universities or to teacher training colleges.†

Maria Grey had long since retired from active work. In 1877, so she wrote, 'an accident I had . . . while out riding with Lord Aberdare . . . began my breakdown'. She did not say whether or not they were riding in a carriage but the mind boggles at the thought of the staid and elderly Mrs Grey on horseback. Lord Aberdare, who was President of the Council of the Company from 1882 until his death in 1895, apparently suffered no ill effects from the accident, but Maria Grey never fully recovered. 'I got patched up again', she wrote, 'and broke down again more than once but, at last, I had to take to my bed . . . and though I recovered from the serious illness which kept me there for three weeks, I never recovered from the nervous prostration which preceded and followed it.' An interesting commentary on the psychosomatic nature of many of the sisters' illnesses is that the moment Maria Grey collapsed Emily Shirreff regained her health – at least to the extent of becoming 'the comparatively able-bodied one [although] she was, as usual, persecuted by her gouty headaches'. In this context, however, it

---

* It later moved to Brondesbury where it still occupies premises, but the main part of the college is now at Twickenham.

† Now colleges of education.

must be remembered that other Victorian women – chief among them Florence Nightingale – took to their beds in times of strain.

The sisters spent several months in Rome, Maria 'crippled by spinal weakness'. In 1878, when the Company presented Maria Grey with a casket and an address of thanks for all her work Emily could give only a poor account of her sister's health. As she wrote to Frances Mary Buss, who had added her own tribute: 'I may honestly say that the receipt of that address, and the additional gratification of seeing yours and Miss Beale's name attached to it, gave my sister the only real pleasure she has felt during the weary months of this year. The less she hopes ever to regain her power of work the more she values that testimony to the worth of her past work. . . . It is not perhaps reasonable, when sixty is long past,* to mourn that an active career is stopped short, but you know better than any one how, in dealing with education, one must still feel that no one worker can be spared – do we not know how all the best are over-worked?'[2]

Princess Louise was very solicitous about the invalid's health. In 1879 she wrote from Canada, where her husband was Governor-General: 'I am so grieved to hear . . . that you have returned from your journey abroad, no better than when you left. This is very sad news, and let me assure how much I feel for you.' She was much touched, she added, by a letter which Mrs Grey had sent her on behalf of the Council. 'Let me assure you, that though away from home, I continue to take a lively interest in the work which has been so well begun, and which has become so powerful and wide spread, and that I shall always be ready to support and help their efforts as much as lies in my power to do so.'

On her return to London the Princess offered some medical advice. 'I have been thinking, and thinking what it could be – I told you, and now I believe it is Sulphonal? for sleeplessness.' She enclosed a prescription and a bottle of the medicine but warned Mrs Grey that she must on no account take it without her doctor's permission.

At that time the Princess must herself have been in need of a sleeping draught. In 1880 she was involved in an extremely unpleasant accident: while in Canada she had half fallen out of a sleigh and was dragged by the hair for several minutes, losing one of her ears. According to the Queen, the shock of the accident produced in the Princess an aversion to married life: from then onwards she spent as much time as she decently could away from her husband.

* Not so very long past: Maria Grey was sixty-two.

Although confined to her bed or her sofa Maria Grey was perpetually busy with needlework and watercolour sketches. She made a special present for the Princess who wrote to thank her for 'the beautiful book-marker, [of] your own devising and made by your own dear hands'. The Princess added that she would have come to thank her in person, 'but I am laid up with great pain in bed, from a chill'. She had clearly grown very fond of Mrs Grey, who was thirty years her senior, and called regularly on the sisters when she was in London.

Mrs Grey must have sent out a whole batch of watercolour sketches as Christmas presents in 1891. One went to the Princess, who apologized for not acknowledging it at once. She had, she said, been too ill to write straight away, and when she recovered too busy designing scenery for some tableaux to be performed before the Queen. Other sketches were sent to the headmistresses of the Company's schools. 'Dear Mrs Grey your little sketch is sweet and fresh in itself', wrote Miss Neligan from Croydon High School, 'but the fact that you remember me so well . . . is a very grateful thought.'

The following year, having noticed from the *Chronicle** of Liverpool's Belvedere School that photographs and drawings were needed, Mrs Grey sent the headmistress a photograph of the Forum at Rome and a drawing made from a sketch which she had painted forty-six years earlier on the spot. 'I hope the girls will care for it', she wrote, 'not for its artistic merit certainly – but as done for them on my bed which I never leave now, by my shaky old hand of seventy-six, to give them a lasting remembrance of my affectionate interest in them and the School . . .'

Until the late 1880s Mrs Grey had continued to write. She provided a lengthy chapter, 'The Women's Educational Movement', for a symposium on *The Woman Question in Europe* which was published in 1883; and in 1888 she completed a book of her own, *Last Words to Girls*. Her reflections, she admitted, 'have no pretensions to originality, for they are only the statement of well-known truths and principles, I might say the re-statement, for there is nothing here, so far as principles are concerned, which was not laid down by my sister, Emily Shirreff, and myself, in our joint work, *Thoughts on Self-Culture*, published nearly forty years ago'.[3]

Even though the book is 'the mixture as before' it shows how well the sisters' original thinking had stood the test of time. It is

* Most of the schools started magazines of their own in the early days which reveal glimpses of a vanished school world. Some have produced their own histories.

also, as the work of an elderly woman, a combination of optimism and nostalgia. 'The increased independence of women, and the present fashion of camaraderie between the sexes in games and sports', she wrote, 'has pretty well exploded the absurdities of my young days, when the affectation of weakness and cowardice, if you had them not, was supposed to be the surest of feminine wiles to win masculine favour. We have now the exactly opposite affectation of mannishness, adoption – as far as possible without absolute abandonment of the sacred petticoat – of masculine fashions of attire, of habits, including smoking and slang, of sports such as hunting and shooting.' She was uncertain, she continued, if the young men preferred this 'to the mysterious charm that stirred their fathers' pulses' but she inferred that 'while the female chum suits very well to play with, they want a womanly woman in the serious relations of life'.[4] She disliked the modern habit of over-indulging children and encouraging them to interrupt adult conversation but, in homes with adequate domestic staff, she felt it was quite right for mothers who wished to do so to undertake part-time work. Every woman, she added, should prepare herself by study, and by social work where possible, for the day when at long last she would qualify for the vote.

Copies of *Last Words to Girls* were despatched to all the schools. Headmistresses hastened to reply, most of them paying the author the doubtful compliment of assuring her that as yet they had had no time to do more than dip into it. One or two of them had read it thoroughly. The headmistress of Wimbledon High School, Miss Edith Hastings, wrote that the book 'embodies all that I should most wish to impress on the girls, and what I have often and often felt I had failed to bring home to them. It is most precious, too, as being a clear declaration from the first founder of the Schools, of the high aim that we mistresses are expected to keep before us – we are much tempted to lose sight of it in eagerness for success and distinctions belonging to scholarship only.' The headmistresses all enquired affectionately after Mrs Grey's health and regretted that she was no longer well enough to visit them. In fact, her last appearance seems to have been in 1884 when she was present at the prize-giving at Bromley High School and spoke with her usual conviction of the importance of continuing education. 'I have heard that some connected with the School . . . have talked about "finishing" here, of coming to this school "to be finished",' she said. 'All I can say is that anything that can be finished in the few short years of school life must be so poor and mean a thing that it might as well not have been begun. . . .' By 1888, however, Mrs

Grey had returned to her strict seclusion: as Miss Alger of Dulwich High School phrased it – somewhat infelicitously in the circumstances, 'Your words and your work can never die. May I hope that this thought will console you when you can only rest or suffer.'

Among the letters Mrs Grey received was one from Miss M. E. Bishop, headmistress in turn of Chelsea and Oxford, and now Principal of the Royal Holloway College. Miss Bishop, who had only enjoyed 'a surreptitious dip' into *Last Words*, wrote that Holloway had 'quite an exceptionally nice set of students, mostly from High Schools. If any one maintains that High Schools don't train morally as well as mentally let them come to me to be enlightened.'

Some nine years later Maria Grey took part (from her sofa) in a fierce debate on the future of the Royal Holloway College. The College owed its existence to the generosity of Thomas Holloway, a wealthy pill maker who, so he had told Mrs Grey in 1875, had bought a site near Egham in Surrey for a 'Ladies' University' which he proposed to build 'in a style and size superior to anything of the kind to be found in Europe – and this regardless of expense'. Any one who has seen Holloway College will agree that Mr Holloway was as good as his word. He did not, he added, intend to endow the college, for he did not wish it to be said that 'the ladies are paupers'. His intention was that his 'Ladies' University', which was opened by Queen Victoria in 1886, should be an independent institution, conferring its own degrees. For the first ten years of its existence students at Holloway were prepared for the degrees of London University and also for the Oxford examinations: but in 1897 an attempt was made to transform it into a separate university for women. A conference was therefore convened by the governors of the College to consider the question.

The chairman was that true friend of girls' education, James Bryce. He had been an Assistant Commissioner on the Schools' Inquiry Commission of 1864 and more recently, in 1894, as Chairman of a Royal Commission (the Bryce Commission) set up to consider the best means of establishing a well-organized system of secondary education in England, he had paid a tribute to the Girls' Public Day School Company.

The Company together with the Church Schools Company, was invited to send representatives to the conference which was to be held in December 1897. On July 1st a letter appeared in *The Times* signed by 151 members of the Association of Head Mistresses including the heads of the high schools, deploring the proposal to turn the college into a university. Millicent Fawcett, the suffrage leader, who strongly opposed the proposal, urged Mary Gurney, one of the Company's representatives (the other being the Chairman of the Council), to ask Maria Grey to intervene. Mrs Grey agreed and sent a letter to James Bryce. 'I venture to hope', she wrote, 'that you still remember my name . . . and will, therefore, understand how anxiously I am watching the movement in favour of a University for women. I look on this proposal as fatal to the best interests of women's education and as such would oppose it to the utmost; but my bed-ridden condition now and for years past leaves me only the use of my pen.' The creation of a women's university, she continued, could 'only make the higher education of women simply ridiculous in the eyes of all those who really understand what a University means and what gives value to its degrees. I venture to think that this is, in fact, the chief recommendation of the proposal to a large number of its male supporters, besides the additional argument it gives them for excluding women from the degrees of the Universities for Men . . .'*

James Bryce replied that he would read the letter aloud at the conference, 'for no one has better earned the right to speak with authority on this question than you have. I may say between ourselves that my own view . . . quite agrees with that you have so forcibly expressed.'

Mrs Grey's letter was duly read and, as Mary Gurney wrote to her, 'loudly applauded'. James Bryce spoke against the proposal, and its supporters showed a most welcome divergence of opinion. 'Mrs Fawcett opened the debate excellently . . . saying how resolved Cambridge friends of women's education are to adhere to present lines . . .' Mary Gurney herself took part in the discussion. 'I referred to the position of *our* girls at Holloway, the students, and the need of *recognized* examinations for them, and also to the work of the Women's Education Union towards opening universities.' All in all, she concluded delightedly, 'it was thought that the proposals are *doomed*'. And so they were: the decision was made to perpetuate the connection with the University of London.

By the end of the century the era of the founders of the Girls' Public Day School Company was coming to an end. Alone among the quartette Mary Gurney had many working years ahead, to be remembered well into the 1900s as 'an active elderly lady who entertained Head Mistresses to tea, who occasionally appeared on the platform at prize-givings and who frequently visited [Portsmouth

* Although the degrees of London University were open to women Oxford and Cambridge still lagged behind. Oxford came into line in 1920 but Cambridge did not admit women to degrees on equal terms with men until 1948.

High] School and took a keen interest in all its activities,' as she did indeed in the activities of all the other schools.

Lady Stanley died in 1895: she was in her late eighties and, as Maria Grey wrote, had been 'the dearest of those [friends] made late in life'. She had kept her seat on the Council until her death, and had served assiduously on the Company's committees, including one on physical exercises to which she was elected at the age of eighty-one.

In 1897 Emily Shirreff died. Despite all the years of ill-health – real and imaginary – she had lived to the age of eighty-three, when her mind, wrote her sister, 'broke down under the stress of bodily disease, and the cloud settled upon it not to lift again on this side of the grave'. Among the many wreaths which covered the coffin at her funeral was one which Mrs Grey found especially touching: it was from Kensington High School, where three of her great-nieces were pupils. In a letter to the school she referred to Emily as an example and an encouragement to the young. 'She had none of the educational advantages you enjoy . . . She had no home facilities or helps for study . . . but she made the opportunities she did not find and her work remains to show to what purpose she studied . . .' One of the three great-nieces recalled her great-aunts Emily and Minnie (as Maria was called) as recently as 1969: Emily, her favourite, was entertaining and amusing, a wonderful companion to children; Minnie, in bed or on the sofa, was more remote.

Among the many letters of condolence was one from Princess Louise, who wrote touchingly of the loss of 'your dear, and constant loving companion'. Maria Grey felt the loss acutely, and after her sister's death she never left her bedroom. At eighty-one, she was convinced that her own death was imminent. In fact she lived almost ten years longer, feebler in body but with an unclouded mind and a face which had softened and mellowed with age. In the autumn of 1905 she wrote in her own hand to one of her great-nieces, enclosing a birthday present of 10s 6d. 'I hope to hear . . . that you have received it,' she added. 'It goes with the dear love and the heart's blessings of your old, old Great Aunt Minnie.'

A year later, she died in her ninety-first year. And, as the *Guardian* correspondent aptly wrote: 'Few have been permitted to see so large an ingathering from the seed they have sown.' All the many friends who were present at the funeral 'rejoiced in the midst of their mourning as they realized how truly it might be said of her that her "labour had not been in vain in the Lord".'

Chapter 8

Company into Trust

The Girls' Public Day School Company greeted the twentieth century with a monster prize-giving at the Albert Hall in May 1900. Princess Louise, who was to have presented the awards, was in mourning for her father-in-law the Duke of Argyll and her place was taken by the Princess of Wales, who was accompanied by her husband and their daughter Princess Victoria. 'The prettiest sight possible to be seen,' the *Daily Graphic* reported. 'As the Princess passed through the avenue of her welcomers the white frocks on either side of her curtsied, as the yellow corn curtsies when the breeze sweeps through it! And how they sang the National Anthem! They sang it right through – "frustrate their knavish tricks, confound their politics!" – there were no pro-Boers at this meeting – and the full-throated loyalty was a pleasant sound to hear.' A more sober report, in the *Daily Telegraph*, mentions the 'large badges in the distinctive colours of each school . . . worn by every girl on her shoulder. The whole of the vast arena was occupied by the girls who were presently to be rewarded.' The largest single contingent – eighty-seven prize-winners – came from Notting Hill High School; Blackheath, 'now the biggest institution under the Company', sent sixty-nine; and Kensington, Croydon, Clapham, South Hampstead, Highbury, Paddington, Dulwich, Wimbledon, Bromley, Sutton, Streatham Hill, Sydenham and East Putney together mustered six hundred. As each group of prize-winners came forward their head-mistress was presented to the Princess by Lady Frederick Cavendish, who had been a member of the Council for nearly thirty years. 'Only once', the *Telegraph* continued, 'was there a break in the long line of white-clad girls passing before the Princess, who had the sweetest smile for each one', and that was an unfortunate child dressed in deep mourning. 'One of the winners was of Parsee extraction.* And last of all came the one representative of the male

* No comment was passed on this phenomenon; nor is it likely that the Prince and Princess of Wales remembered a blunder made by the Prince at a prize-giving at the North London Collegiate School in 1879. 'Miss Buss, is not she

95

sex in an exceedingly tiny boy from a kindergarten class, and the Princess laughingly stooped to pat him on the shoulder and to call him a good little fellow.'

The vote of thanks was proposed by the President of the Company, Lord Spencer, seconded by the Chairman of the Council, Mr (later Sir William) Bousfield, and supported by Sir Alfred Lyall. 'I do not think I can say anything to you which is new', said the Prince of Wales when he rose to reply, 'especially after what has already been said by the speakers preceding me.' However, he bravely embarked on his prepared speech about the achievements of the Company and its schools. 'Young ladies', he concluded, 'I have nothing more to say to you, either in the name of the Princess or myself, save that we sincerely hope that you will all go forward in the world happy, and with the knowledge that you have been well instructed in those branches of education which will be of such value in later life.' In conclusion the Prince reminded them of the Company's motto, the quotation from Tennyson's *The Princess*: 'Knowledge is now no more a fountain sealed.'

At the beginning of the century the Company was responsible for thirty-three schools with upwards of seven thousand pupils. There was one school still to come, Birkenhead High School, opened in 1901 and soon to keep pace with the older establishments; while four had been closed – Weymouth, Newton Abbot, Hackney and Clapton, and Swansea – partly owing to competition from other schools but chiefly because of the migratory nature of the population. 'Quite marvellous has been the effect of the movement,'[2] wrote Dorothea Beale in the last year of her life. She was right: it had fulfilled its founders' highest hopes.

The success and popularity of the schools was, however, involving the Company in additional financial problems. The highly qualified teachers now available had to be adequately paid. New buildings were needed, for houses acquired in the 1870s and 1880s were antiquated and far too small. Better equipment was also needed, science laboratories and gymnasia, to say nothing of cloakroom and lavatory accommodation. The Company was ready to increase its nominal capital, but even so it was clear that there would never be enough to go round unless school fees were raised, a step which the Council were very reluctant to take. They therefore decided to apply for grants from public funds.

Certain grants for educational purposes had been available since

Indian?' he asked the headmistress as a dark-skinned girl passed in the procession. 'She comes from Jamaica,' replied Miss Buss. 'Oh, West Indian, then!' exclaimed the Prince, not at all put out by his mistake.[1]

the middle of the nineteenth century. In 1841 the Board of Trade began to give financial help to Schools of Design, and in 1853 this help was extended to science instruction, the grants being administered by the Department of Science and Art which had been set up for the purpose by the Board of Trade. Three years later this Department was transferred to the newly-formed Education Department but in 1864, under a separate charter, it was allowed to resume responsibility for the administration of the grants.

By 1895 schools receiving grants for science teaching were also required to provide a certain amount of literary and other instruction. In 1897 the restriction which had previously confined the award of grants to the industrial sections of the community was lifted; and this meant that many schools offering more advanced education began to qualify for grants in respect of their science teaching, although grants were not available to schools carried on for private profit. On the other hand, schools owned by companies paying dividends of 5 per cent or less were eligible, and in 1898 the Articles of Association of the Girls' Public Day School Company were amended to preclude the payment of dividends of over 4 per cent, a change unlikely to cause hardship to shareholders who had never expected – and seldom received – any more. The Council then proceeded to make a successful application for grants to the schools in respect of the science teaching, which included mathematics. Twelve schools qualified for grant in 1899, the total sum amounting to £280; twenty-seven qualified in 1900; twenty-nine in 1903. In order to qualify a school had to be equipped with a committee of managers, but in the case of the Company's schools the Department was asked to recognize the Council as the relevant committee. By 1903 grants were also being awarded in respect of the teaching of art and these too were earned by the Company's schools.

The grants were no longer paid by the old Science and Art Department. It will be remembered that the Bryce Commission of 1894 had considered the problems of creating an integrated system of secondary education. Its recommendations had resulted in 1899 in the establishment of a single central authority – the Board of Education – to direct public education as a whole and to co-ordinate the work of the various agencies supplying it, including the Education and the Science and Art Departments. Grants to schools were in future to depend on inspection by the new Board of Education's Inspectors.

In January 1901, the Board indicated that if formal applications were submitted an inspection of each of the schools of the Girls'

Public Day School Company would be conducted. The cost would not exceed 2s per pupil, and the Board were willing to spread the inspections over three years if the Company considered that the total cost would be too heavy to bear in a single year. The arrangement was accepted and the first inspections were arranged on this basis.

In future, in place of the basically friendly and helpful inspections by the Company's nominee, the Rev. Mr Jowitt, the schools had to face a searching and exhaustive official investigation, lasting three days in the case of the larger schools, two days in the smaller. 'The inspection will cover the administration of the School, the condition of the School buildings, and the Education given throughout the School,' wrote the Board's representative to Mr Bousfield on January 30th. The Administrative Inspection would include a conference between the Inspectors and the Council which, it was later explained, 'would not be primarily for the purpose of enabling the Council to put questions to the Inspectors' but was really an integral part of the Inspection itself and it would therefore 'be proper that the Council should be prepared accordingly'. Inspection of the school buildings would include a sanitary inspection, for which purpose the local sanitary inspector might have to be called in, an inspection of all boarding establishments, and of the provision made for recreation. The Educational Inspection would cover all the subjects contained in the normal school curriculum in which instruction was covered by the ordinary fee. The report on the efficiency of a school would be sent to the Council and to the headmistress concerned.

On the face of it these demands seemed perfectly reasonable, but there were several points which did not seem clear to the Council and one or two to which they took violent exception. They objected most strongly, for example, to the Board's assumption that the Administrative Inspection would comprise an investigation of the Company's financial position, together with details of the salaries paid to members of the staff in every school. Such an enquiry, wrote the Council to the Board, 'was much to be deprecated' and the information was omitted from the returns submitted in advance in respect of the first batch of schools to be inspected. The Council also objected to the Board's demand for information on the age and previous training and experience of the teachers, and for exhaustive details about the pupils. They had anticipated a report which would deal solely with the educational work of the schools inspected and the suitability of the buildings, not one which would also affect the administration of the Company and its relations with the staff. They disliked the idea of wasting headmistresses' time with unnecessary form-filling and were most reluctant to publicize financial details, including those of salaries.

The Board seemed ready to compromise, and the first inspections duly took place without a demand being made for precise information. But the passage of the Education Act of 1902, which reorganized education on a municipal basis and brought the recently established County and County Borough Councils* under the supervision of the Board of Education for educational purposes, brought about a radical change in the situation. When, therefore, the Council protested that the Board were demanding information which they had previously agreed to forgo, they were reminded of their changed position. 'We must answer civilly but quite firmly', wrote one Board official to a colleague, 'that the Schools are on an entirely different footing with respect to the Board from that of 1902, and that the Board must be furnished with the same information as to Salaries as that which is furnished by all other Schools recognized under the *Regulations for Secondary Schools*.'[4] A letter to this effect was signed by the Principal Assistant Secretary and sent to the Chairman of the Council with a reminder that 'the salaries of individual teachers must be given in the Return asked for'.

At the same time the relationship between the Council – the Central Authority – and the provincial schools was also coming under review. The Board's Inspectors, who appreciated the need for a focal point, had expected to find local committees of management in operation. There had apparently been a committee of this kind at Oxford but it had recently been dissolved and the Inspectors may well have confused it with one of the committees of shareholders which still existed. The Board considered that it was a mistake for supreme authority to remain with the Council. In a tactful letter to the Chairman a senior official wrote: 'Elaborate measures are taken, and steadily carried out, in order to maintain touch between the Schools and the Central Body, which indeed – in some respects – exercises a more effective supervision than any single local committee could do.' The Council had the advantage of long experience and of the help of able workers in education as well as knowledge of the experiments tried in the different schools. 'If one School is defective at any point, whether in finance or equipment,

---

* The Councils were given the duty of 'providing and aiding elementary education, and statutory powers to provide and aid education higher than elementary'.[3] For purposes of the Act they became Local Education Authorities, or L.E.A.s as they are usually called.

its shortcomings may be made good from the superfluities of other Schools. All this goes to show that the Schools do now derive and are likely to continue to derive, much good from a centralized administration such as the Council provides. The Headmistresses whom I have consulted prefer the system as it stands, even ... where there is no local committee of any kind.' At the same time it seemed probable that 'any School which is entirely without local representatives, and therefore without a living nucleus for local interest and local support, may find itself at a disadvantage in the discussion of the large financial and administrative questions which are bound to come up before the new educational authorities.' The Board official went on to suggest to the Company that it seemed 'well worth the consideration of the Council whether they might not ... arrange to delegate, with all proper safeguards, some of their functions to provincial bodies'.[5]

The Council were averse to relinquishing control over their provincial schools unless forced to do so by the Board's *Regulations*. Nevertheless during the next few years several local committees of management were, in fact, set up although this seems to have been an *ad hoc* arrangement.

Relations between the Company and the Board had begun to improve when a curious situation developed. Mrs Withiel, the second mistress at Notting Hill, who had hoped to succeed the great Miss Jones as headmistress, was not offered the headship of Notting Hill nor of any other school. She resigned, to re-emerge as the first woman permanently appointed an Inspector of Secondary Schools, with a place on the list of H.M.I.s who were to inspect the Company's schools. The Council would have liked her name to be withdrawn: the Board would not agree, although they were tactful enough not to send her to Notting Hill. Headmistresses remained wary of a possible bias. '*Must* we have her?' Miss Gadesden of Blackheath asked the Secretary of the Trust in 1914, and went on to suggest that the Board were fielding 'a rather Second Eleven lot'.

If Mrs Withiel bore a grudge against the Council her reports did not show it, and she remained on the list until the early 1920s. Her initial visit was to Liverpool High School. The Inspectors' reports on that occasion were eulogistic. 'The School clearly deserves the reputation it enjoys', they wrote, 'and forms for past as well as present pupils a centre of wholesome, happy and vigorous life.' They found the discipline and manners of the pupils excellent, a striking contrast to Mr Jowitt's 1882 report which had referred to 'an exceedingly unsatisfactory condition as to tone, discipline and

100

unity'. The girls were in excellent health, reacting well to the stimulus of 'swimming, bicycling, tennis, rounders, cricket and hockey'.

During the early years of the century the Inspectors' reports, while critical in some respects, were generally favourable. Sheffield High School, for example, was found to be 'one of the most successful' of the high schools, although it lacked an adequate library and the Inspectors 'noted with regret that, though a grant of £8 odd was made to the library . . . in 1907, in 1908 the accounts show no such grant'. Sutton High School was regarded as 'highly satisfactory'. Newcastle (Central) which ingested the original Gateshead High School in 1907, was reported the same year to be 'in a position to carry out all that is expected of it' although scholarship was being temporarily 'sacrificed to the natural desire to increase by any means the number of scholars. . . .' And Birkenhead, the youngest of the schools, within five years of its opening in 1901, was 'a thoroughly good one . . . doing excellent public service in the neighbourhood', and giving 'a very pleasant impression of harmonious relations, unity of aim, and lofty educational ideas. . . .' Among other schools making satisfactory headway were Sydenham and Streatham Hill, for whose success the Council 'are warmly to be congratulated'.

During the same period the Council continued to show sound common sense and wisdom in its choice of heads: this is revealed in the reports of the Inspectors which are full of praise for individual headmistresses. Miss E. Gavin, for instance, formerly headmistress of Shrewsbury High School, who succeeded Miss Jones at Notting Hill in 1900,* was 'an able teacher' who appeared to do her work 'efficiently and successfully . . .' Miss E. M. Leahy, the benign, diplomatic headmistress of Croydon High School who seems to have accepted calmly and philosophically her transfer first from Dover to Oxford and then from Oxford to Croydon, was complimented as 'highly qualified for her post by academic attainment and ripened experience'.

'The whole tone is excellent and does credit to the Headmistress', wrote the Inspectors of Miss L. Gadesden of Norwich,† who retired in 1907 after more than twenty years as headmistress. Miss Gadesden, wrote one who knew her, 'did not hold any degrees, but she was the wisest woman I have ever known; she never uttered any platitudes and never talked down to the young'. She is also affectionately remembered by former pupils for her refreshingly

---

* She was transferred to Wimbledon in 1908.
† Previously headmistress of Newton Abbot High School.

matter-of-fact attitude towards her ill-fitting wig which slipped out of place whenever she laughed.*

Miss Gadesden was overshadowed by her more famous sister Florence, who ruled Blackheath for over thirty years and organized 'not only the studies but the life of the School'. The Inspectors also praised her for 'her knowledge and command of detail . . . the spirit she infused . . . her manner with the girls and assistant mistresses [which revealed] quite exceptional aptitude and competence'. Small wonder that the educationist Professor Sir Michael Sadler remarked on his second visit to the school in 1909, 'I think of the Blackheath High School as a place where the sun is always shining!' Florence Gadesden influenced her pupils strongly. 'What a wonderful headmistress she was!' wrote one of them, Miss Margaret E. Popham, the well-known Principal of Cheltenham Ladies' College. 'What a character! What personality: still today, the sound of heels clicking across a parquet floor brings back memories of her clicking across the Big Hall and the old deep affection I had for her surges up anew!'[6] Miss Gadesden is remembered by one of her pupils, Miss D. F. P. Hiley, herself a headmistress of great distinction, as 'a notable person' with the brain of a statesman 'and a leader of the first rank. In appearance and manner she was dark, compact, brisk, decisive. . . . She was in fact rather like a bird, perhaps a robin . . . firm, abrupt, even combative on her own ground . . .' When Miss Gadesden retired in 1919 the *Times Educational Supplement* referred to her appointment as 'an act of incalculable wisdom'. Among many with good reason to remember Miss Gadesden was a shrewd and humorous but somewhat irascible barrister, Alick Maclean O.B.E., Assistant Secretary to the Trust from 1904–10 and Secretary until 1939.† He understood the headmistresses and their foibles and his memories, if mildly irreverent, are extremely apt. Of Miss Gadesden he wrote:

'It's time', a bold Committee said,

* There is, however, on record the case of a persistently naughty little boy whose parents were asked to remove him after an unidentified missile which he had thrown at Miss Gadesden lodged in her wig.

† In his legal capacity he acted for the Trust when it was summoned by the L.C.C. in 1909 for employing a male servant at Kensington High School without a licence. According to *The Times* of August 19th, the evidence showed that the duties of the man in question were 'to see that the girls passed to and fro without molestation . . . also to clean the knives, carry messages for the principal, and open the front door in the absence of the maids'. Maclean's plea that no licence was needed because the man 'was kept more as a policeman than as a house servant' was rejected: the magistrate ruled in favour of the L.C.C. and imposed a 20s fine.

'We took Miss G in hand.
We'll send for her and give her here
A quiet reprimand.'
She came with jaunty mien. They spoke.
She tossed her head with scorn;
And tripped away with saucy smile.
They wished they'd not been born.

Another headmistress celebrated in verse by Mr Maclean was
Miss Edith Hastings of Wimbledon High School:*

A dame she is of high renown,
As gentle as you'd wish to see,
But, when at times she isn't pleased
She lays about her lustily.
How happy we should be if we
Could always be as young as she.

Miss Hastings, known to her contemporaries as a 'gentle but
spirited autocrat [who] gave the greater part of her long life to
education', made a most favourable impression on the Board of
Education Inspectors, who wrote that she 'deserves very well
indeed at the hands of the Governing Body. . . . The organization,
discipline, and tone of the School reflect the very highest credit on
[her]. The School is very efficient . . . and the general setting and
character of the work as a whole are highly satisfactory . . .' Miss
Hastings, a tigress when roused, once refused to admit or give any
information to a Sanitary Inspector who called 'in order to test a
report that a Class-room was over-crowded', thus involving the
Company in legal proceedings.

Congestion and overcrowding were noted by the Inspectors in a
number of schools, which also lacked all but the most elementary
facilities for the teaching of science. At East Putney High School,
for instance, at a time when the Council were vainly negotiating for
the purchase of new premises, a basement room had been 'simply
fitted up for science teaching but cannot be regarded as really
adequate for the purpose, as there is insufficient room for more
than a few girls to do practical work, and the benches at which
they sit are far too narrow. There is no proper provision for dining,
the few girls who stay having to take their meal on a trestle table in
the science room, while the Mistresses are accommodated in the
conservatory. . . .' At Brighton and Hove, too, efficiency was
'seriously hampered by inadequate accommodation'. The Inspectors

* Formerly headmistress of Nottingham High School.

were, however, disarmed by the pretty, youthful headmistress, Miss A. C. P. Lunn* who appeared 'to be thoroughly in sympathy with her staff and with her pupils, a result that is largely due to her tact and to the singular charm of her manner . . .'

There was constant criticism of the salary scale of assistant teachers, criticism which the Council had clearly anticipated. 'It is notorious, and the Council . . . would admit it', wrote an official of the Board of Education to a colleague in 1908, 'that in spite of the improvements which have been recently made their Assistant Staffs are still underpaid.'[7] A few months later the Council felt obliged to send the Board a memorandum 'showing the large increase in these salaries in the last ten years, and the impossibility of doing more than is now annually done in raising them, or of arranging a Scale for automatic annual increase'.

The Inspectors continued to criticize the salary scales, and with justification, In 1909, for example, they argued that the salaries at South Hampstead High School which ranged from £100 to £140 a year 'had much to do with an inadequate staff'. But they found that the headmistress, Miss M. S. Benton, had 'high qualifications for the important post she has held for more than twenty years'. and realized that it was 'in large measure due to her that the School owes its tone and the reputation it enjoys'. Miss Benton, wrote one who knew her well, belonged 'to the great tradition of English eccentrics, if the word can be applied to some one with such sturdy commonsense. . . . Her appearance was . . . individual and rather masculine. . . . She invariably wore a well-cut coat and skirt, a plain shirt with a stiff collar and tie, and a Homburg hat. One tradition says that when she was a student [at Newnham] Miss Clough, feeling this get-up slightly unfeminine, offered her an ostrich "tip" to enliven the hat.' Known to Mr Maclean as the Brigadier-General, Miss Benton was renowned for a kind heart and an awesome directness which enabled her to order recalcitrant parents out of her office. Her abilities were recognized by her election in two separate periods as Chairman of the Executive Committee of the Association of Head Mistresses, the second time during the Presidency of Miss F. Gadesden.

If the Inspectors complained that salaries were low at South Hampstead, they found them 'deplorably low' at Ipswich. The school was ruled at the time by Miss M. Gale, a dynamic woman who 'lived life at top speed', first at Ipswich, then at Blackheath,

* Subsequently headmistress of Sheffield High School. After her marriage she became a Governor of the School and remained on the Committee until her death in 1959.

and finally at Oxford. She was, wrote a Council member, Mrs V. H. Galbraith, 'consumed by an inward fire. I always used to think that if one day I saw a flame of fire on her head I should not have been surprised. She was the only person I have ever known struck by lightning, and one felt it a possible thing to have happened to her.' But what Miss Gale achieved, most notably at Oxford where Mrs Galbraith knew her best, 'for the parents, the girls, the staff, the School, cannot be measured, and will remain'.

Shrewsbury High School was ruled for nearly thirty years by Miss Gale's less forceful sister, a woman who possessed 'something of the dignity of an elder stateman'. Shrewsbury was not geared to so high an academic standard as the majority of the Trust schools, and Miss Gale's predecessor Miss Wise* had spoken of 'a grave danger of weakening mental and moral fibre' if girls were allowed to give up Latin ' "because it is so hard" '. It was, she added, 'one of the best things about a High School training that the girls were taught to tackle a difficult piece of work'. It was obvious, however, that for the less academically inclined girls the pace was too fast, and the Inspectors noted with approval that the Council had reduced 'the weight of the general curriculum'.

One of Miss Gale's finest achievements was the way in which she harnessed 'the old idea of an exclusive fee-paying school to the new idea of equal opportunity bringing, through scholarships, girls into the school who would not otherwise have been able to obtain their education there'. This task was more difficult in an area dominated by the county than, say, in a busy London district. Miss Gale's efforts were appreciated by the Inspectors, who would have liked, there as elsewhere, to see staff salaries on a higher scale. At the same time they awarded full marks to the headmistress of Sydenham High School, Miss H. M. Sheldon,† for making 'successful efforts . . . to secure suitable increases of salary for her Staff', two of whom now earned £150 and two £140. In one of his slightly irreverent verses Maclean describes Miss Sheldon as having 'at times a grumpy way of saying what she had to say'; but the Inspectors remarked admiringly that she was 'in every way exceptionally well fitted' for her post.

The Council were well aware that by now their salaries compared unfavourably with those in other schools: in fact they were a good deal lower than the salaries commanded by teachers in the new municipal and county secondary schools which were being opened all over the country. The teachers themselves, who longed for higher

* Also headmistress of Norwich.
† Formerly headmistress of Dover High School.

starting salaries and a fixed scale of increments, had agreed in 1905 that, 'for the present, the special advantages of being in the Company's schools would outweigh the financial disadvantage'. The Council and the headmistresses were, however, alarmed by the problem of 'obtaining and retaining the best teachers in our schools, owing to the higher initial salaries and regular increments offered by the County and City Authorities'.

The Council were also conscious that they were being outclassed in the way of buildings and equipment by the new schools which owed their existence to the Education Act of 1902. The Act empowered the municipal and county authorities to create secondary schools maintained out of the local rates and aided by grants from the Board of Education. This financial help, which included provision for teacher training, did not extend to the universites nor to the independent schools.*

The new dispensation led to a rapid increase in the number of secondary schools. It also led to a reappraisal of the position of existing schools such as those of the Girls' Public Day School Company. In 1902 the possibility of applying for grants in aid from the Local Education Authorities was considered by the Council, but it was rejected because it would have entailed L.E.A. representation. The Company continued to rely, however, on aid from the Board of Education.

In the same year the Council discovered that a founder member, George Bartley M.P., was, in the words of the Chairman, William Bousfield, actively campaigning 'to obtain a reversal of the policy under which public grants have been made to the Company's Schools'. George Bartley, it may be remembered, had warned the Council as far back as 1873 that their handling of staff appointments would 'not fail to land the Company in Ruin'. Now, it seemed that he himself was doing his utmost to achieve that end.

He opened his campaign by asking a question in the House of Commons and on May 26, 1902, when the House went into Committee, his spoke in the debate on the Education Estimates. The inspection of schools, he said, should be a matter of course, the cost being paid out of taxation, but he failed to see why the Board of Education 'should now be forcing grants upon all schools'. Parents of the middle classes were ready and willing to pay for education, but he understood 'that the demand was that all these schools

---

* Political pressure led to certain modifications in the scheme. In some areas non-county and urban district councils were transformed into L.E.A.s, with powers over elementary but not over secondary education.

106

should get extra grants. It was a mistake for the State to take upon itself, as it was gradually doing, the whole cost of secondary education.'

Bartley referred to the Girls' Public Day School Company by name in a letter to *The Times* on May 31st, as a company which charged an average fee of £15 15s per year per day pupil, educated girls of all classes, paid its way, gave its shareholders 4 per cent 'and yet last year received over £1,000 of public money from the taxes'. Under the new *Regulations for Secondary Schools* 'the State is to give out of taxes up to £9 a year per head for four years on each student, according to the Inspector's report. These grants are, it would appear', he added belligerently, 'from now to be made to schools conducted for private profit.' He had always been opposed to the provision of universal free education even at the elementary level,* but he was concerned now with the grave possibility that secondary education might also be made free. 'Is the country prepared for an additional cost of many millions each year in the near future on expenditure already increasing by alarming leaps and bounds?'

The Council were rightly incensed. Apart from anything else, as George Bartley knew perfectly well, the grants did not go to swell the Company's dividend but were spent on the schools themselves. William Bousfield wrote a letter to *The Times*, published on June 23rd, and a memorandum to the Board of Education explaining this fact but emphasizing that the shareholders had minimal rights. The schools had never been endowed and the capital on which they had been built and equipped had been subscribed 'principally in small sums, by a large number of persons, many of them of very moderate means, who could not afford, nor be expected, to give their money without interest. . . . If educational authorities are not allowed to recognize and encourage such Schools a vastly greater cost must eventually be thrown on the payers of rates and taxes, as it is hopeless to expect that private enterprise, unaided financially from public sources, can cope with the supply of good secondary education, where the fees of scholars have to be kept within the means of the poorer middle-class parent.' The Company had limited its dividend to 4 per cent, and the grants it had received had all 'been expended, together with greatly larger sums, upon the development of science teaching'. If the grants were withdrawn the Company would be forced to raise its fees and so 'throw upon the public educational authorities the onus of providing new

* By 1891 with the help of grants the majority of elementary schools had stopped charging fees but fees were not entirely abolished until 1918.

schools for the large number of girls excluded by the inability of their parents to pay increased charges'.

At the same time Bousfield wrote a strong letter of protest to the offending George Bartley, complaining that he had abused his position as a member of the Council and had made use of confidential information to reinforce his case. He was not, he added, unmindful of Bartley's past help but thought his present attitude made it desirable for him to resign.

He received a pugnacious reply. Bartley stood by everything he had said and refused to resign, but if the Council wished to remove him they could do so when his name next came up for re-election. This was not for another eighteen months. Meanwhile, Bartley remained a member of the Council, appearing occasionally at meetings to the discomfiture of his colleagues.

By the end of 1902 the Council had received a warning that grants to the Company's schools might be withdrawn. The question was raised in the House of Commons on July 9, 1903, when Sir William Anson M.P., Parliamentary Secretary to the Board of Education, expressed his hope that in due course the practice of awarding grants to dividend-paying companies would be 'altogether discontinued'.

A member of the Opposition, Lord Edmond Fitzmaurice M.P., who indicated his disapproval of the practice, thought that the Girls' Public Day School Company had the right to know where it stood and asked for a clear statement of Government intentions. This he did not receive; and the Company remained in suspense until the following year.

On March 10, 1904, a deputation from the Company was received by the Lord President of the Council, the Marquess of Londonderry, who was accompanied by Sir William Anson and Mr (later Sir Robert) Morant, Permanent Secretary to the Board of Education. The President of the Company, Earl Spencer, who led the deputation, based his plea for continued recognition of the schools on the provision they were making for improved education and the training of teachers for elementary and secondary schools. 'If we lost those Grants, which I think last year – I forget the amount – amounted to something like £2,500* . . . we should have to close some of our poorer schools [which] are paid for really by the large profit on certain other schools in the better districts. . . .' Then, again, they might have to raise the fees, with the result that they would exclude 'many of the poorer scholars who are now able to come to us. That would be a great mistake. Our pupils would become less and less. If we were unable to pay interest on our capital which has been

* The figure was £2,836.

108

raised . . . really in the interests of education we should be in the position of not being able to raise any more capital for the extension of our schools.'

Among others who supported Lord Spencer were the Duke of Argyll, who referred to his wife's long connection with the Company, and Sir Kenelm Digby, whose wife had been a member of the Council for many years. Mrs Fawcett, the suffragist leader, spoke of her debt to the Company 'for providing and placing within my means, at very small cost, a system of excellent secondary education for my daughter'. (Her daughter, Philippa Garrett Fawcett, was educated first at Clapham Middle and then at Clapham High School. She completed her education at Newnham College, Cambridge, where she achieved the signal distinction of being the first woman to be placed above the Senior Wrangler. In 1905 she was put in charge of the Higher Education Branch of the L.C.C., becoming the first woman to hold so high an administrative post under the Council.)

In his reply Lord Londonderry, who conceded that 'it would be a national calamity if the schools were closed,' noted that there was no requirement for public representation on the Governing Body – the Council; and that one of the points for which the Government was 'most chiefly denounced' both inside and outside Parliament was that 'we carried through the principle of giving public money without representation'. It was urged on the Company's behalf that profits from the schools were spent on buildings and not on dividends, and if this were so it was a strong point in the Company's favour. On the other hand, if grants were awarded to one company, other company-owned schools, denominational as well as undenominational, would have a right to be treated in the same way. And even if the Girls' Public Day School Company continued to receive grants, 'what security had the Treasury that the schools would be permanent?' Lord Spencer had intimated that schools would be closed without the grant; 'but would it not be possible to lower the dividend and increase the fees?' Lord Londonderry promised, however, that if 'satisfactory answers' were forthcoming to these and other questions he would 'at once communicate with the Chancellor of the Exchequer'.

Sir William Anson slyly reminded Lord Spencer that with a grant approaching £3,000 and the sum of £5,331 available the previous year for dividend 'it is always open to a critic to say that the Government is finding the dividend for the Shareholders'. The income from fees amounted to £112,000, and he thought that a 2 per cent increase in the fees 'adjusted in accordance with the

109

wealthier localities in which the schools are placed, might meet the requirements. If we are told that if this Government grant . . . was withdrawn that schools would have to be closed and disaster would fall upon the higher education of girls throughout the country, I cannot help thinking that it is somewhat exaggerated.' Sir William proceeded, however, to suggest a solution to the problem, possibly by the creation of a trust. He had already announced that the grants would be discontinued, but when he received the Company's suggestions he would re-examine the question.

On July 26, 1904, the persistently hostile George Bartley (now Sir George) asked the Secretary to the Board of Education whether public grants to dividend-paying companies were to be continued 'and, if so, whether they would be extended to other educational adventures for private profit'.

Sir William Anson replied that in the future a school owned or conducted by a company 'will only be eligible for recognition if the company is wound up and its property vested in trustees on trust for the purpose of secondary education. The amount of the share capital so far as actually expended on sites, buildings, or equipment can in such cases be treated as a charge on the property, subject to the repayment of principal with interest at the rate of not more than 4 per cent within a limited period of time.' It might be necessary to allow companies already taking steps to comply with these conditions another year to make the required alterations in their constitution. The new *Regulations for Secondary Schools* laid down, however, as a condition of recognition 'that a school must not be conducted for private profit'.

The Girls' Public Day School Company was already working towards the desired end. A letter from the Board of Education pointed out that the 'limited period of time' referred to must not exceed fifty years from the winding-up. The determination of the method to be used for the redemption of the mortgages on the Company's property 'will be deferred until the greater part of the Share Capital has been paid off. In the meantime the mortgage debt may remain on its present footing.' In order to give the Company adequate time to carry out the necessary financial rearrangements the Board were willing to consider the schools already in receipt of grants as eligible for recognition until July 31, 1905.

The Company's Memorandum and Articles of Association were duly amended in consultation with the Board of Education. The amendments were confirmed by an Order in Council of January 16, 1906, and the name of the Company was changed to the Girls' Public Day School Trust, Ltd.

By the end of 1906 the position of the Trust schools had been regularized. With a single exception – Carlisle High School – application for recognition had been made and accepted for them all.

The general situation remained somewhat complicated. In 1911 the Council were advised that the provision made in the scheme of 1906 for the repayment of share capital was contrary to the law relating to companies and could only be rectified by further re-construction. This involved the conversion of all previous classes of shares into £5 Preference Shares, and the creation of 100 'New' shares of nominal value (1s each) to be vested in certain members of the Council approved by the Board of Education as Trustees. Under the terms of the reconstruction provision was made in certain circumstances for the Trust to be wound up as a Limited Company not later than January 1956, in the confident hope that the schools could then be transferred to a new Trust without share-holders. 'Thus', wrote Mr Laurie Magnus, a future Chairman of the Trust, in 1923, 'it will happen, so far as can be foreseen, and so far as provisions can be made, that the Company, which was registered in 1872, and reserved dividends till 1898, which voluntarily decided in that year to limit its interest to 4 per cent, in order to qualify for the Grant of the old Science and Art Department, which proceeded in 1906 to devise a scheme for its conversion into a Trust, and which completed that scheme to the satisfaction of the Board of Education in 1912 . . . will be transferred . . . into a purely educational Trust.' The culmination, he added, might well be realized 'in a form not foreseen by our founders, but not out of harmony with their intention'.[8]*

* See Chapter 17.

Chapter 9
Competition

The opening of the twentieth century coincided with a growing sense of partnership between the Council and headmistresses. In the past the headmistresses had been subservient; but as the old restrictions were relaxed they emerged with a very considerable measure of freedom, notably in the arrangement of the curriculum and timetables. This freedom and the trust reposed in headmistresses has produced a harmonious relationship between heads and governors which has become widely recognized as an ideal to be sought after in all schools.

Initially, headmistresses belonged as individuals to the Association of Head Mistresses, founded in 1874 by Miss Buss and Miss Beale, of which Miss Jones of Notting Hill was a founder member. Shortly before Mrs Grey and her sister went to Rome they were the guests of honour at a luncheon given by the Association at which, wrote Mrs Grey, their health was proposed 'in a most cordial and affectionate speech by Miss Buss and drunk with three times three by the sixty-two Headmistresses present'.

In 1901 the Trust headmistresses formed their own association: thereafter, in conference, they passed resolutions for submission to the Council and drafted memoranda for submission to the Board of Education. They have met annually ever since and their small Standing Committee meets frequently. They have always counted their opportunities to consult together as one of the great educational advantages of membership of the Trust.*

In the early years of the century every dispute – and there were a number – found the Council and the headmistresses ranged on one side, the Board of Education on the other. These disputes were not necessarily confined to the Trust schools: most were of equal concern to other secondary schools, notably to those which, like the Trust schools, received a direct grant from the Board and from 1926 onwards were known as 'direct grant' schools.

* In recent years there have been annual conferences for all the staff teaching a certain subject and also Junior School conferences.

112

The Education Act of 1902, which gave rise both to problems and opportunities, brought special benefits to girls. The Board was determined that secondary education should be made available to as many children as possible, and girls whose schooling had formerly been confined to the elementary were now enabled to continue their education. In 1897 only 20,000 girls were being educated in recognized secondary schools: in a little over twenty years the number had grown to 185,000.

To begin with nobody had a very clear idea of what constituted a 'secondary' school. In 1904 it was defined by the Board as 'a Day or Boarding School offering to each of its scholars, up to and beyond the age of sixteen, a general education, physical, mental and moral, given through a complete graded course of instruction, of wider scope and more advanced degree than that given in Elementary Schools'. The course, which had to last four years or more, included English subjects, one, or possibly two, foreign languages, one of which could be Latin, mathematics, science, and drawing, with facilities for physical education and manual training.

As a consequence of the Education Act a great many county and municipal secondary schools soon came into being, some evolving from existing higher grade elementary schools, others from science classes, or the pupil-teacher centres which had been set up to provide a better system of training than had been available when pupil-teachers were apprenticed to the heads of elementary schools. The new secondary schools were founded and maintained by the Local Education Authorities who were empowered to spend out of rates no more than 2d in the £ without special permission from the Local Government Board. They drew the vast majority of their pupils from the public elementary schools, on scholarships or at fees averaging £6 a year. They differed from the high schools (with average fees of £16 a year) and the endowed schools which drew their pupils from a variety of educational sources, not excluding the elementary schools. Under the old dispensation Board of Education grants were dependent on science and art teaching: in 1904 the Board's *Regulations for Secondary Schools* substituted block grants in respect of the curriculum as a whole.

The Board recognized that the high schools had been designed primarily for middle-class girls and held a special position in the educational hierarchy. For their part, the Council of the Girls' Public Day School Trust, chronically short of funds, were determined to get as much help as they could from the State without compromising the education and standing of their schools. Ever since 1873 the schools had taken limited numbers of girls from the

H

public elementary schools. By 1893 the counties of Nottingham-shire and Surrey were sending girls with technical education scholar-ships to the schools, and the following year Norwich High School took two county scholars and Brighton and Hove four. By 1902 there were fifteen county scholars at Brighton and Hove out of a total of some two hundred pupils. The father of one was an elementary schoolmaster; the other parents included a milkman, a baker, a plasterer, a cab-driver and a railway guard. These scholars, wrote their headmistress approvingly, 'do remarkably well, and in cases where the scholarship is extended have sat in Form VI'. She found them 'delightful to teach', adaptable and intelligent. 'They begin most subjects with avidity; they show themselves grateful to the County Council to whose generosity they owe their advan-tages . . . They are sent very tidy to School, and are gentle in their manners.'

By that time several of the Company's schools had been recognized by the Board of Education as training centres for teachers in secondary schools. The Council were anxious to co-operate in the national work of training teachers for elementary as well as secondary schools, but in order to safeguard 'the status, character and general curriculum' of their schools and to ward off potential parental opposition they were reluctant to accept as pupil-teachers many elementary school girls. In 1904 they accepted a suggestion from the London County Council that two-year scholarships should be held in the schools by girls between the ages of fourteen and sixteen who intended to become elementary school teachers. They agreed, wherever there was room, to take scholars who had already spent some years in a secondary school, and scholars from elementary schools up to 2 per cent of the total intake. The Council were willing for the same percentage of elementary school scholars to be taken in all the schools. If it seems small it must be remembered that in the light of contemporary opinion their readiness to accept girls of all classes and to collaborate in any way at all with the state system marked a very considerable advance.

Despite every care in the selection of scholars the Council received a number of parental complaints. 'These parents', the Council informed the headmistresses, 'fear that there will be increased danger of the introduction of such pupils, who will often have brothers and sisters still attending elementary schools where they might contract infectious diseases; and further that some of the pupils so admitted might be girls with whom they would not like their daughters to associate even in class.' Headmistresses should have no difficulty in persuading parents 'that the former fear is groundless, owing to the precautions taken in regard to cases of infectious disorders in elementary schools, which are very stringent'. But they were warned not only to be selective but to be on their guard against the appearance in the scholars of 'anything un-desirable . . . in manners, dress, or language'.

The headmistresses realized that if they were not very careful the bulk of the middle-class children might well be removed. In most schools the situation was highly satisfactory. In 1907, for example, Miss Minasi, for twenty-eight years headmistress of Highbury and Islington High School, was complimented by H.M. Inspectors 'on the excellent tone and civilizing influence of the School' and on the ability and neat appearance of the L.C.C. scholars who were indistinguishable from the rest. In a few schools, however, there was a marked reduction in the number of middle-class girls for whom, as at least one Inspector pointed out, the high schools were primarily intended.

In 1907 the Council co-operated in a new scheme, by which secondary school pupils intending to teach could become bursars and remain at school until the age of seventeen or eighteen. They could then go to a training college or, alternatively, as student teachers spend half their time in teaching practice in an elementary school.* At the request of the London County Council the bursary system was successfully introduced into three of the schools of the Company (by now the Trust) – Highbury and Islington, Paddington, and Streatham Hill.

In the same year – 1907 – a system was introduced to enable bright children from the elementary schools to proceed to secondary education. In future there were to be two kinds of grant, a higher and a lower. Schools applying for the higher grant had to receive 25 per cent or more of their total entry as free-place scholars, these children having spent not less than two years in a public elementary school. In order to prevent any depression of the educational standard, candidates for the free places had to pass an entrance test. This was meant to be a qualifying test: in fact, owing to pressure on places, it became fiercely competitive.

There were several other conditions attached to the higher grant. The most important was that the Local Education Authority should have majority representation on the committee of manage-ment or governing body of the school. This condition could be waived or modified at the instance of the L.E.A.: but the 25 per cent intake could be modified only by the Board of Education. 'If

* In the country as a whole the system led to a much larger number of pupils staying on at school until the age of seventeen or eighteen.

115

these conditions are not observed, or waived or modified as the case may be,' the Education Committee of the Trust informed the Council, 'the Lower Scale will be applied, provided the School is on the Grant List for 1906–7.' The Committee also reminded the Council that the Board's figure of 25 per cent was in respect of the whole school, including its preparatory and junior departments, for which no grant at all was paid.

The Council conferred with the headmistresses. There were three courses open to them: to accept the higher grant with its conditions, to remain on the lower scale, or to cut adrift from state aid and become independent which would, of course, entail an increase in fees. When asked for their advice representatives of the Board of Education suggested that the Council would be right 'in refusing to take a large number of Public Elementary School Scholars; if they refused to take *any* such', they would be faced with the *Regulations* which stipulated that no pupil 'may be refused admission except on reasonable grounds'. To refuse a scholar merely because she had attended an elementary school would be regarded 'as not reasonable'. There was no reason, however, why the Trust schools should not stiffen the entrance examination 'so as to admit only exceptionally qualified Scholarship holders'.

Initially it seemed to the Board of Education that the Council were trying to get the best of both worlds. Sir William Bousfield, the Chairman, called at the Board without prior notice in December 1908 to discuss the minimum percentage of free placers the schools would be required to accept in order to qualify for the higher grant. He was reminded of the stipulation that County Councils should be represented on the Governing Body, and further informed that the Board, on whose discretion the decision rested, had 'so far invariably declined to reduce the percentage of free places required from any school below 10 per cent. As the official concerned minuted a colleague, Sir William 'confessed that this would be a serious obstacle'. It appeared to one official, however, that the Trust had 'not sufficiently realized that the function which they have so admirably performed as pioneers of the supply of Secondary Schools for Girls' had been made by the Education Act of 1902 'a function of local government, and that in consequence [the Trust] should try to find other directions in which their energies as pioneers and their great educational knowledge might be of use to the country without fear of harmful competition'.[1] If fees were raised and the number of schools reduced it might be possible for the excellent work to be continued at the lower rate of grant or even without any grant at all.

116

Sir William remained hopeful that some concession would be made, but in the spring of 1909 he was told by the President of the Board of Education that this was unlikely. The President mentioned a suggestion that the nine London schools might qualify jointly for the higher grant. This idea was very strongly advocated at a slightly later stage by Sir William's successor as Chairman, the broad-minded, forward-looking Prebendary J. S. Northcote.

The upshot of Bousfield's interviews at the Board of Education had been a decision not to apply for the higher grant since, in the Council's opinion, 'the conditions prescribed would interfere with their desire to maintain their Schools as Secondary Schools of the highest grade'. This decision was modified in 1908 in the case of Carlisle High School where the Local Education Authority waived its right to majority representation and the school accepted a 25 per cent intake of girls from the elementary schools.

After Sir William's death in 1910 Prebendary Northcote pressed for further co-operation with Local Authority schools. The conservative element on the Council were dubious: they could point to financial difficulties and the loss of middle-class pupils at Carlisle High School and its consequent transfer to the L.E.A. in 1909 as the Carlisle and County High School for Girls. Nevertheless Highbury and Islington, and Paddington and Maida Vale High Schools agreed to receive up to a third of their total intake from L.C.C. schools. In each case negotiations broke down because the L.C.C. refused to waive its right to majority representation on the Governing Body. Paddington was therefore transferred to the L.C.C. in 1912 to become the Paddington and Maida Vale High School for Girls. Highbury and Islington was also offered to the L.C.C. who refused to take it over owing to acute financial difficulties: it was closed in 1911, despite strong and anguished protests from parents and pupils, but it remains alive in the memories of a small but devoted band of former pupils who still keep in touch with one another by means of a newsletter.

Elsewhere the Trust schools were losing many of the brighter girls from the public elementary schools to the municipal and county secondary schools, which offered additional financial inducements. In some cases, of which Wimbledon was one, the L.E.A. was not represented on the Council – the Governing Body – and refused to send any of its county scholars to the school. 'This is a most unfortunate decision', said an Inspector in 1907, 'as the school is by this means precluded from affording that opportunity for the development of local talent that it could well supply, where inability to pay fees is an absolute bar to entrance.' The same situation prevailed at the other Surrey schools, Croydon and Sutton; and the H.M.I.s stressed the desirability of some arrangement being made between the Council and the L.E.A. Elsewhere – at Kensington and South Hampstead, for example – the Inspectors made pointed remarks about the tiny proportion of elementary school pupils admitted.

Competition with other secondary schools was, therefore, growing acute, and the Trust schools were also losing to the private schools girls whose parents objected to the smallest leavening of pupils from the working classes. If they were to continue to compete with their rivals, it would be necessary to raise salaries in order to attract highly qualified staff: if salaries were raised, then fees must be raised also, but if the schools were to remain state-aided any increase in fees must be sanctioned by the Board of Education.

Despite an ominous drop in numbers in the Trust schools the Council sanctioned a small salary increase all round in 1910: but at the same time they instructed headmistresses to reduce costs wherever possible, pointing out that the cost per pupil per year should not exceed £7 5s.*

By that time the Trust was also facing competition from new secondary schools which were being opened in the vicinity of its own. In 1908, for instance, the headmistress of Tunbridge Wells High School was able to report that she had maintained her numbers notwithstanding the existence of the county school. Three years later numbers had fallen steeply and the Council, which had adopted the policy of using some of the profits from the more prosperous schools to help the less successful, reluctantly decided that in no circumstances could a school be carried on at a continuing loss. The existence of Tunbridge Wells was in the balance: it survived the crisis and remained in being.

In 1909 the L.C.C. sought to reconcile the Council to the presence of a new secondary school at Clapham: they pointed out that the fees would be lower than those in the High School and that

---

* They also advised other economies, some of them fundamental, such as the dismissal of superfluous staff. Others, the installation of telephones, for instance, were trivial. In 1913 the Council approved a request by the headmistress of Notting Hill to pay half the cost of a telephone provided that she herself 'was really willing to risk the disadvantages of the School having one'. The headmistress installed a telephone for her private use and did not ask the Council for a contribution. Three years later they approved the installation of a telephone at the Belvedere School on the understanding that it would cost the Trust nothing: and as a result of further enquiries seven more were installed in other schools, presumably on the same terms.

the new school was 'intended to meet the needs of a different class'. The Council, which protested in vain, protested also against the erection of new secondary schools at Tulse Hill in the vicinity of Dulwich and Streatham Hill High Schools, and at Shrewsbury. Convinced as they were that the existence of their own schools was threatened they put little credence in the Board of Education's assertion 'that the interests of the Trust [would] not be prejudicially affected to any degree . . .'

Streatham Hill and Shrewsbury survived but in 1913, to the accompaniment of despairing protests from parents and pupils, Dulwich High School was transferred to the Church Schools Company. In the meantime the position of the London schools had been causing anxiety. With the exception of Clapham and East Putney, wrote a Board of Education official, they 'were steadily going down in the number of pupils, and . . . were . . . carried on at an aggregate loss'. Profits from a successful school were used to bolster up others which seemed to be failing but, on balance, the facts pointed 'to the extinction of the Trust Schools, which calamity could only be avoided by the adoption of some decided policy before it was too late . . .'.

There were further hints of impending doom in 1914. 'Every feature of the business is dark,' reported the Finance Committee. Trust property was mortgaged to the extent of £106,000 and the sum of £25,000 had to be borrowed from the bank three times a year to foot the salary bill. 'The only proposal by which the Trust can be saved from disaster and since the money [to reduce the mortgage] can only be raised by the sale of some of the Schools, the Committee recommend the Council to consider without delay which Schools it would be advisable to sell.'

The Council did not panic, and no schools were sold. In any event, with war on the horizon, it was no time to think of sales.

Unlike the Second World War the 1914–18 war caused no major upheaval in the schools of the Trust. Certain changes and modifications were made. There was, for instance, a temporary ban on increases in staff salaries, a saving which was offset by the reduction of fees for girls whose fathers had joined the Armed Forces. After their morning's work many teachers spent their afternoons teaching in boys' schools, replacing masters who had joined up. Prize days were abandoned and instead of prizes pupils were awarded certificates. The girls organized sales of work and performances in aid of war charities and there were few, as the headmistress of Tunbridge Wells remarked in 1916, who did not 'contribute the whole of their pocket money for war purposes'. Belgian refugees were admitted without fees to a number of schools: on a practical level, the girls of Putney High School grew vegetables in the school garden, and several schools arranged special clerical courses to prepare girls to take the places of men in Government and other offices. There was some very minor air-raid damage to buildings, and a disastrous fire at Wimbledon in February 1917, which had nothing to do with the war but which, according to the *Wimbledon Boro' News*, 'caused the utmost alarm and concern in Wimbledon and neighbourhood'. Fortunately the school was empty except for the caretaker and his wife who escaped 'safely and at ease' from the burning building.

Miss Gavin,* the headmistress, a highly disciplined woman who kept a strong temper well in check, replied in characteristic vein to some one who went to commiserate with her after the fire. 'We must have no regrets, it is the chance to build newer and better school premises.'

The school was housed elsewhere while the premises were rebuilt. Meanwhile, Miss Gavin had been driven to the point of distraction by the Board of Education official who demanded that the burnt registers should be reconstructed without delay. They excused her however, from submitting returns in respect of children under eleven, for whom no grants were payable. 'Surely', as she had remarked to the Trust Secretary, 'we might be let off this silliness now.' The new premises of Wimbledon High School were opened in the autumn of 1920 by a former pupil, the Duchess of Atholl M.P. who later, as Parliamentary Secretary to the Board of Education, became the second woman to hold Government office.

The principal war casualties were the German-born members of staff. Animosity towards everything German was a feature of the First World War, and as a result of complaints from parents a number of German teachers were forced to look for other work. This animosity even extended to the girls. In 1917 owing, it must be supposed, to information supplied by a parent, the *Daily Mail* asked the Council for details about the award of Senior Trust Scholarships to two girls with German-born fathers, one from Putney, the other from Notting Hill, when 'among the competitors were daughters of men who had thrown up civil appointments in order to join the Army, and whose families were, therefore, in straitened circumstances'. The Council replied that both girls had by this time left school, that there had been no such candidates in 1915 when the second scholarship was awarded, and that both had been awarded on the results of an external examination by a university body. They resolved, nevertheless, that in

* Also headmistress of Shrewsbury and Notting Hill High Schools.

future girls with German-born fathers would not be eligible for Trust scholarships, a resolution which did not apparently apply to girls with English fathers and German-born mothers.

Public intolerance persisted even when the war was over. In December 1918 the Council received complaints from parents over the choice of a head girl for Streatham Hill High School. The girl's mother was English; her father, a naturalized German, had lived in England for twenty-five years and had been called up for National Service, and her brother had served in the R.A.F. She had been elected by the assistant mistresses and senior girls, and the Council, advised by the Education Committee, saw 'no ground for interfering with the election'.

The war brought to a close the Trust's long association with Mary Gurney, the last of the founders. To those who knew her only in old age she seemed a somewhat remote figure, upright and indefatigable. 'Her great ability and the force of her personality', wrote the Council in a memorial tribute, 'together with her thorough knowledge both of the Schools and of the business of the Trust made her through a long course of years probably the most influential Member of the Council and it always relied on her wisdom.' Miss Gurney had taken an intense and motherly interest in all the schools and Wimbledon High School was largely her creation. In later years, while the overall number of pupils increased, it became necessary slowly to reduce the number of schools from thirty-eight to twenty-three, one of them – Kensington – now a junior school only: and this number stands in 1970 with approximately 14,500 pupils. It has been recorded that it would have seemed like manslaughter to Mary Gurney to have voted for a single closure yet, at the last, she would not actually oppose it. Forcefulness was the keynote of her personality. A few years before her death when it was suggested that as the title 'High School' was used indiscriminately the Trust schools might be renamed after Princess Louise or Mary Gurney, Mrs Woodhouse, headmistress of Clapham High School, remarked that the use of Miss Gurney's name would not be an advantage 'because in the course of her excellent work she must have made enemies'. No change of title was made, but Mary Gurney's memory is perpetuated in a 'Gurney' house in several schools, and in the Gurney Scholarship, which is competed for by all sixth-form Trust scholars. Those who knew her best – the headmistresses and the Council – also remembered her unselfishness, her unfailing sympathy, 'and a wonderful tenderness rare in so forceful a character'.

It had been laid down in the original Constitution of the Company

121

that there should be women members of the Council. One of the best known was Lady Savory, who served on the Council for more than thirty years. Lady Savory, widow of a former Lord Mayor of London, was an upright Victorian figure and something of an autocrat. She took a personal interest in the headmistresses and often invited them to dine or stay in her house. She also acquired an unrivalled knowledge of Trust affairs. When she visited a school she revealed a disconcerting amount of information about each member of the staff, and she never wavered in her conviction that any headmistress worth her salt must be a good woman *and* a gentlewoman. She remained devoted to the Trust until the end of her life. As she wrote to the Secretary on the outbreak of war in 1939: 'I meant to have written before now to say that I had – poor-spiritedly – fled from London . . . so I fear I cannot be of much use. But I would always come up for a meeting if there was anything special.'

Another outstanding woman member of the Council was Miss Henriette Dent, a former pupil of Sydenham High School, who was Head of the Postgraduate Department of Clapham High School from 1915–33 and afterwards Principal of the Cambridge Training College for Women, later known as Hughes Hall. Wise and experienced in educational matters, Miss Dent was a Council member for nearly twenty years and the headmistresses, who relied on her judgment, also prized her friendship. Among others are Mrs V. H. Galbraith, a former pupil of Portsmouth High School, a vigorous, far-sighted member of Committees or of the Council for over forty years and originator of a number of innovations, and Dame Kitty Anderson, the present Chairman, formerly headmistress of Miss Buss's North London Collegiate School. Dame Kitty, a member of the University Grants Committee and of the Robbins Committee on Higher Education, holds Honorary Doctorates from the Universities of Hull and York. She was the first woman to become Chairman of the Council, an office which she fills with distinction, her immediate predecessor having been Dr H. F. Collins C.M.G., Officer of the Legion d'honneur, a former H.M.I. whose wide educational experience and personal interest in the schools had been of the utmost value.

Chapter 10
The Higher Grant

In 1918, when the issue of the war was still uncertain, a new Education Act became law. Known as the Fisher Act, after the President of the Board of Education, the historian and politician H. A. L. Fisher, it was chiefly concerned with elementary education* but, as Fisher pointed out in the House of Commons on May 9th, it was hoped that the L.E.A.s, whose powers under the Act were considerably increased, would be encouraged to provide more secondary schools, apply for grants, and 'as a natural consequence', offer free places at those schools. It was also hoped that L.E.A.s would prepare schemes to 'ensure means whereby children and young persons shall not be debarred by poverty from the benefits of higher education'.

The Local Education Authorities were soon busy with their plans. 'The Trust Schools will, or should, under such schemes provide the highest education, leading to the Universities,' announced the Trust's Education Committee: and if the schools fulfilled the necessary requirements they would qualify for local authority aid as well as for state aid. In order to qualify the schools would not only have to accept a fixed percentage of ex-elementary schoolgirls but also agree to local authority representation on the governing body. Although the Board of Education stated categorically that this need not be a majority representation the Council and headmistresses remained nervously apprehensive. They had not yet made up their minds to apply for the Board's higher grant: the new proposition merely served to increase their fears.

The need to come to a decision about the higher grant became more urgent than ever in the light of the post-war salary review. In 1917 H. A. L. Fisher had obtained an increased contribution from the Exchequer for teachers' salaries and two years later he set up a committee – the Burnham Committee – under the chairmanship of Lord Burnham to work out the necessary scales. The Committee

---

* It abolished fees and among other things fixed the school-leaving age at fourteen, giving L.E.A.s power to raise it to fifteen.

was composed of two panels, one representing the L.E.A.s, the other the teaching profession: it served as a permanent negotiating body on salary scales. The new scales, if adopted by the Trust, would mean that salaries must go up and be further increased by regular increments: among other things superannuation contributions would have to be paid. The Council were aware, as a Board of Education official had pointed out, that 'the consequences of the Trust not receiving the Board's Higher Grant or Aid from Local Education Authorities were that [it] had not as much money available for salaries or pensions as schools receiving such grants or aid, and . . . the effect on [the schools] efficiency . . . would be serious'.

Circumstances had driven the Council to the brink of a decision, yet still they hesitated. In 1920 the Conference of Trust Headmistresses urged them to adopt the new salary scale for assistant staff without delay to ensure a constant supply of well-qualified teachers. In view of the extra financial burden involved they gave an assurance that 'in any decision they may make to accept further State aid or even Local Rate Aid, with the conditions attendant upon both, they may rely upon the loyal and cheerful support of their Headmistresses'.

In the meantime the Board had reiterated the undertaking that in schools such as those of the Trust they would not insist on a 25 per cent intake from the public elementary schools but would be prepared to agree to 10 per cent, the figure to be based on the total intake for the previous year. The figure included children entering the preparatory departments for whom no grants were paid and this, coupled with the fact that girls from the elementary schools tended to stay longer than fee-paying girls, meant that over the years the percentage would be nearer sixteen or seventeen.

All the same, the Board had made a considerable concession: it did not pass unnoticed. The probability that the Trust would apply for the higher grant provoked the National Democratic Party* to send a deputation to the President of the Board of Education in January 1919, asking him to re-establish the rule that secondary schools in receipt of Government aid must take 25 per cent non-paying pupils from elementary schools; to give an assurance that in no circumstances would grants be made to schools unwilling to accept the obligation; to observe the regulation that the governing body of a school receiving Government aid must contain a majority of representative governors; and to secure an early opportunity for

* Founded in 1918 to unite support within the Labour movement for Lloyd George's Coalition Government.

a discussion in the House of Commons of the whole question of grants in aid of secondary schools.

Mr Fisher replied that he did not think it desirable to insist on a rigid rule with regard to the percentage of free-place pupils admitted to secondary schools and that in his opinion the best way to ensure that as many pupils as possible from elementary schools received the benefit of secondary school education was to make the rule as elastic as possible.

The Council were still vacillating when they received an unequivocal memorandum for submission to the Board drawn up by two retired headmistresses, Mrs Woodhouse (Sheffield and Clapham), now a member of the Council, and Miss Hastings (Nottingham and Wimbledon), who later succeeded her as a member of the Council. Both were convinced that the 10 per cent intake was too high. They were in 'entire sympathy' with the aim 'of extending the fullest advantages' of secondary education to ex-elementary scholars but felt most strongly that the high standing of the Trust schools would be fatally injured if they were largely composed of girls whose previous education had been on different lines. They therefore suggested that pupils under eleven should be omitted from the percentage calculations and, further, that the proportion of ex-elementary school children should at no time exceed 8 per cent of the other pupils above the age of twelve.

The Council modified the memorandum before submitting it to the Board. They did not seek to reduce the percentage: instead, they suggested that girls from schools of all kinds should be allowed to compete with the children from the elementary schools for the free places. At a subsequent conference at the Board of Education a deputation from the Council was told that the figure of 10 per cent was in itself 'a considerable concession . . . and was moreover liable to be challenged', but that children from the elementary schools who had progressed to municipal or county secondary schools need not be excluded from the percentage. The deputation was further informed that the representative governors on the governing body of a school in receipt of the higher grant need not necessarily be in the majority.

After further heart-searching and deliberation a pertinent memorandum was drawn up in 1919 by a prominent Council member and future Chairman, Mr Laurie Magnus. If 'we elect to stand on our own feet', he wrote, the Council would have to provide teachers' pensions as well as increasing fees by something approaching 50 per cent. The alternative to precarious independence was the acceptance of the Board's higher grant and, where available,

L.E.A. rate-aid. 'Are the Council prepared to stand aside from the main stream of educational reform, and to attempt to maintain twenty to twenty-five Schools distinguished by anti-social marks and cut off from the beneficent irrigation of State-grants and State-pensions?' Or, as Mr Maclean, the Secretary, put it more succinctly: 'Refusal of Government and Municipal Aid would mean detaching the Schools from the National Scheme and be contrary to the democratic spirit of the age.'

By this time the majority of headmistresses had withdrawn from their former entrenched position. 'Very few', they informed the Council, 'fear any ill effect of a 10 per cent admission of Ex-Elementary Scholars on the character of their Schools. Nearly all say that the effect of a 25 per cent admission would be disastrous.' They were aware that the higher percentage might be imposed at any time, especially with a Labour government in power, but in the light of changing opinion they felt that while due care must be taken in the selection of the free placers – 'we must not be accused of selecting for "class" '. The alternative – to become independent – seemed 'retrograde and against the trend of public opinion. We must not stand outside a great national scheme.'

In March 1920 the Trust sent a deputation to the Board of Education: it included the Chairman, Llewelyn Davies, nephew of the redoubtable Emily and a man of the utmost integrity, Mr Magnus, and Mr Maclean. An official of the Board asked what the Trust intended to do about the higher grant. He explained that although many parents could afford to pay higher fees 'all could not' and the Board were anxious to avoid the necessity of authorizing an increase. 'It was hardly a sufficient answer that the schools could be filled with children of parents who could afford to pay.' Acceptance of the higher grant 'would not only show that [the Council] were ready to take advantage of other means of finding the required additional income, but also that by the provision of free places they were prepared to do something to meet the needs of poorer parents. . . '. The meeting passed off well. The deputation, wrote an official, 'were extremely friendly and struck [us] as being genuinely desirous of progressing towards a more definite part in the local provision of secondary education . . .'.[1]

Three months later the Chairman received a letter from the Board expressing satisfaction 'that the Trust have definitely announced their intention to apply for the higher rate of grant'.

Acceptance of the grant resulted in an appreciable increase of the total received which went up by approximately £15,000 a year; but taking into account the fact that the fees of the free placers were by

126

no means always paid by the Local Education Authorities, Maclean reckoned that the gain throughout the school would be about £1 10s a year per pupil. At the same time, with the Board's permission, fees were increased from an average of £16 to an average of £20 a year, and in 1921 the Council placed all the salaries in their schools and training departments on the Burnham Scale.

By this time the schools had begun to arrange entrance examinations for the free placers. Payment of fees and local authority representation on governing bodies were settled by individual L.E.A.s. In some cases they took no financial responsibility and the cost had to be borne by the schools; in others they paid full fees for a proportion of the free placers or part fees for them all; in only a few cases were they prepared to foot the whole bill.

In the case of two schools alone – Croydon and Ipswich – did the L.E.A.s grant cover more than the payment of fees. Croydon had been in a special category ever since 1914 when, for purposes of administration, it had been transferred to a governing body which consisted originally of nine members, five of them, including the Chairman, nominated by the Borough Council, four by the Council of the Trust. The school remained the property of the Trust; the Governors undertook 'to preserve intact the status and traditions and the general scheme of education . . .' and the school received a maintenance grant from the Borough Council. Although initially the L.E.A. had majority representation, by 1920 numbers were even. At Ipswich rate aid was granted in 1921 after protracted negotiations ('though the delay does not arise at this end', as the Council tartly remarked), on condition that six of the eleven members of the Governing Body were nominated by the L.E.A., the Chairman being among the Council's five nominees. The closer administrative co-operation with the L.E.A.s which followed the acceptance of the higher grant was achieved with far less trouble than had been anticipated. Many L.E.A.s appointed as their local representatives on the governing bodies of the schools distinguished men and women who were already members of the Council: in every case, with the exception of Croydon and Ipswich, the Council's own nominees remained in the majority, the L.E.A. representation averaging one-third.

The applications for free places varied from school to school. At some there were as many as a hundred candidates for ten places and one or two schools admitted more than their quota. Others had difficulty in finding enough applicants of a suitable standard. Headmistresses were instructed by the Council to hold the examination for the free placers themselves, 'but if this cannot be amicably arranged with the L.E.A., then the L.E.A.s should be asked to send a sufficient number of their successful candidates to enable Head-mistresses to make a choice . . .'. If the quota still remained unfilled L.E.A.s were to be invited to submit additional candidates. They were not, however, always willing to do so.

Nevertheless the main issue had at long last been resolved. It had been debated at a time when the social climate was very different from the climate of today; yet, if the advice of the forward-looking members of the Council had been heeded, it would have been settled very much sooner.

In the course of negotiations between the Trust, the Board of Education and the L.E.A.s which subsequently took place the few local school committees which the Trust had set up were dissolved and Committees of Management or Governing Bodies were established in their place. Many distinguished men and women have served – and continue to serve – on these bodies. They work closely with the Council and with the schools concerned and have always been of the greatest possible help to headmistresses.

Chapter 11

Innovations

In 1920 the Trust was approaching its Golden Jubilee. Despite certain gloomy prognostications of previous years, twenty-five of the thirty-eight schools had survived. In the face of the ultra-conservative views of some of its members and headmistresses, the Council had contrived to steer the schools into the mainstream of educational development without abrogating their ideals and principles. The schools were open to girls of all classes and types, to a minimum of 10 per cent from the elementary schools, to the intellectually backward as well as the advanced: while the general academic standard remained high the schools had, in fact, become multilateral.

It is, perhaps, appropriate at this point to look at some of the ways in which their reputation for excellence and originality had been gained. Through the years their teaching methods had been highly praised by successive Board of Education Inspectors. In 1910, for example, the Secretary of the Trust had been asked if selected groups of promising young teachers might pay two-week visits to schools 'where they may be able to see teaching work of unusual merit or interest in their special subject or subjects'. Visits to two of the Trust's most academic schools – Clapham and Oxford High Schools – were accordingly arranged, with very useful results.

The health and well-being of the children had always been guarded with scrupulous care. In the early days of Wimbledon High School, it will be remembered, a girl in Form II 'had some delicacy and was allowed a muff for her feet'. A little later the Trust was in the forefront of the movement to introduce medical inspection and to equip its schools with gymnasia and playgrounds. Facilities were often primitive or inadequate but the girls were enthusiastic and well coached, facts which the Board acknowledged in 1913 with a request for a group of Inspectors of elementary and secondary schools to visit Blackheath High School 'where the Physical Training is thoroughly well done ... in order to see a lesson or lessons given by your Mistress of Physical Training'. In the 1920s

I

when there was a general demand for playing fields – something which had not been contemplated when the schools were founded – individual schools raised large sums of money for the purchase of suitable sites. Perhaps the most interesting of these was acquired by Wimbledon High School which bought the famous All England Tennis ground which the school still uses.

From the very first the Council had been eager to promote the finest possible teaching in music and art. Here, too, their efforts won the approval of the Board of Education. In 1914, to give one example, the Secretary was asked if he 'could spare us one or two copies of the list of approved music which the Trust supplies to all its Schools. Our Inspectors find this list extremely helpful and if you are able to meet us we should be grateful.'

The Trust's special interest in music dated from 1902 when the Council decided to set up a Music Advisory Board of three distinguished Doctors of Music – Lloyd, Eaton Faning and Ernest Walker – to inspect music and class singing in the schools and to submit written reports.

Music had been taught – and well taught – in a number of schools for a good many years, but from 1901 onwards Kensington was pre-eminent. The High School was ruled from 1901 until 1931 by Miss E. Home, a woman of intense determination and demanding energy. A musician of high quality and imagination, Miss Home organized the teaching and established a Music Training Department.

By 1909 music was included in the General Inspection of the Board of Education and in that year the Board's Inspector, Dr (later Sir Arthur) Somervell, Professor at the Royal College of Music, wrote a eulogistic report on the music at Kensington. 'The Head Mistress . . . who takes a large share of the teaching, has organized the work on original lines. The idea is to place Music on the same footing as other School subjects, and thus to enable the pupils to acquire a knowledge of the musical "language" to the same degree as that of any other language; that is to train them to read at sight, write from dictation in time and tune, to understand what they hear, and thus to prepare them for the study of the literature of the language. Upon this basis all the musical work of the School is built. . . .' Dr Somervell was equally impressed with the 'unique' course in the Training Department and the benefit to the students 'of constantly watching the Classes at work in the School, and of teaching under supervision some of the beginners . . .'. To sum up, it was 'a pleasure to visit a School where there is so much enthusiasm and so keen a sense of the importance and value of Music, both in itself, and as a means of general education'.

The music scheme arranged for Kensington was approved by the Music Advisory Board, as were similar schemes arranged for Streatham Hill and Wimbledon High Schools; in 1911 Dr Lloyd referred to the music at Kensington 'in the highest terms.'

The Council, anxious to provide the best possible course of instruction, appointed Dr Yorke Trotter, Principal of the London Academy of Music, as a visiting lecturer and arranged for a member of his staff to teach the piano in the Training Department. After an initial inspection of the teaching Dr Trotter came to the conclusion that his own methods had been adopted without any acknowledgment. He was incensed when a report in *The Times* in July 1909 of a demonstration of the music teaching in the school referred in glowing terms to Miss Home's 'system'. Although Miss Home repudiated the suggestion and explained that the system was in fact 'the result of the investigations of others', Dr Trotter resigned in dudgeon, taking his assistant with him. The Council referred the matter to the Music Advisory Board, who poured oil on the troubled waters. Miss Home, they declared, had 'a real claim to distinction', and neither side had acted unfairly towards the other. Dr Yorke Trotter and his assistant were therefore thanked for their 'valuable services' and informed that the Council accepted 'without reserve' the statement that Dr Trotter and his assistant 'employed in their music lessons the methods in use at the London Academy of Music'*.

Kensington High School retained its reputation for music. 'The results of the work are the most remarkable that I have yet come across in Secondary Schools,' wrote Dr Somervell in 1916. In 1925, in the early days of sound radio, the Education Committee of the Trust proudly reported to the Council that Miss Home had been 'invited to "broadcast" a discourse on Music Teaching'; in 1931, shortly before her retirement, the school was visited by Mr (now Sir Robert) Mayer, whose Children's Concerts have been a delight to thousands. Afterwards he wrote to congratulate Miss Home on her 'amazingly good' work, 'and lucky indeed are the children who have the advantage of coming under your tutelage'. Among Kensington pupils who became professional musicians were the cellist Antonia Butler and, in a later generation, Marion, Countess of Harewood (née Stein), now President of The Friends of the Trust. The Music Training Department was closed in 1935 in the face of competition from the recognized Schools of Music.

* In 1923, when Miss Home was asked for a copy of the original prospectus for her Training Department, she underlined the words, 'Lectures and Lessons are given by T. H. Yorke Trotter, Esq., Mus. Doc', adding: 'I am appalled at this relic of the past!'

Kensington was not the only good music school. Among others were – and still are – Bath, Brighton, Bromley (where the present headmistress has high hopes for a young violinist), Croydon (where the cellist Jacqueline du Pré was educated until the demands of her music became paramount), Newcastle (Central), Notting Hill and Ealing, South Hampstead, and Wimbledon, where in 1952 an opera written by Hugo Cole and commissioned and performed by the school under the direction of Miss Lenore Reynell, was highly praised in the press.

The music syllabus in the schools was based largely on Miss Home's scheme for Kensington. Girls were prepared for the recognized examinations: their work was not examined by the Music Advisory Board whose duties were confined to inspection and advice. The eminent members of the Board worked in harmony with the headmistresses and the Council, unlike their opposite numbers on the Trust's Art Advisory Board.

From 1882 until the beginning of the twentieth century the art work in the schools had been examined by Mr T. R. Ablett, a pioneer in the development of art education and founder of the Royal Drawing Society, who drew up the syllabus and selected work for the Society's annual exhibition. By 1909 the 'Ablett System' was being criticized by the Board of Education for its lack of disciplined methods. The headmistresses were also tired of a system which, they felt, failed to bring the syllabus in line 'with the most modern educational requirements' and so, acting as usual from the highest motives, the Council decided to set up an expert and independent Art Advisory Board and to discontinue the practice of entering girls for the examinations of the Royal Drawing Society.

Imaginative drawing and drawing from memory had been fostered by the Ablett System. These facilities were anathema to Mr (later Sir George) Clausen R.A., and Professor Henry Tonks of the Slade School (later Professor of Fine Art in the University of London), the best known members of the new Board.* 'We propose a system which we consider to be sound', they wrote, 'and one which, whether the pupils carry their studies further or no, will . . . give them an understanding of the principles underlying the representation of things in Art.' There was, they maintained, only one kind of teaching: it applied alike to artists and to children.

The Board's ideas seemed revolutionary to long-established teachers of art. One of them (she had taught for many years at Kensington) asked for an interview at the Board of Education. She

---

* Despite repeated urging by the headmistresses, the Council declined to appoint any women members either of the Music or of the Art Advisory Board.

explained that in her opinion in dispensing with Ablett the Council were 'going to the other extreme, that while the Ablett system was objectionable as being trivial, superficial and not productive of a real habit of work in the pupils, the new Committee (sic) are too academic and inclined to look for too high a standard of accuracy and to disregard the needs of those who have no particular gift for Art...'. The Board of Education, which had sanctioned the establishment of the Art Advisory Board, were thankful not to be asked to intervene. 'It seems to me', wrote one official to another, 'that the Council of the Trust while it is to be congratulated on its escape from Mr Ablett, has not very much advanced matters by the appointment of its Advisory Committee....'[1]

By 1911 the Board of Education had given its approval to a revised curriculum prepared by the Art Advisory Board, which had also begun to issue its own certificates of proficiency. The members of the Art Advisory Board took their duties very seriously but many art teachers felt cramped by their emphasis on meticulous drawing and could not accept the idea that genuine artists and ordinary children should be taught on precisely the same lines. When told of these objections Clausen replied that the standard in the schools was improving beyond all recognition, but that 'nothing worth having is done without concentration and hard work and these are not to be cultivated without discipline'.

Four of the five members of the Art Advisory Board signed a memorandum to the Council condemning 'go-as-you-please' methods and 'so-called imagination drawings'. The Board, they added, 'is prepared to stand by the teaching it advocates'. The fifth member declined to sign. He was not, he declared, 'so enamoured' by the suggestions of the Board 'as to be prepared to fight for them'.

The Council, which took due note of the memorandum, advised no action; but they were well aware that opposition to the continued existence of the Board was mounting. 'There is evidently a movement agin the government,' remarked Clausen in 1926: he had no intention of modifying his requirements. Five years later the Board's annual report was fiercely criticized by Miss D. F. P. Hiley, the brilliant and outspoken headmistress of Newcastle (Central) High School. 'Can we learn from an art that is well and truly dead?' she demanded. Poster art, which the Board professed to despise, was 'absolutely alive and essentially modern'.

It was left to an equally outspoken new member of the Council, Mrs V. H. Galbraith, to deliver the *coup de grâce*. She proposed that the Art Advisory Board be abolished; and it was dissolved in

133

1932. 'All good things come to an end,' declared the Board in a valedictory report. In private, however, one member expressed his injured feelings. 'If the Council imagine that the Public Authorities will preserve and continue the work as initiated', he wrote, 'they are mistaken. It will deteriorate . . . I go down with the ship!'

If he chanced to read press reports of an exhibition of the art work of the Trust schools held six years later he must have wondered if his worst fears had not materialized. The exhibition was evidently a great success, the *Queen* congratulating the Council and the staff of the schools on the quality of the drawings and the craftwork displayed. 'A high standard of skill is shown with a certain number of examples of outstanding talent' and there was a special word of praise for 'some more or less "impressionist" sketches, a theatre queue, a market scene, a bus stop, the interior of a draper's shop'. The wide variety and range of subjects indicated that 'the young artists are permitted to choose what pleases them. . . . This variety is perhaps due to the fact that in the schools of the Trust there is no one system of teaching art. . . . There is considerably more spontaneity and freedom . . . than in former years. It is clear that the art teachers are realizing the immense value, educationally and psychologically, of self-expression. . . .'

The Music Advisory Board, which had never aroused the same passionate intensity, was kept in being. Its activities were suspended during the Second World War and after the war, although an attempt was made to revive it, the surviving members were elderly and disinclined for further service. The Board was therefore allowed to die a natural death.

During the 1930s the Trust took the lead in an educational experiment which had far-reaching results. In Trust schools, as in a number of others, introductory lectures on physiology had already been started. In 1932, for example, the mothers of girls at Croydon High School were invited to a talk by a member of the British Social Hygiene Council 'on the instruction to be given to girls developing from childhood to adolescence'. Miss Gwatkin, the headmistress of Streatham Hill, went a step further and arranged 'some very successful lectures to the Sixth Form on the Biological Foundations of Human Life'.

The link between physiological and psychological development had not yet been established. In 1929 the Council had rejected an appeal from the Trust Headmistresses' Conference for specialist advice on the handling of difficult children. In 1933 the Conference put in a definite request for the appointment, on an experimental basis, of an experienced woman psychologist who would visit each of the schools in turn and, after consultation with the headmistress and staff, make general recommendations. An experiment of this kind, they said, 'would be a piece of pioneer work in educational research which the Council with its unique opportunities . . . and its past record of notable contributions to educational policy . . . is specially qualified to undertake'. The upshot of this request was the appointment in 1934 of Mrs Marion Milner as visiting psychologist. She was able to study only a few schools during the year at her disposal, but her findings were so significant that the appointment was renewed.

One of the most important and significant points to emerge from Mrs Milner's investigation was that the problem children about whom she had primarily been consulted came from educationally deprived homes. The social changes of the past half-century had opened the secondary schools to a number of children whose parents were quite unable to help them to formulate or give expression to their ideas. For these children – and also for all the others who were slow in learning – the ordinary curriculum was far too academic. Mrs Milner recommended the substitution of an Intelligence Quotient test at entry for the usual test of achievement which seemed to her to be unrealistic in schools with pupils from such widely differing backgrounds; and she emphasized the value of group work in which all would have a part to play. For the non-academic girls she recommended that in place of the standard lecture-type lesson there should be lessons with plenty of practical group activity. In this way the girls would become totally involved in their work and thereby acquire the skill and confidence to express themselves freely: they would also be greatly helped by the way in which practical activity acted as a spur to memory. This would not, of course, enable them to pass the academic examinations they found so difficult and Mrs Milner felt that an attempt should be made to persuade parents and employers that public examinations were not the be-all and end-all of school life but that character and personal qualities were more valuable than examination qualifications. Among her other recommendations were the appointment of a member of staff as careers mistress, adequate time for relaxation for both staff and pupils, the keeping of individual record cards which would provide a guide to each child's background and development, an increase in the number of free study periods, the election of form leaders, and an assurance that the girls would be equipped with a full knowledge of the facts of human reproduction by the time they reached the age of puberty.

Mrs Milner's recommendations had a mixed reception at

successive Headmistresses' Conferences. Some were rejected on the ground of insufficient evidence or because Mrs Milner, who had had no teaching experience herself, could not appreciate the practical difficulties in the way of introducing activity lessons without an increase in staff, or persuading parents to modify their faith in the importance of examination results. It was generally agreed, however, that there was a need for more consultation and co-operation with parents. There was also a need for sex education. The keeping of individual record cards was approved by some but not all the headmistresses. They recognized the usefulness of the I.Q. test but they did not think that it should be used as the sole criterion. They were in favour of appointing form leaders, but divided on the question of appointing a careers mistress, some of them maintaining that they themselves were best fitted to advise. Some headmistresses introduced group or project methods in related subjects, giving history and geography adjacent places in the time-table instead of keeping them in watertight compartments; and in a number of junior schools 'discovery' subjects were started in which history and geography were combined in a single lesson. In several schools free study periods were initiated and the system was kept up for a number of years. In 1942, for instance, when Miss M. D. Yardley became headmistress of Sydenham High School she found that her predecessor, Dr M. S. Smith, had set aside certain days on which the girls were free to choose the subjects they wished to study and to consult the subject mistresses when they needed help. 'It was an exhausting day', Miss Yardley remembers, 'and had to be carefully planned beforehand.' The girls enjoyed it but ultimately the staff lost faith in it and the free study days were dropped.

Much of what Mrs Milner advocated has long since passed into the normal currency of school life. In the 1930s some of her suggestions were revolutionary and the Trust headmistresses, even though they were not always in agreement and felt that in many ways she was too critical, pressed for her visits to be continued. 'We all feel', they wrote in 1937, 'that . . . the Trust Schools have led the way with a most interesting piece of pioneer work which may have results far outside our Schools.'

The Council extended the length of Mrs Milner's appointment and also gave her permission to make use of her findings in a book, *The Human Problem in Schools*. In a preface to the book, which was published in 1938,* Dr Susan Isaacs, the Head of the Department of Child Development at the Institute of Education, wrote: 'The Girls' Public Day School Trust Headmistresses have

* By Methuen.

performed a very great service to girls' education as a whole by their courage and enterprise in raising the question which led to Mrs Milner's experiment and by inviting a first class psychologist to enter their sacred preserves and report upon what she found. They have placed in their debt all who are concerned with the problems of mental development and of education in the life of adolescent girls.'

The book was very well received by the educational press. 'The statement on the jacket that "it embodies the results of one of the most interesting and important experiments undertaken in this country" is no exaggeration,' wrote *Mother and Child*. 'What is perhaps a little surprising is that such an investigation should not have been undertaken by the department of education of one of our universities but should have had to await the initiative of a governing body and a group of headmistresses.' *Education* described Mrs Milner as 'a psychologist with both feet on the ground' and praised her modest manner and the fact that her statements were 'tentative rather than dogmatic'. Other journals referred to her candour, sincerity and common sense, and compared the book with 'a clean wind' blowing through the schools.

The Council of the Trust, well satisfied with the experiment they had initiated, sent a copy of the book to each of the schools. When the Chairman referred to the investigation at the Annual General Meeting in 1939 the voice of a solitary shareholder was raised against it. Headmistresses, he said, were the best psychologists: there was no need for educational psychologists as such. He received no support and the continuance of Mrs Milner's appointment was confirmed. Unfortunately the exigencies of the Second World War put an end to her visits and after the war they were not revived. By that time it was usual to consult child guidance clinics and the Council encouraged headmistresses to go to them for psychological help in the case of difficult children. There is no doubt, however, of the value of the work which the Trust had initiated and supported.

Chapter 12
Golden Jubilee

1922 was the fiftieth anniversary of the Girls' Public Day School Trust. The plan to celebrate it fittingly was not ready in time but, as the organizing committee remarked enigmatically, 'so leisurely and movable a festival is difficult to fix in time; it is also difficult to fix in space'.

The Trust was in the midst of a financial crisis during Jubilee Year. The Council had reluctantly come to the conclusion that a building fund with a target of £50,000 which had been launched in 1912 and was still open was unlikely to exceed £9,000. An ambitious programme had been planned which was to have included a magnificent new purpose-built school for Putney. The school was, indeed, one of the two principal beneficiaries (Brighton and Hove was the other) but it only benefited to the extent of one additional house, a new assembly hall, laboratory and studio: the plan for the new building remains on the drawing-board to this day.

Jubilee Year coincided with the early days of the financial depression which severely affected the educational world. Despite the gathering gloom the Jubilee was celebrated on June 1, 1923 with a solemn service of thanksgiving in St Paul's Cathedral, 'a reassuring report as to [its] safety' having been received by the Council. More than 3,000 people attended the service: among them were between eight and nine hundred representatives of the 9,000 girls in the schools at the time. They had come from Trust schools in various parts of the country, from Newcastle in the north to Portsmouth in the south. They were dressed in white, with straw hats, school hatbands and rosettes in the school colours and, wrote the *Yorkshire Post*, 'delightful they looked'. The vast majority of the congregation were elderly women, former members of staff and representatives of the 100,000 pupils who had passed through the schools during the past fifty years.* On their lined faces the reporter claimed to see written 'something of the strenuous early days of the high school teaching'.

* For some of the many distinguished pupils see Appendix 3.

138

To the older members of the congregation the most moving of the prayers recited was one which commemorated the 'service and steadfastness' of the founders of the Trust, Maria Grey, Emily Shirreff, Henrietta Stanley and Mary Gurney. The sermon was preached by Dean Inge, who took as his text Isaiah 54:13 – 'And all thy children shall be taught of the Lord and great shall be the peace of thy children.' According to the *East Anglian Daily Times* the 'gloomy' Dean addressed his remarks exclusively to the elderly people present. He touched on various points of religion which he considered unsatisfactorily taught in some of the schools, and expressed the hope that 'there would be more unity of thought'. It was 'a matter of regret', the article concluded, that the Dean 'made no reference whatever to the occasion of the service'. It was, perhaps, as well that his remarks were inaudible to all but a few. The organizing committee had intended to print his sermon, but came to the conclusion that it was not 'sufficiently appropriate to make it worth while'. After the service there were a number of reunions with 1,600 former pupils meeting for tea in the City Halls.

The retiring headmistress of Streatham Hill High School, Miss Oldham, a past President of the Association of Head Mistresses, had written to the Board of Education suggesting that Jubilee Year might be the right moment to honour the Chairman of the Council, Mr Llewelyn Davies, and a representative of the headmistresses. The suggestion reached Sir Edmund Phipps, who had once been Assistant Secretary of the Trust but had gravitated to the Board where he became Principal Assistant Secretary for Elementary Education and, later, Deputy Secretary, and who was also a member of the Council of the Trust. Sir Edmund thought that if anybody deserved an honour it was Miss Oldham herself.

Miss Oldham has been described by one of her pupils, Elizabeth Hamilton, in her book *A River Full of Stars*, as small and square. 'Her large head, set low on her wide shoulders, gave her a bull-like appearance which was accentuated by the curls resting on her broad forehead, and by a habit when displeased of thrusting her head forward as though about to charge.' She was a truly great teacher, 'a big-hearted woman with interests that extended far beyond the School'. She had a taste for music and the theatre, for women's suffrage and social reform. 'She sat on committees, addressed societies and took a busy part in all that had to do with citizenship.'[1]

This being so, it seems a pity that Sir Edmund was overruled by his superior at the Board, who did not consider that there was a headmistress 'of sufficient note to merit special distinction'. The

Trust, he added, had undoubtedly 'done a most valuable work for the Higher Education of girls' but Llewelyn Davies, though keenly interested in the welfare of the Trust', was a comparative newcomer to the educational world. He was 'a reasonable person to deal with [but] as you would expect he (or perhaps his Council) are not inclined to move forward with great speed . . .'.[2]

It was agreed, however, that the President of the Board of Education would receive a copy of the recently published *Jubilee Book of the Girls' Public Day School Trust* and that an appreciative letter should be drafted for his signature, which the Trust should be empowered to make public. The *Jubilee Book* was a composite work. Each school had contributed a brief account of its origin and history: these were edited by the Vice-Chairman of the Council, Laurie Magnus, who himself wrote chapters on the history of women's education both before and after the foundation of the Trust.

Mr Magnus was Chairman from 1929 until his early death in 1933. By appointing a practising Jew and disregarding the subsequent spate of offensive anti-Semitic postcards sent to them anonymously through the post, the Council showed their liberal religious principles. Mr Magnus is remembered today as gay, friendly, highly intelligent, intuitive and extremely tactful. As Maclean wrote:

He steers us safely through the shoals,
And gets us out of awkward holes . . .
Reluctantly he gives the sack
To girls whose sins are very black.
In polished phrases he assuages
Parents whom the 'Sec.' enrages.
Now and then he has a bunch
Of high-brow mistresses to lunch;
But when a teacher's got to go,
'Tis he who has to tell her so;
And no one can with greater skill
Administer a gilded pill.

The *Jubilee Book* contained one or two understandably critical comments on the dictatorial habits of the Board of Education: there were references to 'vexatious *Regulations*' and to the recurrence of the 'minatory refrain . . . "subject to the approval of the Board" '. Nevertheless, as Mr Magnus conceded, 'if we wanted certain benefits, we had to accept certain conditions'.[3] These references did not escape the notice of Sir Edmund Phipps, but the letter from the President of the Board of Education, Mr Edward

Wood (later Lord Halifax) was kind and laudatory. 'Records such as this', he wrote, 'are well worth making, if only because they serve to remind us of the immense changes which have occurred in the popular conception of girls' education, a development in which the Trust and the teachers have played so honourable a part.'

Within the charmed circle of the Trust there was a moving little ceremony at the annual conference of headmistresses which on this occasion was also attended by former headmistresses and members of the Council. At the end of the formal proceedings Miss Florence Gadesden stepped forward to read an address on behalf of her colleagues past and present. 'We . . . wish to place on record our deep sense of the great service rendered by our Council to the cause of national education,' she said. 'Through fifty years of very mingled fortunes the Council have laboured steadily and devotedly for the advancement of the secondary education of English girls, and we, the nature of whose work places us in a position to estimate the result of that devoted service, cannot refrain from offering to them our tribute of appreciation and gratitude. . . . [We] recognize also that the principles which have guided the educational administration of the Trust have been not only right in themselves, but have proved of great value in raising the status and developing the efficiency of the teaching profession. To the fullest extent compatible with a firm central control the Council have allowed freedom of development to the individual schools. . . . We have learned to count on our Council's encouragement in anxiety, help in trouble, and support in need. . . .'

Miss Gadesden spoke truly. The change in the relations between the Council and the headmistresses was now complete and the headmistresses were confidently aware that their right of independent action, once recognized, would always be respected. There would inevitably be differences of opinion in the future, and individual Council members might deplore a particular course of action, yet through it all the Council remained – and has continued to remain – firmly behind them.

As a memento of Jubilee Year the headmistresses presented the Council with a walnut wood chair for the use of the Chairman, and Mr Maclean with a clock, inscribed in Latin verse 'to one . . . to whose punctual care we have owed it if we were punctual ourselves'. Llewelyn Davies and Maclean made suitable replies but there is no record that Maclean delivered his in verse. A tribute by the headmistresses to the hard-working office staff brought the proceedings and the memorable year to a close.

Chapter 13
'Vexatious Regulations'

The 'vexatious *Regulations*' imposed by the Board of Education and mentioned by Magnus in his *Jubilee Book* applied, of course, to all secondary schools and caused general resentment, not least in the direct grant schools which prided themselves on their freedom of action. As far as the Trust schools were concerned, officials of the Board were often too rigid in their endeavour to fit them neatly into the educational pattern. The Council and the headmistresses, on the other hand, were sometimes suspicious and arrogant in their determination to preserve their standards and the right to admit girls of all types. As Maclean wrote to Phipps at the Board in 1923: 'Of course we are aware that we do not pass whole battalions of girls through Matriculation in the wonderful way that some of the best County Schools do; but their girls live mainly for that, and our girls essentially do not. Moreover, their Schools consist chiefly of picked girls from the Elementary Schools, whereas we take in the backward and stupid, in order to give them a chance in life which they deserve as much as any one else.'[1]

Examinations had been a sore point since 1918 when, at the Board's request, the university examining bodies had co-operated to produce two standard examinations – the 'First' and 'Second'. The First – School Certificate – was to be taken at sixteen after five years' general education; the Second – Higher School Certificate – was to follow two years later after more specialized study.* The Board were rightly opposed to the system of cramming, and in pursuance of a policy first enunciated in 1911 that examinations 'should not be concerned only with picked pupils', stipulated that 'except with the concurrence of the Board a pupil may only be entered for a First Examination as one of a form so entered'. Initially – to the fury of headmasters and headmistresses and of

---

* In a further attempt to standardize examinations the Board ruled that no external examinations below the standard of the First should be taken by pupils in grant-earning schools. In due course, however, they agreed to recognize the normal examinations of several universities as First and Second Examinations.

parents who knew in advance that their children had little or no hope of success – the Board insisted on strict compliance even though they realized that it would 'frequently involve a considerable proportion of failures, partial or complete'. They offered a grant of £2 per candidate but only on condition that a whole form was entered; and in the event of failure they were normally prepared to pay for a second entry.

Application for the rule to be waived had to be made through local Inspectors whose interpretation of it varied. In 1919, for instance, Miss Bell, the headmistress of Sutton High School, applied for exemption for four of her girls. It was refused, and she was obliged to enter one girl who was just recovering from concussion, one who came from a family with two mental defectives, one who was still deeply disturbed by the death during the war of a brother, and one who had not been long enough in the school to come anywhere near the required standard.

The regulation insisting on the entry of an entire form remained in force until 1928. By that time it had proved so unworkable that the Board were induced to admit that a form could be divided into parallel streams, only one of which need be entered for an examination. This was a reversal of the egalitarian policy on which it had been based and reintroduced the system of cramming. Next year wiser counsels prevailed. The regulation was dropped, the Board relying 'on school authorities to take steps to ensure that attention is not concentrated unduly on pupils to be entered for the examination to the neglect of those who are thought likely to fail if presented'.

Intimately bound up with the question of examinations was the question of the curriculum and timetable, which the headmistresses considered should be settled by themselves. Neither they nor the Council were prepared to rescind the rule which made work compulsory only in the mornings, stubbornly clinging to the idea – real or illusory – of the civilizing influence of afternoons spent at home. Provision had been made for voluntary afternoon attendance for preparation, extra subjects and physical training, but the Board of Education, which listed the subjects for study and the hours to be allotted to each, were convinced that without compulsory afternoon school it would be impossible to comply with their *Regulations*. The headmistresses and the Council refused to comply: that morning school only had proved 'no bar to intellectual progress', they declared, was proved by the continuing success of pupils from Trust schools in the public examinations.

The Board was not appeased. H.M.I.s, the Council were informed, often complained of 'the crowded state of the curriculum' and the fact that important subjects 'had to be taken at break-neck speed, with the result that girls were "fagged" at the end of the morning'. The Board did not insist on the introduction of compulsory afternoon school although they strongly advised it. It was in fact gradually introduced, although not for ordinary form purposes, at the Council's discretion, particularly after 1925 when Miss Beard, the headmistress of Putney High School, complained that many of her pupils came from 'uncultivated homes and parents who could not control their daughters' movements if left at home in the afternoon'. In essence, however, the rule remained in force until the Second World War when a complete timetable for afternoon work was generally adopted.

A number of minor disputes arose from the Trust's refusal to introduce compulsory afternoon school. Headmistresses were under the impression (they were soon disabused) that the 'sole duty' of an H.M.I. 'should be to inspect and to give advice'. They were annoyed when Inspectors suggested among other things that more time should be made for housewifery, a subject which they had never taken very seriously. In most of the schools – and in other high schools as well – 'housewifery' was construed as needlework and taught only in the lower forms. The Board wanted a comprehensive course, including practical and theoretical cookery and hygiene as well as needlework. When this demand was put to the Council in 1906 the Board were 'respectfully' informed that the schools of the Trust were 'designed to give the highest type of teaching for girls [looking] forward to form educated members of society, or preparing for work in life as teachers, or for other posts requiring culture and systemized training'. The Council would, they said, endeavour to introduce hygiene into the curriculum but thought that an extended housewifery course 'would make a serious alteration in the aim and work of the Schools'. Parents were worried lest compliance with the Board's requirements would bring about a change in the character of the schools. Some girls had already been removed, others who had been entered had been sent elsewhere: and if this feeling spread it would involve the Trust in serious financial loss and damage the educational prospects of the girls sent to inferior private schools. Finally, with a grandiloquent gesture, the Council threatened to raise the fees, abandon state aid and announce their independence, 'rather than acquiesce in altering the curriculum so as to make it what would in their opinion be a lower description of School'.

In view of this threat which they may – or may not – have taken at its face value the Board modified their demands very slightly. They were willing, they said, for one of the three branches of housewifery to be dropped. The headmistresses thankfully opted for cookery and needlework, since most of them felt that hygiene 'was not always a desirable subject . . . especially if it included physiology', and could in any event 'be more easily provided if it could be included in the science curriculum, or given . . . in summer in place of drill . . .'.

In actual fact headmistresses seem to have taken very little notice of the Board's demands. The Inspectors who visited Kensington High School in 1909 pointed out that while the curriculum contained 'most of the subjects usually taught in a first-grade secondary school' a significant omission was 'the lack of a course of Housewifery, either practical or theoretical, or anything, except Needlework, which would generally be described as a definite preparation for home life'.

To meet this complaint the Council instituted in a number of schools a one-year post-scholastic course in domestic economy (or home-life) for girls from seventeen to twenty-one, previously high school pupils, with the emphasis on 'Household Management, seeing that the Students will probably become Mistresses of Households'. Since the majority would already have had 'an excellent course of Physics and Chemistry the opportunity might now be given of showing the practical bearing of these subjects on the ordinary work of the household and on the various processes of cookery and laundry-work'.

The Board approved, especially when the Inspectors found at Streatham Hill High School, for example, that girls were staying at school longer than they would otherwise have done in order to take the course. The classes were very popular in some schools. The Clapham class, opening with seven students, reached more than fifty by 1909, the students subsequently taking posts as housekeepers and school matrons. At Croydon, however, the aim was said to be 'entirely practical', the girls being trained exclusively for the duties of home life. As the headmistress Miss Leahy explained in 1913, when well over a hundred girls had taken the course, 'the difficulties of modern housekeeping will be met with more cheerful courage by a mistress who is not helpless'.

Miss Leahy, herself a historian and a mathematician, was typical of a new generation of headmistresses. The question of academic achievements had not arisen in the case of the first Trust headmistresses 'whose striking personalities and strong opinions had more than compensated for their almost inevitable lack of paper

K

145

qualifications' but by the end of the century the Council were in a position 'to serve the growing intellectual traditions of our schools by the appointment of University women at their head'.

The post-scholastic home-life courses which had been introduced into a number of schools ranked for purposes of grant as Day Technical Classes,* provided the students were distinct from pupils taking the ordinary school curriculum, and they were governed by the Board's *Regulations for Technical Schools*. The headmistresses were irritated by the distinction: the courses formed an integral part of the school, they argued, so why should they not be eligible for secondary school grant in the ordinary way?† 'The arrangements . . . have always been a mystery to me,' wrote Miss Leahy to Mr McDowall. 'As they come under the Day Technical Classes it seems difficult to discover what is happening.' McDowall confessed himself equally baffled. There were innumerable complaints at the immense amount of paper work involved. 'I think it is outrageous that prompt replies should be expected to *all* communications,' wrote Miss Leahy in 1911.

A bureaucratic Board official gleefully noted that year that an examination of the Croydon register furnished 'evidence of considerable carelessness on the part of the officers responsible . . .' He also discovered irregularities in the registers for Kensington and Notting Hill and took the opportunity of reminding the Secretary (now Maclean) that grants from public funds depended directly on the entries in the registers and on the claim forms and that it was essential 'that such entries should be entirely trustworthy'. 'I am sick of protesting to the B. of E.', wrote Maclean to Miss Leahy; and to Miss Paul,‡ the headmistress of Notting Hill: 'I propose to send them the usual answer: that their forms are so complicated that it is impossible to guarantee accuracy.' Miss Paul, a most endearing woman, tolerant, understanding and humorous, replied that she had no objection to filling up forms 'but I can't guarantee accuracy because I don't understand them'. When the headmistress of Norwich wrote in the same vein Maclean answered that there were some 'obstructive fossils' at the Board who needed strangling.

The scheme was intricate enough to confuse even Sir Edmund Phipps. 'I find', he wrote to Maclean in 1910, 'that a difficulty has

---

* Schools of Art also ranked as Day Technical Classes.

† Special courses were also introduced for younger girls with a practical rather than an intellectual bent. These were recognized as part of the school curriculum provided there was a reasonable amount of instruction in ordinary subjects.

‡ She was appointed headmistress of Clapham High School in 1913.

arisen upon the claim for the Notting Hill Day Technical Classes (Domestic Science) which has raised a question of principle affecting the recognition for the current year. . . . These points will be settled between the Secondary and Technical Branches as soon as possible: meantime I am afraid we can only wait.' He went on to explain that work at the Board had been disrupted 'by our arrangements for the Funeral Procession [of King Edward VII] which occupied us all last week'.

A few weeks later the Board announced that no new courses would be recognized for grant as Day Technical Classes: those already in being would continue to qualify provided conditions and numbers were satisfactory. There was, of course, no reason why a course, once recognized, should continue to qualify again automatically, and the threat hung like a sword of Damocles over the schools.

The threat of non-recognition was of special concern to schools with fully-fledged training departments. Chief among these was Clapham, where the dynamic Mrs Woodhouse, who became headmistress in 1898, founded a training college with four departments: a postgraduate department for the training of teachers in secondary schools, a kindergarten (Froebel) department, an art department and one for domestic science. Teacher training was Mrs Woodhouse's great joy. She believed that teachers must have 'a professional outlook and definite educational aims' and that children must be safeguarded 'from the incompetence of unqualified practitioners'. As a pioneer headmistress, Mrs Woodhouse was renowned in the wider educational world. Her interest in further education was reflected in the training departments, known collectively as the Training College. The Postgraduate Department was for nearly twenty years in the capable hands of Miss Henriette Dent, and the Training College as a whole produced teachers of a very high order who were in great demand in secondary schools and training colleges all over the country. Yet Mrs Woodhouse and her successors were constantly harassed by changing Board of Education *Regulations*,* and frustrated during the years when recognition was withdrawn from one or other of the departments on the grounds of insufficient numbers or inadequate facilities.

Withdrawal of recognition, wherever it might occur, was a serious

* A regulation which caused particular hardship and was generally resented laid down that no grant should be paid for any group containing fewer than five students. It also stipulated that the grant should be paid only in respect of multiples of five: thus, if a group contained fourteen students the grant was only paid in respect of ten.

matter. A special source of trouble (not, of course, in Trust schools alone) was the Board's Advanced Course system. In 1917, with the object of stimulating advanced work among pupils who stayed on at school after the age of sixteen, the Board launched a scheme by which certain schools were recognized as centres for Advanced Courses in the upper fifth and sixth forms. Recognition ensured a grant of up to £400 a year, the greater part of which had to be spent on increased salaries for suitably qualified teachers. In return, the school authorities undertook certain obligations with regard to maintenance allowance and exemption from fees for pupils who would not otherwise be able to remain at school to follow the course. They also had to ensure a required number of pupils and teachers with suitable qualifications, conform to stated requirements of syllabus, and provide suitable equipment, notably for the teaching of science.

There were three Advanced Courses: science and mathematics, modern studies, and classics. The schools of the Trust at once began to reorganize the work of their senior pupils to meet the Board's requirements. Much depended on the opinion of individual Inspectors and, as usual, these appeared inconsistent. Judging by the views of her local Inspector, grumbled Miss Leahy, 'which he claimed to be those of the Board . . . it appeared that only very abnormal girls could take a course such as he specified and those girls would be unable to take it who had to specialize for the existing School Examinations held by the Universities'. By the end of 1917 the Board had recognized courses in three schools only: science and mathematics at Clapham, and modern studies at Notting Hill and Streatham Hill. Applications from the other schools had been turned down because of insufficient numbers (the normal minimum was nine) or an inadequate syllabus.

Headmistresses of schools which had been slighted were justifiably indignant. Miss Gadesden of Blackheath maintained that her sixth-form girls had been doing 'advanced work' in modern studies for years, 'and year after year we have sent girls to the Universities, all of whom have taken up "Honours" work. My difficulty is not saying that advanced work . . . will be carried on but in stating definitely that a *certain* number of girls can be produced each year for any particular group of subjects.' Blackheath did, in fact, qualify for science and mathematics, and modern studies in 1918, but in 1920 Miss Gadesden's successor Miss Gale was warned that recognition would be withdrawn unless the numbers were maintained.

Six more schools were recognized in 1918: Croydon (science and mathematics), Kensington (modern studies), the Belvedere, Liverpool (science and mathematics, and modern studies), Tunbridge Wells jointly with the City School (science and mathematics), Sheffield (science and mathematics) and Ipswich (science and mathematics). Miss Gale, who was headmistress of Ipswich High School at the time, was proud that hers was the only school in the area to institute an advanced course. She had a struggle to raise the requisite number of pupils but the Council had empowered her to offer exhibitions to girls from the municipal schools. 'Rather a triumph to get their Headmistress to agree to a scheme of transfer!' she remarked. The Borough was also offering scholarships and she herself was offering two to girls from the county. The Council enquired if it was really necessary to take county girls on scholarships, to which the Machiavellian woman replied that she must have them in order to get the course started, but 'once I have got [the] course going, [the] offer of places need not be renewed'.

Sheffield High School's recognition was withheld in 1920 owing to lack of scientific apparatus. This seemed a most arbitrary decision since equipment for a new laboratory was on order. Llewelyn Davies, who called at the Board with Maclean, referred to it as 'a piece of harsh administration'. Maclean suggested that it was the result of a change of Inspectors and might have been a mistake, especially as the girls had obtained extraordinarily good results in science in the Higher Certificate examination. He was stiffly told that there had been no mistake. The grant had been withheld owing 'to a clear failure to satisfy the express conditions'.[2] At Sheffield and elsewhere, although application for recognition had been made in good time, the Board's decision was delayed until all the arrangements had been made and the course had actually started.

Tunbridge Wells lost its grant in 1921 because the standard of the pupils was not high enough, and Streatham Hill's grant was withheld the following year. This proved something of a relief to Miss Oldham, the headmistress. 'The only regret I feel', she said, 'is for the financial loss to the Council. Educationally I am convinced that we shall gain now that we shall have the liberty to plan each girl's curriculum and her time so as to fit her abilities and needs.' The Board's insistence that numbers should be guaranteed in advance meant that a headmistress sometimes had to try and induce girls to take a recognized course, something she was naturally averse to doing. In 1923 Miss Sanders, headmistress of Sydenham,* explained to the Council that she was applying for reasons of prestige and finance alone. 'The staff and I give due weight to what

* Previously headmistress of Tunbridge Wells.

149

our experienced and friendly Inspectors have said and we will leave no effort unmade to improve the work, but I do deprecate with all my strengh a "speeding up" to a regulation standard, set, after all, by the new municipal schools . . . I believe that the reason for "the manner and bearing" of the girls and "the energy and enthusiasm over their games and other interests" which pleased the Inspectors, is that they are not over-pressed. . . .'

During the years of the economic depression the problem became even more acute, for many girls left school early. In 1935, however, the Board of Education changed over to a system of capitation grants awarded in respect of sixth formers who had passed the First Examination. The change was greeted with relief both by the Association of Head Mistresses and the Trust headmistresses: they considered it sound. in principle even though they realized that some schools might lose financially. But they continued to resent the petty as well as the major demands and restrictions, some of which seemed to them to be frivolous or irrelevant.

A demand which drove several Trust headmistresses to the point of rebellion was for details of the further education and occupation of girls who had left school. This information, as the Board rightly pointed out, was 'likely to preserve a relationship between the School and its old pupils, and thus to react favourably on the corporate life of the School'. In schools such as Kensington where, as Miss Home explained, parents often went abroad and removed their children without saying where they were going, the information 'could only be pure guesswork'. The population of Putney, said the headmistress, Miss Hewetson, appeared 'to be more than usually migratory. . . . In the majority of cases . . . the girls live at home and have no careers.' Most annoyed of all was Miss D. F. P. Hiley of Newcastle (Central) who had raised the school to a position of great importance among the schools of the north of England. She supposed, she wrote to Maclean in 1918, that 'it would be misunderstood for contempt of court if I sent a courteous note [to the Board] to say that I was so glad that Mr X had come safely through the war and was happily at work with all his old vigour. He is making enquiries about children who left years ago!' If only the Board could be persuaded to accept a few obvious suggestions 'you could save hours, even days, of time to the schools of the country, not to mention that extravagant expenditure of temper which is the result of being compelled to do work which one knows to be entirely useless and unreasonable, but of course I don't want to throw Mr X out of employment. Perhaps he could be educated to do something better.'

150

Miss Hiley,* wrote one of her pupils, 'with her scholarly mind and quick intelligence, her ready wit and hatred of all sham and shoddiness, might have been a very alarming headmistress, but these qualities were balanced by a strong sense of justice, utter lack of pettiness . . . and her deep interest in people and a faculty for getting the best out of them'.

Mr Maclean was alternately soothing and brisk. 'Kindly note that I [alone] am the sacred medium for correspondence with the B. of E.', he wrote to one headmistress who had been trying to put her own case to the Board.

The irritation and frustration were general. 'The complicated and ever-spreading network of local and central bureaucratic control is destroying the individuality of the schools', declared the Association of Headmasters in 1922, 'crippling the powers of governing bodies, alienating local interest and deadening the enthusiasm of the teachers.' Officialdom run mad was the verdict of the *Times Educational Supplement*. In an article published in January 1923 it accused the Board of becoming an office 'whose aim is restricted, as far as possible, to the minute allocation of Parliamentary Grants . . .'. A system of correspondence and filing of papers was in use 'which no business office would tolerate' and the basis on which grants were allocated lacked 'both uniformity and simplicity'.

Perhaps the worst storm which blew up during the early 1920s between the Board of Education on the one hand and the Associations of Headmasters and Head Mistresses and, among other bodies, the Council of the Trust on the other, concerned the relationship between the preparatory and junior departments and the senior school. The dispute threatened the schools of the Trust in particular, for their preparatory departments were a direct legacy from Emily Shirreff. The primary object of the Trust, as the Council saw it, was 'general education and not the winning of distinctions in Examinations'. Children who entered the preparatory department at five passed almost automatically through the junior school to enter the senior school at eleven, and many of those originally regarded as backward soon made up for lost time. There was an examination for outsiders wishing to enter the senior school: for fee-payers it was based more on general knowledge than achievement, for free placers it was stiffer but more limited in scope. There was, however, an ever growing pressure on secondary school places, and the Board naturally considered that fee payers had an advantage over

* After her retirement in 1935 she summed up her experiences in a lively, wise and entertaining little book, *Pedagogue Pie*.

free placers and preparatory department children had an advantage over both. They were anxious for the Trust to introduce a similar test for children of all types, based on the probability of a candidate's passing the 'First' Examination at the age of sixteen. They could – and did – point to at least one instance of injustice towards the free placers. In 1922 Miss Bell of Sutton rejected seven out of nine applicants for free places, 'as being not of the right type and as not showing a satisfactory attitude towards work'. An Inspector who had seen the examination papers set for the free placers and fee payers respectively and the written answers of both groups said that it should have been possible to admit six of the seven and that 'a lower standard had been accepted by Miss Bell for fee payers than for free placers of the same age'. Questioned by the Council, Miss Bell insisted that fee-paying children should be given every chance of entering the school and added that, in her opinion, the Board's *Regulations* were 'growing so oppressive that she could not continue to work under them'. The Chairman, Llewelyn Davies, claimed that the Trust had no wish 'to apply fanciful tests to free placers and . . . the matter would no doubt be put right'. But, as the Council and headmistresses saw it, the chief difficulty was the Board's insistence on a written examination in two subjects – English and arithmetic. Children from elementary schools concentrated on these subjects which would given them an advantage over children whose curriculum, like that of their own juniors, was more widely based.

The headmistresses in conference then passed a resolution deploring the 'rigid conditions' which the Board sought to impose, because they would 'inevitably exclude from the Schools of the Trust many who are fully capable of profiting by education in a Secondary School'. They suggested that even if a satisfactory entrance test could be devised it 'would fall very harshly on children, who, lacking the sharpness which sometimes accompanies shallow wits, are slower in development and are, therefore, more in need of the kind of education which the Schools of the Trust are founded to supply'.

A deputation from the Council which called at the Board was told that, despite the complexity of the question 'and the hardship for backward girls, public money could not be wasted on girls who would not profit'. The selection of pupils 'could not be left solely to the individual judgment of headmistresses. There must be a genuine test, which would be virtually competitive in crowded Schools . . .'. Provided, however, it 'did not exclude the children of the poor in favour of the children of the rich; or result in a number of unsatisfactory pupils being retained in the Schools, it might be a wide one . . .'. The children in the preparatory and junior departments, the Board argued in 1922, 'should not be regarded as having a vested right to proceed to the main school and . . . these children should be subjected to a test at the age of eleven to secure that only those who were fitted to proceed were allowed to enter the main school, and . . . were not given preference over better qualified girls from outside'.[3]

The Association of Head Mistresses was equally worried by this decision. It might result, said a former President, Miss Sara Burstall, headmistress of Manchester High School,* in 'selecting the wrong type of child, the precocious, quick, "clever", voluble eleven-year-old who is not really able and does not later justify the selection'.

There was a distinct possibility in 1922 that secondary schools would be compelled to close their preparatory departments for children under ten. The idea, which did not materialize, was strongly resisted by the Associations of Headmasters and Head Mistresses and by the Council of the Trust. The Council, convinced of the importance of ensuring 'the unbroken education of a girl from the Kindergarten upwards in the same school with its continuous tradition', were willing to compromise. They would 'submit their children of ten to a test with a view to the elimination of those who certainly would not profit by further education at the school'. This did not imply that it would be a written examination or based on the likelihood of a girl passing the Board's First Examination five years later. 'Nor will it be entirely an intellectual test. Administrative capacity and practical gifts are not revealed in an intellectual test at eleven.'

The test was extremely elastic, and children from the preparatory departments continued to pass almost automatically into the senior school as fee-paying pupils. But the Council and the Association of Head Mistresses thought that the tests applied by L.E.A.s for the award of free places were far too narrow. There should be room in the secondary schools of the country for girls of varying degrees of ability, declared a spokesman for the Association of Head Mistresses in 1934, but while 'the present keen competition for secondary school places persists, either free or at less than the education costs', the entrance examinations would continue to be framed to suit the majority of schools in the area, 'that is with curriculum of the elementary school in mind. Children who have followed the wide curriculum and more leisurely work of good preparatory schools

* Not a Trust school.

153

are being almost entirely excluded; and yet similar children have in the past proved to be some of the most promising material . . .'.

By that time the majority of secondary school pupils were non-fee-paying but the change to universal free education with all it implied was yet to come.

Chapter 14
Problems

The economic depression of the 1920s was, of course, reflected in the educational world, and teachers were among the principal sufferers. Under the Teachers Superannuation Act of 1918 followed by the Act of 1925, teachers in State-aided schools qualified for pensions based on salary and length of service.*

The nation's difficulties and the 'axe' with which Sir Eric Geddes was empowered to cut departmental spending not only nullified many of the enlightened reforms embodied in the Fisher Act but had a direct effect on teachers' salaries. In 1923 a 5 per cent cut for twelve months was made in the salaries of all teachers in L.E.A. schools. The Council of the Trust were unwilling to enforce the cut in their own schools and asked if they were affected. They were told that neither the Board of Education 'nor the authorities have any direct financial interest in the abatement being made' in schools which were not maintained by the local authorities, which meant that only Croydon and Ipswich High Schools would be concerned.

On the other hand, the Board imagined 'that just as [you] decided to adopt the Burnham Scales, so [you] may desire to adopt this abatement of them . . . No doubt the abatement is generally represented by the teachers as their contribution towards the national demand for economy. This particular consideration does not apply to your teachers [but] they would have the comfort of knowing that the money they sacrifice . . . would be available for the educational purposes of the schools in which they are serving. I have no doubt that all your schools would like to do a good deal more for their pupils if the money were available.'

The question was put to the Trust headmistresses who were

* The pension was calculated on the salary earned in the last five years of service together with a lump sum calculated on the same basis. The scheme was originally non-contributory, but the teachers were later asked to contribute 5 per cent a year from their salaries towards superannuation, the authorities adding a further 5 per cent. This figure, for both sides, was raised to 6 per cent under the Act of 1956, and in 1966 the authorities' contribution was raised to $8\frac{1}{2}$ per cent.

willing to be guided by the Council although, as Miss Oldham of Streatham Hill, now on the brink of retirement, remarked: 'It would be wholesome if a few pensioned and salaried people in high places (Lord Chancellors, etc.) were to set a good example by voluntarily renouncing 5 per cent of what *they* receive – and better still if the Government could see a better way out of their economic difficulties than by repeated discrimination against one profession in particular – a galling process to those affected.' The assistant staff hoped the cut would not be made but they, too, agreed to abide by the Council's decision. In the event the cut was only made at Ipswich, where the L.E.A. majority was in a position to impose it, but the staff did not suffer as the Council made good the deficit.

This gesture of independence was not repeated: in 1931 the Council complied with the terms of a national salary cut of 10 per cent. The cut was accompanied by a reduction in the standard capitation grant to the schools, though not to an amount nominally equal to the sum by which salaries had been reduced. The net result to the Trust was a saving of about £6,518 but, as the Education Committee pointed out, 'the financial crisis has so far caused a falling-off in the amount of the school fees of at least £2,500'. There was, however, a balance of approximately £4,000 which was placed by the Council in a special reserve account.

In all schools the number of staff was reduced, and the quality of the teaching suffered with the appointment of new teachers with all-round rather than specialist qualifications.

Among other economies effected by the Board of Education was a standstill order on buildings. In the case of the Trust the embargo was partially lifted to allow Notting Hill High School to be transferred to Ealing (under the name of the Notting Hill and Ealing High School) in 1931, and for Sydenham and Norwich to move in 1933 to more suitable accommodation.

The removal of Norwich High School from the congested centre of the city to its present home, Eaton Grove, a large house standing in its own grounds, was only accomplished after a prolonged argument with the Board. The district was prosperous, Eaton Grove was capable of enlargement and the Council, convinced that if this were done the school would attract many more children, submitted plans to accommodate a hundred pupils over and above the existing two hundred and thirty.

At the suggestion of the Board Sir Edmund Phipps, who had a foot in both camps, acted as go-between. As he explained to the Chairman, Mr Laurie Magnus, the authorities 'have had to refuse all L.E.A. new proposals and can't allow a preference to other schools. . . . The Board don't want to refuse to pass our plans, and would like us to help them to get out of the difficulty . . .'. Magnus, whose loyalty was to the Trust, replied that while he appreciated the fact that the Board could not countenance the building of 'more luxurious or more extensive accommodation for children already in the School', this was a question 'of providing places for children who have to be educated' and, as the Council proposed to foot the bill from the proceeds of the sale of the old building and its playing fields, together with contributions promised by parents and, if necessary, by mortgages and low interest loans, 'it seems to me they should welcome such action on our part which postpones expenditure by the L.E.A. . . .'

Since the school received a grant per pupil, replied Phipps, any increase in the total number would automatically mean an increase in the grant. 'It is very annoying; but . . . [if] we don't want our plans refused altogether . . . then isn't the only thing to take what we can get and be ready for the future? . . . If you stand on our dignity, I don't say you are wrong; but I've always tried to get us regarded as allies of the Board. . . . These people really are our friends'.

In view of the many altercations of the past it cannot have been easy for the Chairman and Council of the Trust to look on the Board of Education as a friend. Yet over the years relations had most definitely improved, not only at headquarters level but also between the schools and the Inspectorate. They had in fact reached a stage when the visits of H.M.I.s were no longer regarded as hostile enquiries – when a headmistress could refer to the advice of 'our experienced and friendly Inspectors' or an Inspector could write of 'my old friend the Trust'. But the past had not been forgotten, and the Board of Education official who now wrote to Phipps that 'our relations with your Council have always been so friendly' was either unaware of past disputes or seeking to draw a veil over them. The Board, he went on to explain, were prepared to go some little way towards meeting the Trust's plan but would not agree to any large-scale alterations to the house. The prevailing embargo on secondary school building by L.E.A.s meant that work could be carried out only in the case of schools so old and decrepit as to be a danger to life or health.

It was impossible to press the matter further. As Magnus wrote with typical magnanimity to Phipps: 'I think I fully appreciate the different points of view and values, and no doubt I am rather crusted in G.P.D.S.T. procedure while your experience has been acquired at the Board. The two methods may not always be identical.'

157

During the financially trying years of depression the Trust received one unexpected windfall. It was the result of the optimism and perseverance of a Council member, an astute and ebullient lawyer, Mr G. M. Edwardes Jones K.C., who set himself to discover a way of lightening the burden.

Under the Income Tax Act of 1918 charitable institutions, including public schools, gained exemption from Property Tax (Schedule A), a tax from which Trust schools were not exempt. In 1926 a decision in the High Court denied exemption to a boys' school on the ground that, since it belonged to a limited company with marketable shares and might be wound up at any moment, it was not a permanent body. The Trust's position was different, argued Edwardes Jones: in the event of its winding up, its assets had to be applied to educational purposes. The Finance Committee therefore agreed to his suggestion that he should be allowed to bring a test case in respect of one school – Wimbledon High School.

News that the case was to be heard soon reached the Board of Education. 'It seems to me', wrote one official to another, 'very foolish of the Inland Revenue Authorities to start a fight with the Girls' Public Day School Trust on a very dubious point, with the probability that if they succeed the result will be that pressure will be brought to bear on the Chancellor of the Exchequer to insert provisions in the Finance Act which will mean that not only the Girls' Public Day School Trust but other schools in a similar position will be exempted from income tax.'[1]

This fact was not, of course, lost on Edwardes Jones. His application on behalf of Wimbledon High School was heard in July 1928 by the General Commissioners for Wandsworth and opposed by Counsel on behalf of the Inland Revenue Authorities. The Commissioners ruled that the school was indeed a public school in the meaning of the Act and as such exempt from Schedule A tax. If this decision was allowed to stand it would, of course, affect all the other schools of the Trust and result in a substantial rebate.

As was to be expected, the Commissioners of Inland Revenue refused to accept it. They appealed to the High Court in January 1929, and the decision was reversed.

Edwardes Jones advised a further appeal, offering his services, as one of the Trust's Counsel, without fee. The case was taken to the Court of Appeal but there, too, it failed. The Council would now have let the matter drop but Edwardes Jones, 'having expressed his dissatisfaction with the decision', advised an appeal to the House of Lords. At the same time he recommended the reconstruction of the

Trust on the lines of a scheme which had been drafted in 1905 but subsequently abandoned, which might gain for the schools the benefit of exemption from Income Tax on Profits (Schedule D).

Counsel, asked for an opinion, advised that an appeal to the Lords against Schedule A tax was unlikely to succeed. The Council of the Trust were more ready than ever to retreat although willing to consider altering the constitution in the hope of gaining exemption from Schedule D. Not so Edwardes Jones. By January 1930 he had adduced two new important facts. The first was that colleges were exempt from Schedule A tax, even those Cambridge colleges of which the Masters and Fellows, as proprietors, distributed among the Fellows under the name of dividend the surplus of general income, certain tuition fees apart. The second was that the Report of the 1867 Commission of Enquiry into Education classified as public schools proprietary schools which were the property of an individual or a company carried on 'from the hope of improving Education or (but this is rare if indeed it ever exists) as a directly commercial speculation'.

These new facts, said Edwardes Jones, so strengthened the Trust's case that he was ready to meet the expense of an appeal to the Lords himself if the Council were unwilling to take the risk. Counsel, asked for an opinion again, were cautiously optimistic. 'While we are still doubtful of success we think that there is a prospect which, having regard to the magnitude of the sum at stake, fully justifies the Council in carrying on the appeal.' The Council now agreed that the risk was worth taking. It was at this juncture that Edwardes Jones met an old friend, the statesman-lawyer Sir John (later Viscount) Simon, who had just completed his work as head of the Statutory Commission for India. Edwardes Jones persuaded Simon, a man of much greater legal stature than himself, to take the case and undertook to be personally responsible for his fees.

The Appeal was heard in July and unanimous judgment was given in favour of the Trust. Interest at 5 per cent on the tax paid in respect of Wimbledon High School for 1920–1 onwards was awarded, the refund amounting to £1,148. The magnitude of the sum at stake could now be seen. When applications for refunds in respect of all the other Trust schools were made a total of slightly more than £20,000 was recovered, a very large sum indeed in those days. 'For this highly satisfactory issue the shareholders are largely indebted to Mr Edwardes Jones K.C.,' the Council reported. His advice had been invaluable: he had given his time and his professional services gratuitously, and without him the Council would undoubtedly have abandoned the case after its failure in the Court

159

of Appeal. In acknowledgment of all he had done Edwardes Jones was made a Vice-President of the Trust, continuing at the same time as a member of Council.

The House of Lords decision was generally accepted as wise. It demonstrated, according to *The Times*, 'that the best common sense is the best common law'. The money recovered 'will be used only for educational purposes, and so good will have come out of much tiresome litigation'. *The Journal of Education* welcomed the decision 'not only on general educational grounds, but also as freeing from embarrassment an Institution which ever since its foundation has been among the pioneers of educational progress in this country'.

The £20,000 was placed in the Trust's Special Reserve Account, where it was soon being eyed covetously by a small group of disgruntled shareholders. The Council then turned to the question of Schedule D tax but found that under the Finance Act of 1927, exemption was only permissible if profits were 'applied solely to purposes of charity' and that in order to claim exemption it would be necessary to revise the constitution of the Trust to get rid of the shareholders' right to dividends. They were also warned by the Inland Revenue Authorities that exemption from Schedule D would, in all probability, nullify their exemption from Schedule A. This, said Edwardes Jones, was a preposterous suggestion. Nevertheless the Council declined to go on with the fight and so the schools remained liable for a tax on profits even though these – apart from the 4 per cent dividend to which shareholders were entitled but seldom received – were devoted exclusively to educational purposes.

The years of the depression took a heavy toll of the population of the schools. With a few exceptions – notably Bath, Bromley, Nottingham and Sutton – numbers dropped considerably. This was attributable in part to early leaving but there were a number of contributory factors, among them population migration, a falling birth-rate and the continued growth and reputation of the maintained schools.

In 1932 the Government's economy measures resulted in an increase in the number of ex-elementary children in the L.E.A. secondary schools. The old system of free places was replaced by 'special' places for which L.E.A.s were authorized to apply a means test to parents and exact full or part fees from those parents who could afford to pay. Fees in the maintained schools were extremely low: even so, there were many parents whose income was below the fixed level and whose fees were remitted.

Direct grant schools were still admitting their quota of 10 per cent or more of free placers from the elementary schools, but it seemed possible that the system of special places might redound to their advantage. In 1936 Sir Edmund Phipps, looking at the question from both sides, heard that the L.C.C. were so hard pressed for room that they would soon be obliged to provide additional secondary school accommodation. 'This suggests to me', he informed the Council, 'that we might make some arrangement with them which would enable them to use our schools instead of building in competition with us. It ought not to be beyond the wit of man to find possible terms by which we might get "aid", perhaps all our "deficiency" in each school concerned, in return for more free places and perhaps for lower fees.' This might, he thought, solve the problem in the three south London schools, Clapham, Streatham Hill and Sydenham, in which – largely owing to the shifting nature of the population – the drop in numbers was most pronounced. 'The character of the population has changed so much that we can't hope anything for the schools but a long losing battle with all its miseries for us and for the Headmistresses.' Unless the L.C.C. offered aid 'we should do well to close them. After all we have plenty of other schools in London to do us credit and keep our type in evidence. . . . Our main business is not, I submit, to keep a fixed number of schools alive but to provide schools of a certain type.' The real failure in duty would be to let the standards of the Trust schools deteriorate. 'The Council have a natural reluctance to close a school. Their predecessors had to close many or there would have been few today. It seems to me that we must now face the facts at last. If we act, let us act boldly and make a good job of it by putting the schools out of anxiety.'

Sir Edmund was hopeful that with help from the L.C.C. it might be possible to save at least one of the schools. The alternative – to raise the fees – was unthinkable. The Council, as they stated in a memorandum on the subject to the L.C.C., 'have prided themselves on the fact that there is probably a greater mixture of all "classes" in their schools than in any others in the country'. Any increase in fees 'would therefore be distasteful to them, as a retrograde step', and they wished to do nothing which could result 'in the exclusion, from any of the Schools, of the children of the less well-to-do parents for whom the Schools have hitherto been available'.

The plan which was finally agreed between the L.C.C. and the Council was for the provision by the L.C.C. of thirty special places to be divided among the seven London schools. These were to be over and above the 10 per cent of free places open to ex-elementary

L

school girls, and the holders could be drawn from schools of all types including the elementary, the selection being made by the headmistresses on the strength of an examination of their own devising.

It was reckoned that over a period of five years there would be an increase of about a hundred and fifty pupils and an approximate net gain in income to the Trust of £3,000 a year. This was a most generous gesture on the part of the L.C.C. Without it there is a strong probability that the Council would have had to close the three south London schools. Even as things were some sacrifice was necessary, and after much thought and lengthy discussions the Council decided to keep Sydenham in being but to merge Clapham with Streatham Hill and dispose of the Clapham premises.

'I come to a school which imperiously cries for a superlative,' Laurie Magnus had written of Clapham High School in 1923. 'Perhaps the right epithet is wonderful; for, indeed, there was something like a touch of magic in the growth of [the School] out of a mixture of types, into a single, homogeneous pattern of educational effort and efficiency.'[2]

Clapham High, for so long one of the most famous of the schools, was renowned in the educational world as a 'nursery' for headmistresses, and also for a distinguished list of former pupils. Teachers from all the schools had become heads of Trust, and of other aided and maintained schools, but the impetus of Mrs Woodhouse had placed Clapham in the forefront. Mrs Woodhouse had a towering personality. 'A genius she!' wrote the irrepressible Maclean:

> But how her words
> Came streaming breathlessly
> When she put forth for 'Clapham High'
> Some new impassioned plea!
> Intricate schemes were joy to her.
> On giant tasks she thrived.
> But, Oh, her faithful, panting Staff –
> They only just survived!

'To us', writes Miss Potter, herself a distinguished headmistress and old pupil, 'she had many of the attributes of royalty, a dignified, gracious, handsome presence, the habit of command, severity tempered by kindness and courtesy and an unfailing memory.'

Few women could have kept up the pace Mrs Woodhouse had set: her immediate successors, though competent, lacked her dynamism and breadth of vision, and the last headmistress arrived too late to prevent the decline. Numbers had fallen from five to less than two hundred, a drop which could be partly accounted for by the depression and the fact that the district had been going down in the world. It was the same story in the Training College, particularly in the Art Training Department which was unable to meet competition from other, better organized, institutions and was closed in 1937. In the same year, after an abortive request to the L.C.C. to take over and maintain the school, the Council decided most reluctantly on the merger with Streatham Hill, to take effect from the end of July 1938. There would be room at Streatham for a hundred pupils: the remainder would have to be transferred to other schools, among them Putney and Wimbledon High Schools. The two surviving departments of the Training College, the postgraduate and kindergarten, would also be transferred to Streatham as soon as suitable premises could be found.

It is highly improbable that the Council had any idea of the violent emotions their announcement would unleash. Professor Alfred Hughes, who had succeeded Mr Magnus as Chairman, was inundated with letters of protest and petitions for the decision to be rescinded. They came from parents, staff and pupils – past and present, from educational bodies and from representatives of local organizations. To all of them the amalgamation could have only one result: the death of Clapham. 'In view of the wide reputation and fine history of this school', as the Chairman of the Governors of the National Froebel Union wrote, 'it appears little short of disaster that it should lose its identity. I have to say that the closing of Clapham Training College would be a blow to all that we stand for.'

Among the letters which Professor Hughes received from every form in the school was one from the head girl: 'Please, Mr Chairman, will you beg of your Council to save our School.' The headmistress and head of the Training College, Miss M. Jarrett, who had been in office only three years and felt, as did others, that she had not been given a chance to resolve the dilemma, was shocked and distressed. 'It seems most tragic', she wrote, 'that such an end should come to Clapham with its distinguished record and it will, I know, be most deeply felt by many who have loved Clapham and still love her, for through her many years of vigorous life, she has won much affection and loyalty and her old girls and old students are scattered everywhere.'

The protests continued to pour in. The Clapham Chamber of Commerce offered to support the Trust 'in any effort made to retain the school in Clapham'; the Clapham and District Ratepayers'

163

Association passed a resolution asking for the decision to be reconsidered; Sir John Leigh, the local Member of Parliament, appealed against the decision and offered to give the Council any help in his power. The former Prime Minister, David Lloyd George, two of whose daughters had been educated at Clapham, wrote of his 'dismay' in view 'of the great prestige of the school and the place it has won for itself in educational circles. It is a pity that such a fine institution should not be able to continue its work, especially as this work embraces the training of teachers for the future, a branch of education which I consider of paramount importance.'

Amid the welter of protests and appeals there was only one which showed any sympathy for the unfortunate Council. The President of the Association of Head Mistresses, Miss E. M. Tanner, who recalled Clapham's 'pioneer work' in the higher education of girls and the training of teachers, and 'the far-reaching influence of the School, not only in education, but also in public and private life', felt sure that, 'though the school itself may pass away, the traditions it has made have become part of the permanent heritage of English education. May I add how deeply I personally regret the necessity of closing the school, but how much I admire the courage of the Trust in coming to what must have been for them a very hard decision to make.'

At the request of the parents, old girls and former students, the Council agreed to receive a deputation in December 1937. The deputation put forward a scheme which they hoped might yet save the school, suggesting an increase in fees and offering to make good an annual deficit of up to £2,000. The Council promised sympathetic consideration but, with other factors involved, they held to their original decision. Sir Edmund Phipps admitted that he must be regarded 'as the villain of the piece'. He was a far more forceful figure than the elderly Chairman and may well have over-persuaded him. Yet today it is impossible to think of the decision as anything but a mistake.

The merger, now inevitable, produced a leading article in the *Times Educational Supplement*. It referred to 'the cold blast of migration' which the Trust had felt in its south London schools and a loss amounting to about £8,000 a year which it had experienced in administering Blackheath, Clapham, Putney, Streatham Hill, and Sydenham High Schools. It congratulated the L.C.C. for its award of thirty local special places, and ended on a note of farewell: 'The closure will be regretted by many people . . . but it is hoped that through the far-seeing and liberal spirit displayed by the London

County Council, the existing London schools of the Trust will be able to continue their valuable labours, and that the provision for the training of teachers which has always been a feature of the work of the Trust will also be maintained.'

The merger was duly carried out as arranged. The headmistress of Streatham Hill was about to retire. The headship of the school which in future was to be known by the cumbersome title of the 'Streatham Hill and Clapham High School' was offered to Miss Jarrett. She hesitated for a long time before accepting the post since, as she said, she had been 'both a witness of and a participator in the great distress caused by the closing of Clapham', but she was prepared to do her best to integrate the two schools and to heal the hurt feelings of the Clapham girls.

The two surviving departments of the Training College were moved to spacious premises near the school. The postgraduate department was carried on until the war brought teacher training almost to a standstill and in 1942, with only three applications for places, it was closed. The kindergarten (Froebel) department remained a viable concern. It survived the war and in 1949 was taken over by the L.C.C., to re-emerge in 1953 as the Philippa Fawcett Training College, named after Clapham's famous alumna. In company with other closed schools, Clapham survives today in the form of a flourishing association of old girls.

Chapter 15
The Second World War

During the European crisis of 1938 the Trust prepared itself for a second world war. The schools, though varied in type and scattered all over the country, shared the same traditions and were happily interdependent; the headmistresses, as varied as the schools they served, rose splendidly to the occasion.

Plans for the instant evacuation of schools in the danger areas had already been made, and staff and girls had to be ready to set off at a moment's notice for an unknown destination. The Council had arranged that as far as possible pupils should be accommodated in other Trust schools where the atmosphere would be congenial and not altogether unfamiliar. This arrangement placed a burden on the headmistresses of schools in the so-called safe areas. 'As an instance by no means unique', reported the Chairman, Mr H. J. Simmonds, 'Bath received by September 27th applications from other Trust schools to take two hundred and fifty pupils; and by the 29th the headmistress [Miss E. M. Cull] had arranged with parents to accommodate two hundred of them.'

Mr Simmonds, Chairman from 1938–44, had previously been legal adviser to the Board of Education. Wise, humorous and level-headed, wrote a member of the Council, he combined 'the clarity of thought and objectivity of the best kind of lawyer, with great personal charm and warmth of heart in his relations with the Schools and headmistresses'. Typical of this attitude is the letter he wrote to the headmistress of Kensington High School, Miss M. M. Burke, who had apologized for taking some action without his prior consent: 'I do not know which of us is the more guilty, you for not asking, or I for not knowing that I should have been asked.' Mr Simmonds was renowned for his 'superb grasp of the essentials of any problem' and for his 'persuasive skill in bringing others . . . to his point of view', for his unswerving courage in making decisions and his support of the principles in which he believed. In the immediate pre-war period there were many people who thought that the Trust could not possibly survive in wartime conditions.

166

This belief he utterly rejected and during the most critical years of the war he proved to be the ideal pilot. The Trust also owed a great deal to the selfless labours of Mr Maclean's successor as Secretary, Mr A. C. Lightfoot, who had been a member of the staff since 1925.

After Munich, evacuation plans were put in cold storage and life in the schools returned to uneasy normality. There was one significant change of policy: the ban on the award of Trust Scholarships to girls of foreign extraction which had been imposed towards the end of the First World War was lifted and the Council authorized the award of up to sixty entrance scholarships a year to Jewish and other refugees from Nazi persecution. Some parents offered hospitality, and by March 1939 most of the schools had accepted refugee children, either on scholarships or at reduced fees.

As the spring and summer passed and the threat of war became ever more imminent, many girls left schools in the obvious danger areas and the overall number dropped by over three thousand. At that moment the schools were in graver danger of extinction than at any time during their history. Several of them would undoubtedly have perished but for the loyalty, ingenuity and resourcefulness of their headmistresses. In the past, with few exceptions, the Council had shown much wisdom in their choice of heads. They entered the war years with headmistresses of long standing who could bear comparison with the pioneers of old and with newcomers who showed the same qualities of devotion and courage.

As the Council had no idea how many of the schools it would be possible to carry on the headmistresses all received a term's notice on the outbreak of hostilities. In the event this was a mere legal formality: the schools remained in being, but headmistresses and staff had to suffer salary cuts and the number of teachers was severely curtailed.

Thirteen of the schools were in areas scheduled for evacuation, six were in reception areas and the rest in neutral areas where, equipped with air-raid shelters, they were able to continue an existence which, at best, was uncertain. Arrangements had been made to attach six of the schools in the evacuation areas to Trust schools in districts scheduled for reception and for the remainder to be received by non-Trust schools in similar districts. Thus Birkenhead High and the Belvedere School were transferred to Shrewsbury High School, Blackheath to Tunbridge Wells, Kensington to Oxford, Streatham Hill and Clapham, and Sydenham, to Brighton. Of the other schools in the evacuation areas, Putney

167

went to Reading, Croydon to Purley and Eastbourne, Newcastle to Keswick in the Lake District, Nottingham to Ramsdale Park and Daybrook, Sheffield to Calver in Derbyshire, Portsmouth to two villages in Hampshire and South Hampstead to Berkhamsted.

The history of the war years differs from school to school, but the evacuated and the host schools shared such difficulties as a lack of adequate accommodation in school rooms and billets. There are stories of hostesses who accommodated girls in rooms too damp and cheerless to be fit for use, of teachers obliged to sleep two in a bed, of evacuees feeling lonely and lost. The feeling of inter-dependence among the Trust schools was strong enough to surmount most problems. In the course of the war several of them solved their particular problems by turning themselves into fully-fledged boarding schools, a transformation far from simple but carried out with a high degree of success. One of these schools was Portsmouth, a second was Newcastle (Central). Each at a critical period had a change of headmistress: in 1941 Miss E. M. Thorn succeeded Miss G. E. Watt as headmistress of Portsmouth High School, and in 1940 Miss M. Leale succeeded Miss Odell at Newcastle.

For both schools there were peculiar problems to be solved. Portsmouth High School had been evacuated to two country houses in villages thirteen miles apart: one housed the senior school, the other the junior. 'It is not easy', writes the author of the School History,* 'for a day school to adapt itself to being a boarding school overnight with new ways to learn and with only the minimum of equipment. In such moments of crisis one's impressions are often intensified and it is easy to recapture something of the mixed feelings of discomfort, unrest and the occasional moments of unintentional happiness that broke through.'

Portsmouth High School remained in Hampshire until 1945. Not so Newcastle. The beauties of the Lake District were the chief attraction to both staff and pupils who shared the school buildings of the Keswick School, a grammar school for boys and girls. Billets had been found for the High School girls but during the season their rooms were needed for summer visitors, and it was for this reason that Miss Odell, with the Council's permission, found a large empty house, equipped it with the minimum of furniture and opened it as a boarding-house for fifty-two children. Staff and pupils alike now felt that they had a centre and great efforts were made not only by the staff, but also by the mothers of girls who had settled in Keswick to be with their daughters, to make the boarding-house the pivot of the school. 'There were plenty of

* M. E. Howell Ph.D., M.A.

physical discomforts', wrote one of the pupils, 'but this and more was offset by the fun and novelty of a boarding-school life.' Inevitably the older girls found the adjustment hard to make. 'Those of us who spent all our Sixth Form years there missed a good deal', wrote one of them. 'The necessary restrictions on our liberty during non-school hours were extremely irksome to one of my age, from seventeen to almost nineteen. I think not having our own library available was also a great loss.'* Nevertheless the standard of work did not suffer. During the second year of evacuation the numbers remained constant, but Newcastle was little affected by raids and so parents soon began to take their children home. At the instance of Miss Leale† the Council bought a small private school in Gosforth. For six months the school was run in two sections, one at Keswick, the other at Gosforth, but in 1943 the main school building was released by its wartime tenants and the Keswick branch was closed. 'Oh, the delights of being home!' wrote a former pupil excitedly. 'I don't know whether those at the school before 1939 felt as I did, but it seemed to me as if we were a SCHOOL again. There was a past: there was a future. In Keswick, one lived only for the present.'

It was inevitable that many girls uprooted from their homes and their schools should feel homesick. For this reason and also to escape from all the other problems caused by the evacuation, the Council agreed to bring back several schools during what proved to be a deceptive period of calm. Birkenhead and the Belvedere Schools returned home after a single term at Shrewsbury; Putney High School, which had been evacuated to Reading, also returned to London, although not to its own buildings which had been let to the Metropolitan Police.

Kensington High School, which had joined forces with Oxford, was under a new headmistress, Miss M. M. Burke.‡ She had taken over from Miss Lilian Charlesworth – a former pupil at Clapham – who had been transferred to Sutton High School in 1939. Miss Charlesworth, one of the outstanding headmistresses of recent years and a woman of great charm, humanity and breadth of vision, held a number of offices beyond the confines of her own schools. Among them were the chairmanship of the Council for Education in World Citizenship, the Charlotte Mason Schools Company, the Council of Whitelands College and also the directorship of the

---

* *History of Gateshead High School and Central Newcastle High School* by Olive Carter M.A.
† Later headmistress of Bromley High School.
‡ Later headmistress of Wimbledon High School.

169

Thomas Wall Educational Trust. She was President of the Association of Head Mistresses 1948–50* and played an active part in the promotion of education for international understanding.'

By the end of 1939 it had seemed to Miss Burke that there was no assured future for Kensington High School except in London and so, with seriously depleted numbers, the school came home. Early in 1941 the building, which was fortunately empty at the time, was wrecked by a landmine. Within a week the energetic headmistress had found new premises in the neighbourhood and her staff set to work and cleaned the whole house before it was ready for occupation. At this point Miss Burke was horrified to learn that she would not be allowed to open the school without the sanction of His Majesty's Inspector. As she had received no communication from him she wrote in some indignation. In reply he came to see her, sanctioned her plans and became a firm friend.

Several schools were forced to carry on a dual existence with all the attendant discomforts: while the main schools remained in the reception areas, classes were reopened in towns and cities. South Hampstead was one of these schools. The headmistress and her staff divided their time between Berkhamsted and the Hampstead building which was partially occupied by the Fire Service. During the blitz and the raids of the latter part of the war, classes and examinations were held in the dining-room which had been reinforced as a shelter; and with numbers which ebbed and flowed with the tide of war the school remained in existence. It was peculiarly fortunate in its headmistress, Miss M. L. Potter, a teacher of rare quality, a wise and sympathetic woman, whose twenty-six years in office formed an outstanding period in the school's history.

Two other schools – Sydenham and Streatham Hill and Clapham – had their dual existence curtailed after the fall of France when Brighton High School, which had given them hospitality, was no longer considered a safe area.

The school which re-assembled at Sydenham numbered seventy girls, ranging in age from five to eighteen. By January 1942, when Miss M. D. Yardley was appointed headmistress, numbers had crept up to eighty-seven but Miss Yardley found herself the only full-time teacher. In the next two years the total increased to nearly 200, but it dropped to twenty-five during the fly-bomb raids of

* Miss P. R. Bodington of South Hampstead High School was the next Trust headmistress to become President; the latest is Miss J. R. Glover, Miss Charlesworth's successor at Sutton. No fewer than twelve of the Association's thirty-eight Presidents have been Trust headmistresses (see Appendix 4).

1944 and for a few weeks the school was closed. Within two months of its re-opening the school had a miraculous escape. It was in full session when a rocket exploded above the building: had it exploded on, instead of over it there would undoubtedly have been many casualties.

Streatham Hill and Clapham High School, its numbers grown to 333, was a casualty of the fly-bomb raids: in July 1944 a bomb plunged between the school and the house next door, wrecking both buildings. Miss Jarrett, the headmistress, was asleep in the house at the time, as was a member of her staff, the school secretary and the caretakers. None of them was hurt but the building was almost a total loss. 'The familiar background of our lives was wiped out in a second,' wrote Miss Jarrett later. Yet, almost incredibly, in late September the school reassembled in two large houses on Tulse Hill which had been secured, cleared, cleaned and furnished in time for the opening of the autumn term.

Among the schools which remained in their own premises was Wimbledon. During the blitz a stick of bombs fell in the grounds, and later in the fly-bomb raids such heavy damage was caused to the buildings that the school was temporarily closed while essential repairs were made. Under the indomitable leadership of the headmistress, Miss Littlewood, the school carried on, even celebrating some of the lighter aspects of the war in a revue produced by the staff.

Bath might well have been a total casualty. The school, which had welcomed girls from other Trust schools, was crowded and vigorous by the spring of 1942 when, during the holidays, the senior school was destroyed by a bomb and the other buildings, with the exception of the boarding-house, badly damaged. The newly-appointed headmistress, Miss G. S. Blackburn, found 'the most indescribable desolation everywhere, and with the appalling problem of trying to rebuild in the middle of the war, there was a real danger that the school might have to be closed down. That it was not, was of course due to the faith shown by the Trust and to the energy of Mr Lightfoot, its Secretary, and Mr Croston, its Surveyor, who both came down at once and decided to find temporary premises in which to carry on.' Until these were secured the undamaged boarding-house remained the nucleus of the school. Miss Blackburn herself played a notable part in the school's survival. As a member of the Society of Friends she could not contribute to the war effort but the challenge of helping to rebuild a devastated school was one which she could and did accept.

Bath suffered damage during the so-called Baedeker raids. An area almost as vulnerable as London was Croydon. Just before the outbreak of war a new headmistress, Miss M. F. Adams, was appointed to the High School. Before she could survey her new school Miss Adams had to organize the evacuation of her previous school from Liverpool and she reached Croydon after an all-night journey. 'To this day', wrote one of her pupils much later, 'those who were there can recall her silent entry into the Hall, looking on the school she took over. Fifty-four girls instead of eight hundred made up the group and many of them were new entries' because, while the school drew its pupils from a wide area, only those who lived in the borough were eligible for evacuation under the Government scheme. 'When the stage was reached for holding together the pitiful remnant of the School . . . it was the energy and foresight of Miss Adams which drove the scheme forward and made it possible to save something from what looked like total shipwreck.' Croydon High School was evacuated to Eastbourne, but by 1942 there were also groups of children in Purley and in Croydon itself. In 1940 there was a second evacuation – from Eastbourne to Llandilo in South Wales. The school returned home the following year, and by 1943 it numbered four hundred and fifty. Although the building was damaged during the fly-bomb raids the school itself was able to carry on as usual.

Dr Adams is perhaps the most widely experienced as she is certainly the most travelled of all Trust headmistresses. A graduate of the University of Glasgow, from which she holds an Honorary Doctorate, she has spent almost all her professional life away from her native Scotland, first as a member of staff at Manchester High School, then as head of Queen Mary's School, Lytham, from which she came to Croydon on an inauspicious date – September 1, 1939 – to pilot the school through its wartime vicissitudes. Dr Adams, a former President of the Association of Head Mistresses, is well known among teachers all over the world for her work with the teachers' international organizations, especially FIPESO, the International Federation of Secondary Teachers, of which she was President for several years.

A second evacuation had to be organized for several schools besides Croydon but although a few of them, like Sydenham, were temporarily closed, in the end, with two exceptions, they survived the war. The first exception was Kensington, the oldest school of all. Planning permission to rebuild on the old site was refused because the site was considered inadequate. In 1948, after a long and fruitless search for suitable premises, the Council decided with the utmost reluctance to close the senior school. Kensington had

172

always been a neighbourhood in which numbers were liable to fluctuate and the decision, though deeply regretted, was not greeted with the same outcry as the decision to close Clapham. Fortunately the loss was far from total. The junior school survived and has continued to flourish. It retains many of the traditions of the old school, among them the musical tradition inculcated so long ago by the indomitable Miss Home.

The other school that failed to survive the war was Tunbridge Wells: it had weathered more than one financial crisis but had been reprieved in 1936 on the grounds of its great value to the town, and in 1939 was again on the brink of closure when the continued drop in numbers was offset by the arrival of evacuees from Blackheath High School. In 1945, however, when the last evacuees returned to London, it was finally closed; but it remains very much alive today in the memories of its loyal and devoted old girls.

The heat and trials of the day had been valiantly borne by the headmistresses. Their vitality and ingenuity seem never to have flagged. With a display of equanimity which they can seldom have felt they contrived to deal with all the problems that came their way. They helped and encouraged the members of their staff, who themselves showed great fortitude and resourcefulness, and despite all the dangers and discomforts they kept their pupils busy and happy, and even found time for endless correspondence with anxious parents. The brunt, of course, was borne by the headmistresses of schools in the danger areas. Others also played a vital, if less spectacular, part. Among these were the headmistresses of Nottingham and Sheffield High Schools. Nottingham, under the direction of Miss E. M. Merrifield,* moved to Ramsdale Park in 1939 to become a boarding centre; Sheffield, under Miss M. Macaulay,† went to Cliffe College in the Derbyshire village of Calver and 'became a boarding-school overnight – as if by a miracle', but really as a result of wise planning. During the flying bomb attacks both schools gave a welcome in the summer holidays to girls from the southern schools who were suffering from the strain and were thus able to recuperate in peace and safety. 'On the last day of the summer term at Ramsdale', wrote an eyewitness, 'as the last load of girls disappeared down the drive, the first load of Londoners arrived and throughout the summer holidays groups of girls from London Trust Schools found at Ramsdale some respite from the flying bombs.'

At the end of the war the Council placed on record their 'high

* Later headmistress of Notting Hill and Ealing.
† Later headmistress of Streatham Hill and Clapham.

admiration' for all that the headmistresses and their staff had achieved. The work had not been accomplished without heavy strain and it was for this reason that Mrs V. H. Galbraith recommended, in 1946, that every headmistress should be granted a term's leave of absence. This suggestion led to the introduction of a grace term to be spent in travel which is granted to every headmistress of ten years' standing and repeated after a further period of seven years. Senior members of staff in rotation are now also given periods of extended leave.

On their side the headmistresses were deeply grateful to the Chairman, Mr Simmonds, and Mr Stead who succeeded him in 1944, and also to the members of the Council on whose shoulders had rested the final responsibility for each and every decision. They therefore offered the Council their congratulations 'on having safely negotiated the war years'.

Chapter 16

The Trust Schools and the Education Act

Long before the outbreak of the Second World War the Government had given serious thought to the future of secondary education and the need to extend it to the whole of the school population.

In 1923 the special requirements of girls were considered by the Consultative Committee of the Board of Education, which issued a report – *The Differentiation of Curricula between the Sexes in Secondary Schools.* The report noted that the pressure of a crowded time-table in girls' schools coupled with domestic duties at home was causing overstrain in teachers and pupils alike. It recommended, among other things, that headmistresses should be given greater freedom in drawing up the curriculum and permission to plan special courses for the older non-academic girl. As a result examination requirements would have to be modified so that girls could take the School and Higher Certificates a year later than boys. The Committee, on the whole, did not favour drastic changes, on the ground that secondary education for girls was still in some respects in an experimental stage. Its recommendations, though carefully considered, made very little impact on the existing state of affairs, and the education of boys and girls remained essentially the same.

A far-reaching report – the Hadow Report on *The Education of the Adolescent* – published in 1926 recommended a complete overhaul of the system of elementary education in relation to secondary education and the consequent division of schools into primary, for all children between the ages of five and eleven, and post-primary – or secondary – for those between ten and fourteen (or fifteen as soon as the school-leaving age could be raised). The report also recommended the streaming of children at the age of eleven-plus into three types of school – grammar, modern, and junior technical or trade.

The Board of Education approved these recommendations and during the next ten years a number of L.E.A.s attempted to reorganize education along the lines suggested. A different conclusion was, however, reached in 1938 in the Spens Report on *Secondary Education with Special Reference to Grammar Schools and Technical High Schools*. The Spens Committee considered that the long-term effect of the Education Act of 1902 had been to place too much emphasis on academic education. They considered the possibility of tripartite, multilateral schools, in which children could be streamed according to ability, but rejected the Hadow Report's recommendation of three different types of secondary school.

The outbreak of war called a halt to plans for reorganization, but the issue remained very much alive and in 1943 two educational reports and a white paper were published. The controversial Norwood Report on *Curriculum and Examination in Secondary Schools* categorized children into three types: those who were 'interested in learning for its own sake' – the potential intellectuals, those 'whose interests and abilities lie markedly in the field of applied science or applied art . . .', and those who dealt 'more easily with concrete things than ideas'. The report was criticized as an attempt to fit the children into unjustifiable patterns of ability.

The White Paper on *Educational Reconstruction* was more realistic. It advocated the reorganization of public education in progressive stages – primary, secondary, and further education – with the disappearance of the old elementary schools.

The proposed reconstruction, together with a special report on the *Abolition of Tuition Fees in Grant-Aided Secondary Schools*, was of direct interest to the Council of the Trust. This report paid due attention to the schools of the Trust and to the other direct grant schools which could 'claim to have played a very important role in the history of Education in this country. They took part, in fact, in a notable educational experiment and, as in the case of the Grammar Schools, the Board of Education and the Local Education Authorities after 1902 built on the foundations they had laid'. The recommendations were not unanimous. The signatories to the majority report recommended the abolition of fees in all grant-aided schools, and suggested that the direct grant schools might be financed by the Board of Education on a scale sufficient to preserve, or even extend, their educational standards. The total abolition of fees was not, however, approved by the signatories of the minority report, among them the Chairman, Lord Fleming.

A special meeting of the Council of the Trust was called to discuss the implications of the report and of the paper on *Educational Reconstruction*. Discussion of the latter was deferred since, as Mr Lightfoot wrote, it postponed 'a conclusion as to the future of direct grant schools' pending the recommendations of a committee on the public schools, also under the chairmanship of Lord Fleming. The meeting therefore gave its undivided attention to the prospect of the abolition of fees. An experienced educationist, Mr F. B. Stead, formerly the Board of Education's Chief Inspector of Secondary Schools, who succeeded Mr Simmonds as Chairman of the Council in 1944, said that even if the direct grant schools were to be excluded from any scheme to abolish fees it was more than likely in the future that a Labour Government would insist on bringing them into line. He thought in the circumstances that it might be wise to forestall the possibility by accepting the idea in principle 'with a good grace instead of fighting for a *status quo* which would sooner or later have to be surrendered'. He also thought that instead of protesting the Council should endeavour to secure those things which in his opinion mattered most, 'the entity of the Trust Schools as a group (including their Preparatory and Junior Schools); the entity of the Trust itself as a body responsible for financial control and administration'; and financial aid from the Board of Education on the lines suggested in the majority report.

Mr Simmonds felt that his colleague was going too far to meet a situation which might never arise. The proposal to abolish fees in direct grant schools, he said, 'should not be accepted without a fight'. As the proposal was not yet official policy it was agreed that no action should be taken but that an effort should be made to find out from the Board what their attitude towards it was likely to be.

In the event the report was overtaken by the far-reaching Fleming Report of 1944 on *The Public Schools and the General Educational System*. The Fleming Report advocated the division of the schools under review into two types and put forward a scheme for each, Scheme A and Scheme B, both of which dealt with girls' schools as well as boys'. Scheme A was chiefly concerned with the direct grant schools which since 1926 had received a capitation grant direct from the central authority. Scheme B comprised the public boarding-schools which were to be asked to make room in their annual intake for a minimum of 25 per cent of children from the primary schools who would be admitted under a bursary system.

Scheme A, which would replace the direct grant system, would include such schools recognized by the Board of Education as efficient and not conducted for private profit as the Board might agree to accept. In reviewing the claims of a school the Board would consider its financial position, its non-local and other special characteristics, the value and extent of the contribution it could

M

177

make to the national provision of secondary education, including the education of children who had previously attended grant-aided primary schools, and the observations of the L.E.A. The criterion for admission for every pupil would be capacity 'to profit by education in the school', and no pupil should be excluded by reason of parental inability to pay the fees. In the schools admitted to Scheme A tuition fees would either be abolished or graded according to an approved income scale which provided, if necessary, for total remission.

Among the other provisos in respect of the Scheme A schools was the right of L.E.A.s to reserve an agreed number of places for pupils for whom they would be directly responsible. This suggestion alarmed the Council of the Trust as likely to lead to an undesirable measure of L.E.A. control. Mr Simmonds and several of his colleagues who had given evidence before the Fleming Committee had stressed their belief that it would not be in the best interests of national education for all day schools 'providing secondary, i.e. "Grammar School", education [to] be of the same pattern, as they would inevitably tend to be if administered and controlled by Local Authorities', and had added their conviction 'that the Trust Schools have distinctive features which make them worthy of preservation as part of the national system . . .'.

The fate of Schemes A and B depended, of course, on official reaction to the Fleming Report. Its recommendations, like so many others, were a compromise. The report made a genuine attempt to bridge the gulf between the independent schools which catered for the children of the rich and the moderately well-to-do, and the State schools which catered for the children of the poorer classes; it was also an attempt to deal fairly with the direct grant schools which stood midway between the two extremes and catered for rich and poor alike. It was almost inevitable that the report should be criticized by some people for going too far and by others for not going far enough. It is significant that while the principle on which the report was based – that secondary education should be available to all children capable of profiting by it irrespective of parental means – was accepted, its recommendations were ultimately set aside.

The last of the wartime reports, the McNair Report on *Teachers and Youth Leaders*, made a thorough examination of all the problems inherent in recruitment and training. The educational highlight of the war years was, of course, the Education Act of 1944 passed, like the Fisher Act before it, at a moment when the nation's safety was in the gravest danger. The new Act, laid before the

House of Commons by the President of the Board of Education, Mr R. A. (now Lord) Butler, superseded all previous Acts. It transformed the Board into a Ministry of Education* with a Minister authorized 'to promote the education of the people in England and Wales'. It reframed the entire system of public education and provided for the inspection of schools outside the State system. Its provisions reflected the recommendations of the various reports which had preceded it, due weight being given to the Hadow Report of 1926. Education was visualized as one continuous progression from primary, through secondary, to further education, in three successive stages. Between the ages of five and fifteen (sixteen as soon as the school-leaving age could be raised) education was to be free and compulsory, and the secondary schools were to be reorganized on a tripartite basis consisting of grammar, secondary technical, and secondary modern, all maintained by the L.E.A.s. After the reorganization some of the secondary modern schools were amalgamated with grammar schools or with technical secondary schools to become bilateral; others became units of comprehensive schools which provided all forms of secondary education, and which became, of course, the desired end of Labour Government policy.

The direct grant schools, with fee-paying and non fee-paying pupils, acted as a bridge between the independent schools and the maintained and voluntary aided schools which now had no fee-paying pupils. They would be able to enter the scheme at the discretion of the Minister on the advice of the L.E.A.s. The constitution of the governing body of a direct grant school would remain substantially unchanged, but among the conditions attaching to entry was the proviso that preparatory and junior departments (for which no grant had ever been paid) would be regarded for administrative purposes as separate and distinct from the secondary section – or upper school. In the eyes of the Ministry they would be independent; in the eyes of the Trust they would still be an integral part of the school proper.

A second important condition concerned the offer of free places. The governors of every school would be required to offer each year no less than 25 per cent of the previous year's admission to the upper school as free places. These could be offered to the local authority: if they were taken up the local authority would have the right to ask for further free (or 'reserved') places amounting to another 25 per cent. This arrangement would leave a residue of places to be filled in order of merit on the results of a test organized

* Since 1964 the Department of Education and Science.

by the governors. Parents of the pupils who filled these places would have to pay the full approved fees of the schools if they could afford to do so – if not they could apply for rebate on a graduated scale approved by the Minister.

The Minister's failure to bring the direct grant schools in line with the maintained schools disappointed the Association of Head Mistresses which, on so many other issues, had complemented the views of the Trust. The Association expressed regret 'that provision for the abolition of fees has been made only in schools maintained by the L.E.A., since [it] stands for the abolition of fees in all schools in receipt of public money'. The Government, however, had seen no reason why a clean sweep of fees should be made in such a limited group of schools. As Mr R. A. Butler remarked in the House of Commons in January 1944 when he moved the second reading of the Education Bill: 'A heavy-handed insistence on the prohibition of fees in all direct grant schools would be likely to result in the governors of such schools deciding to leave the State system, because we could not stop them. Such a step would . . . inevitably accentuate the social distinctions and widen the gap between the schools.'

The governors of a direct grant school who wished to apply for continued recognition submitted their application to the Minister. Between March 1945 and May 1946 the Ministry of Education compiled a new and revised list of one hundred and sixty-six direct grant schools in England and Wales: it comprised seventy-four boys' schools, two mixed schools and ninety girls' schools, and the number was subsequently increased.

The Council of the Trust made a joint application in respect of their twenty-two schools in April 1945. The letter pointed out that the schools 'of which the Junior and Preparatory sections remain as heretofore integral parts', had been recognized as efficient and conducted since 1905, when the Board of Education first made grants to secondary schools on a capitation basis 'in conformity with the *Regulations for Secondary Schools*. They have in fact been regarded as part of the national system not only by the Ministry but also implicitly by the L.E.A.s'. The Council went on to express their thanks for the consideration the Trust schools had received in the past and in particular for supplementary grants which had been made during the war years 'which have gone far to cover the losses consequent on evacuation . . .'. The Council believed, the letter concluded, 'that the Schools of the Trust have a contribution of their own to make to the national system of education'.

Enquiries were sent by the Ministry to every Local Education

180

Authority and H.M. Inspector concerned. The replies were generally favourable: in fact, with two exceptions, all supported the application. The Minister was recommended to accept, and in November the schools were recognized *en bloc* as a group of secondary grammar schools, thus forming the largest single unit on the direct grant list. By that time a new Burnham Scale of salaries had come into operation and the Ministry had approved a new scale of fees which amounted to £39 a year for Trust schools outside the London area and £42 for the London schools.

Although the direct grant schools were subject to a high degree of government control they were in effect allowed a great deal of freedom. As the Chairman wrote proudly to the headmistresses, the Trust would be free to administer and conduct its schools, the junior departments included, 'on the lines with which we are all familiar'. It was the primary duty of the Council to see that the Trust's limited financial resources were used to the best advantage and interest of the schools: the headmistresses had the vital task of maintaining and improving the educational standards in their own schools. 'Let us each go forward with our common task in that spirit of mutual understanding, which is part of our tradition and the sole guarantee of effective co-operation.'

There was general rejoicing at the issue. The headmistresses thanked the Council 'for having secured the Minister's continued recognition of its Schools for direct grant, so enabling them to make their characteristic contribution to education'. As with the maintained grammar schools, the Trust schools now had a mandate to offer, on a selective basis, the academic training leading to higher education. This they were well equipped to do, and the broadening of the social admixture was an added strength. In the war years the Council had sought to check the drastic fall in numbers by admitting girls of an intellectual calibre they would normally have rejected; by 1945, for the first time in the history of the Trust, the total numbers exceeded ten thousand. Under the new dispensation the schools were open only to grammar school type children: numbers increased, sixth forms were greatly enlarged, and in due course the schools were able to take full advantage of expanding university places.

The new system brought new problems. One, of course, was the imposition of the contentious eleven-plus test of entry. Twenty years earlier the Association of Head Mistresses and the Trust headmistresses had spoken out against a test at the age of ten or eleven as likely to favour the sharp but shallow-witted child at the expense of the slow developer. From 1945 onwards, however, the Trust

181

schools have been academic and selection by ability has followed the pattern imposed on them.

The question of selection came up at the earliest stage. By 1948 a number of Trust headmistresses were finding difficulty in choosing the most suitable children for the preparatory department at the age of five. The children admitted had to be, as far as it was possible to tell, capable of passing into the upper school and be suited by 'age, ability and aptitude' for an academic education. It was inevitable that some children should be rejected who would have done well and that a few would have to leave at eleven because they could not make the grade. This state of affairs, so frustrating to parents and children, deprived the Trust of something it had always valued. The mandate had been accepted, yet there were many who shared Miss Charlesworth's regret that 'the upper schools could not be multilateral in the sense that they were in the past'.

This problem affected all the direct grant schools in varying degrees. Relations between their headmistresses had always been friendly on a personal as well as an educational level. The same friendly relations have, of course, been established among the direct grant and the maintained schools. Among others, Miss Blackburn, formerly headmistress of Bath High School, has spoken with especial warmth of her contacts with her colleagues in the maintained schools. She was particularly anxious that no stigma of 'superiority' should be attached to the High School and for this reason was at pains to ensure that when a girl from a primary school won a scholarship to the High School the names of both schools were mentioned in any subsequent press release.

The ties which bind the Trust schools together are naturally exceedingly close. There are, for example, individual groupings of schools in the area of London and the home counties, between schools in the midlands and between those in the north. Headmistresses are in constant touch with headquarters in London, but they consult most frequently with their own governing bodies and with colleagues in their own area.

Chapter 17

Reconstruction

The immediate post-war period was one of growth and achievement, but in the late 1940s the Trust faced a crisis which threatened to destroy it completely.

It will be remembered that in 1872 the Girls' Public Day School Company was founded by the issue of £5 Preference Shares, this being the only means of raising the capital to provide the wherewithal for the schools which the Company proposed to establish. Over the next thirty years – notably in 1898, 1906, 1911 and 1912 – the Articles of Association were altered with the object of benefiting the Company (later the Trust), of bringing it nearer to the desired goal of charitable status, and of complying with the regulations of the Board of Education concerning the receipt of public money by non-profit-making organizations. It will also be remembered that two far-reaching amendments were made to the Memorandum and Articles of Association in 1911. The first allowed for a stated majority of shareholders to move for the Trust to be wound up as a Limited Company by 1956 if the Council failed to make an acceptable offer to buy the whole of the Preference Share Capital. The second was the creation of 100 1s 'New' Shares, to be held as Trustee Shares, carrying, after January 1956, enormous voting rights of 10,000 votes per share in certain circumstances.

The existence of shareholders had always hampered the efforts of the Trust to gain recognition as a purely educational organization. For many years the shareholders, an educationally minded body, were content with little or no return on their holdings. By 1898 the dividend had been limited to a maximum of 4 per cent, and because the financial security of the Trust and the ever growing needs of the schools were considered paramount, there were many years in which no dividend at all was paid. The shares had a Stock Exchange quotation but in the circumstances their value was very low.

The exigencies of the First World War followed by those of the economic depression placed a very heavy burden on the Trust. The majority of the original shareholders were no longer living and, while the majority of their heirs were willing to make allowances for these difficulties, some were growing restive. It is undeniable that there was a certain amount of hardship, especially among elderly women with small fixed incomes which could not keep pace with the rising cost of living. 'I am more indignant than I can say', wrote one of them in 1922, 'to receive another balance sheet with no dividend (since 1912 nothing received on an Investment of £590). If this was a scheme of Charity . . . that fact ought to have been made clear to Investors – as it is I consider I have been defrauded.' She could not dispose of her shares except at a loss and 'when one sees the reckless expenditure evidenced in the balance sheets . . . it is really exasperating to one of limited means. There is much reason in the complaints of those who view *reckless* expenditure on administration in Education with anger. I ought to have retired from my Profession (Private School) ten years ago, but what chance is there? If the Company is run on altruistic lines, what hindrance is there to one or more of the members buying my Shares? I am in earnest – and I hope there may be someone honourable enough to do it. . . .' Another woman, who had inherited £255 worth of shares from her parents, had been content to forgo the dividend until 'two months ago [when] my husband passed on into the wider life where £sd is of no account. But I am left here and I badly need this money. . . . Could you not send me the £255 with *some* interest? It does not seem asking much of a great Trust, tho' it means a great deal to me.'

To these and other complainants the Council expressed regret that they had been unable to recommend a dividend since 1912 and explained that the doubling of teachers' salaries under the Burnham Scale had made it impossible. It would not, of course, be possible for the Trust to reimburse individual shareholders or to buy back its own shares, and the Council were well aware that after so long a period without a dividend the shares were virtually worthless. The accusation of 'reckless expenditure' was quite another matter. Shareholders would find 'that the cost per pupil when compared with other institutions of a similar kind is extremely low, notwithstanding that we have to pay a large tax on so-called profits, and have to have very small classes at the top of the schools for girls preparing for Universities'.

These were isolated complaints but in 1931 there was a concerted effort by a small but extremely vocal group to get hold of the £20,000 in respect of Schedule A (Property) Tax which, it will be recalled, had been recovered from the Inland Revenue Authorities as a result of the Wimbledon test case. This money, they claimed, should either be used to make up arrears in dividends or, failing that, to pay the full allowable 4 per cent dividend for the current year. At the Annual General Meeting of shareholders one of them underlined this request by remarking, in words which were later (though incompletely) expunged from the minutes: 'We are not interested in education: the Council do that well enough.'

In 1936 the group tried another approach. They suggested, first, that the next vacancy on the Council should be filled by some one who would represent the shareholders' interests and, secondly, that as an economy measure some of the schools should be closed and others moved out of London. In the past shareholders had pressed for representation on the Council but had never been given it. Now (to quote the minutes) one of them 'indulged in a number of very abusive remarks and ignorant comments on certain items in the accounts and asked for a winding up of the Trust'. The remarks were apparently too abusive to be recorded and 'no reply was made to him'. The aggrieved shareholder left the meeting but continued to write letters to the Trust demanding the closure of all the schools which did not show a profit.

The Second World War plunged the Trust into additional financial trouble. The Education Act of 1944 presented it with a new and challenging problem: the need to extend the schools to accommodate the healthy increase in numbers.

The Trust was still financially hamstrung by its liability to pay Schedule D (Profits) Tax, the Wimbledon test case having relieved it only of Schedule A Tax. The available money was devoted to the maintenance of the schools, the profits accruing from any one of them being used for the benefit of them all, but there was never enough to meet their actual needs.

The dissident shareholders were quiescent during the war but at the close of hostilities they emerged as a small but influential group of City men. Their avowed intention – if the provision which had been made for the repayment of their shares was not implemented by 1956 – was to move for the winding up of the Trust and, *ipso facto*, for the sale of the schools.

They opened their campaign at the Annual General Meeting of Shareholders in 1946. The Chairman, said one shareholder, was 'not employed to work for the Ministry of Education or the Government, but to conduct the Trust in such a manner as would provide the shareholders with a return for their money'. The shareholders had received no dividend since 1934 when a low rate was paid and the Council could only deplore the situation. A form of reconstruction mooted by shareholders foundered, as had similar schemes put forward in the past, owing to lack of funds.

In 1947 the leading spirit of the group (known familiarly to some members as the 'gang') made an abortive attempt to oust the Trust's auditors and replace them with a firm of his own choosing. He was, he said, 'disgusted with the general policy of the Council'. The shares were not offered on the open market, he said at the Annual General Meeting, 'and changed hands at much lower than their proper value . . .'.

This meeting was presided over by the newly elected President of the Trust, the distinguished educationist and public servant Miss (now Dame) Lucy Sutherland, Principal of Lady Margaret Hall, Oxford. During the proceedings Miss Sutherland invited the Vice-Chairman, a well-known chartered accountant, Mr (later Sir William) Cash to reply. Over the past few years, he said meaningfully, there had been purchases of shares on the Stock Exchange 'on the prospect of a liquidation of the Trust'. The Trust relied for a large part of its income on grants from the Ministry of Education, part of which had to be paid out again as income tax. In fact, it was 'at the mercy of the Ministry of Education who could at any time amend their rate of grant'. He went on to explain that the premises owned by the Trust were used as schools and if the schools were closed the value of the buildings would be small. Their standard was 'considerably below the requirements of the present time and very far below the standard required by the Ministry of Education for the future'. The Trust was involved in a heavy programme of deferred repairs and plans for essential rebuilding and improvement. In whatever form it might be carried on in the future, 'it would be faced with heavy capital expenditure towards which no assistance could be obtained from the Ministry'. It was 'not an ordinary commercial undertaking, and the schools were direct grant schools and not run with the object of making a profit'. If any profits were made they must be ploughed back into the schools.

It was painfully clear that the 'gang' had no intention of allowing the matter to rest. The Council therefore set to work under Mr Cash, who succeeded Mr Stead as Chairman in 1948, to produce a reconstruction scheme which would both satisfy the shareholders and induce the Inland Revenue Authorities to recognize the Trust as an educational charity exempt alike from Schedules A and D Tax. Miss Sutherland, who presided over the Annual General Meeting of Shareholders in May 1949 explained that the purpose of the meeting was to consider two resolutions, the combined effect of which would ensure continuity of the educational work of the Trust, provide for it a form of constitution best suited to its educational purposes, and at the same time would secure the exemption from income tax to which such a Trust would be entitled.

In essence the proposed reconstruction scheme was simple. The Trust had an issued capital of £153,295 in 30,659 4 per cent tax-free Preference Shares of £5 each, of which 686 had been surrendered by their owners for the benefit of the Trust. These shares had a Stock Exchange quotation and had recently been changing hands in the region of 50s. The remainder of the capital consisted of the so-called 'New' Shares which had been created in the reconstruction of 1911–12. The present scheme would cancel the preference shares which had already been donated to the Trust, and then proceed to write off £2 from each of the remaining £5 Preference Shares, offering in repayment of the £3 outstanding an equal nominal amount of 4 per cent Debenture Stock with a maximum life of twenty-six years.

This offer, declared the leader of the 'gang', indicated 'a magnificent audacity. . . . If I can have the Council of this so-called Trust through the hoop, I shall be delighted to do so.' The Council, added one of his colleagues, 'make great play and reference to charity and education. We shareholders should remind him that charity begins at home, and one of the first and most important principles of education is to honour one's obligations. What sort of education is it to borrow £5 and a little more, and turn round and say: "I am going to give you £3 back in paper money"?'

A woman shareholder who spoke in support of the resolutions guilelessly uncovered the root of the opposition's case. The Trust, she said, 'was not started as a business proposition, and it seems very unfortunate to me that people have come into it, I can only suggest as speculators. Those of us who are really interested in the Trust and in education and wish to see these schools continued, and doing the wonderful and excellent work which they have been doing, are quite satisfied that we are getting a very sound return on the shares that we now hold. I think the whole trouble is that the people who are objecting to this have simply come into this as a speculation. I think the audacity is on their part, and not on the part of the Council.'

Her point was underlined by Mr Cash who warned the speculators that the facts would, if required, have to be placed before the High Court during the hearing of a Petition which the Trust was to bring.

The resolutions before the meeting were carried, but there was an interval before the Petition was presented in July. The result indicated that the dissident shareholders had some cause for

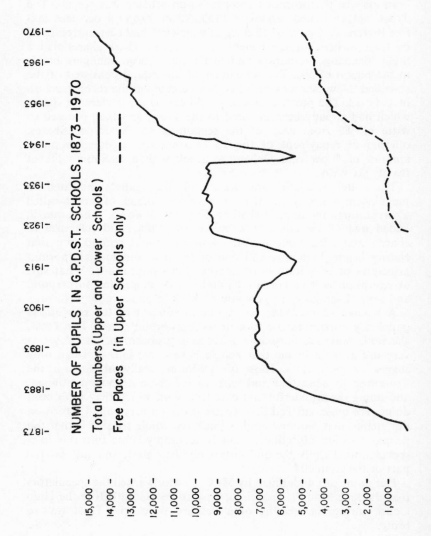

NUMBER OF PUPILS IN G.P.D.S.T. SCHOOLS, 1873–1970

Total numbers (Upper and Lower Schools) ——————

Free Places (in Upper Schools only) — — — —

complaint. Mr Justice Wynn-Parry, who had heard the evidence for and against the proposals, ruled that they were not sufficiently generous to the shareholders.

An alternative scheme was therefore prepared, in order, said Mr Cash, to settle 'this rather vexed question'. In December 1949, while the scheme was still in preparation, it was reported that the price of the shares had rocketed in a single day from 52s 6d to 85s nominal. The scheme was ready in March 1950. In principle it followed the original scheme, but it took into account the suggestions of the Judge and also some which had been put forward by shareholders. It involved the elimination of the Preference Shares by means of reduction and repayment of capital. The nominal amount of the outstanding Preference Shares would, however, be repaid as to one-half in cash and one-half by the issue of equivalent nominal amounts of 4 per cent Debenture Stock, redeemable over twenty years by means of a sinking fund. The Debenture Stock would not be quoted on the Stock Exchange, as the Council attached great importance to the omission of the word 'Limited' from the name of the Trust.

The scheme was approved at an Extraordinary General Meeting of the Trust and was confirmed by an Order of the High Court of Justice in May. As a result the Commissioners of Inland Revenue recognized the Trust as an educational charity and, as such, exempt from the payment of all income tax.

This was a tremendous saving but there was a heavy price to pay. In order to make the necessary cash repayments the sum of £75,000 had to be raised and the Trust's mortgage liability increased by a corresponding amount. The issue of the Debenture Stock represented a debt of another £75,000.* The Council now set up an endowment fund: in response to an appeal for funds a number of shareholders surrendered their cash and debenture rights and a total of nearly £6,000 was raised in this way.

Despite the heavy financial burden it involved, the reconstruction scheme had succeeded in saving the Trust from liquidation. The scheme was the brain-child of William Cash who had also been

---

* This was fully redeemed in annual instalments by 1966. There were several reasons – among them the very high stamp duty which would have been payable had the Trust's properties been transferred to another organization – why the constitution remained that of a limited company, but the Board of Trade gave permission for the word 'Limited' to be omitted from the Trust's name, an exemption granted only to companies not trading for profit. The sole shareholders now are the holders of the 100 New Shares – members of the Council and Chairmen of the Governing Bodies of the schools outside the London area. The holders receive no dividends, bonuses or other remuneration.

responsible for its modifications. His introduction to the affairs of the Trust had come by way of his charming and gifted wife, a former pupil of Oxford High School, a Council member and an admirable chairman of the Education Committee. As a Council member for nearly twenty years William Cash worked tirelessly to ensure the financial stability of the Trust and by his own efforts achieved remarkable results. He was an admired and highly respected figure although in later years some people found him autocratic. The well-earned knighthood conferred on him in 1958 was for services to education, an honour described in the *Times Educational Supplement* as conferred on him personally and also on 'the whole group of schools with which he is associated'. After the reconstruction of the Trust the headmistresses, intensely relieved at the outcome, expressed to Sir William in person and to the Council their 'deep sense of gratitude . . . for the enormous amount of time and energy, wisdom and expert knowledge expended on behalf of the schools'.

When the final details had been settled the Council decided that the way was clear to bring to fruition a scheme which had also originated with Sir William and which had been in their minds for some considerable time. This was the formation of a body known as the Friends of the Girls' Public Day School Trust. Its object was 'to create a strong and widespread fellowship of all those who value the type of education provided by the Trust, including not only those who have been educated or who have taught in Trust Schools, but also parents of pupils and others, both men and women, who know and appreciate the work of the Trust'. The organization was formally launched in a letter to *The Times* in March 1951, signed by its President, the Countess of Harewood, a former pupil of Kensington High School, by Miss Sutherland, as President of the Trust, and Mr Cash, as Chairman of the Council. Under the chairmanship of Miss Charlesworth, the 'Friends' became a flourishing concern: it is a separate body from the Council of the Trust and draws its members from many parts of the British Isles and from overseas. It publishes an annual newsletter, it helps the parent body in a number of ways, among them the award of travelling scholarships to school leavers and gifts to the schools themselves. Its members, wrote a distinguished Trust headmistress, Miss Kathleen D. B. Littlewood* in 1960, 'are unshaken in their loyalty to the Trust and belief in its system of education which, whatever its modern developments, holds the ideals and principles of the first founders'.

* Headmistress of Bromley and Wimbledon High Schools.

Following the reconstruction, plans were set in motion for necessary rebuilding. Bath High School, severely damaged in the war, was still housed in temporary premises. It was restored in cream-coloured Bath stone which – to quote its former headmistress Miss Blackburn – 'combines the graciousness of the old with the free uncluttered lines of the new'. The building was formally reopened in May 1951 by H.R.H. the Duchess of Gloucester, performing her first public act as Patron of the Trust schools.

After Bath, Oxford High School presented the most pressing problem. It was housed in premises built by the Trust under a building lease which had expired and been renewed for a short period. In 1955, on the eve of the school's eightieth birthday, Her Royal Highness laid the foundation stone of a new building which she opened three years later. In its new home the school is described by a former headmistress, Miss V. E. Stack, as 'surrounded everywhere by the beauty of line and shape and colour which its architect . . . has planned with so much imaginative powers. From the quadrangle our exquisite "Deirdre", the bronze figure by Sir Jacob Epstein presented by the Friends of the Trust, gives a serene welcome, a kind of benediction to everyone entering the school, and to every child passing along the corridors. . . .'

Essential rebuilding apart – and Croydon was to come next – there was not a single school which did not urgently need improvement and extension, especially in the provision of science accommodation. In 1955 the Council learned that, largely through Miss Blackburn's efforts to obtain financial help from industrial firms for the provision of additional laboratory accommodation at Bath High School, a new Association of Industrial Firms had been founded to provide grants for new laboratories in independent and direct grant schools. Most of the grants went to boys' schools but Trust schools benefited to the extent of £21,600, the largest single grant – £17,000 – being contributed towards the £43,000 required for the building of a new science block at Croydon.

The Trust was, of course, in need of a great deal more. It had never received anything in the way of endowments or grants for capital purposes and so it was deemed necessary to negotiate for the issue of £600,000 Debenture Stock which was taken up by a consortium of insurance companies and business houses in London. After paying off the previous mortgage and other commitments some £300,000 remained for expenditure on the schools. A programme of essential rebuilding was immediately put in hand and much was achieved during the 1950s. In 1961, eleven schools were given new science blocks, additions which have since been provided for the other schools. The schools themselves have played their part by raising funds for building, for amenities such as the provision of separate sixth-form accommodation, and for the purchase of sites and freehold properties. In the meantime, between 1944 and 1969, the value of the Trust's freehold land and buildings increased by more than £3 million.

By 1962 it had become clear that owing to road-widening and local development schemes Croydon High School would have to move. A ninety-nine year lease was sold to one of the development companies concerned which enabled the Trust to buy a large undulating, wooded site in Selsdon Park, away from the noise and bustle of the town. The foundation stone of the new building was laid by the Duchess of Gloucester in 1964. It was blessed by Dr Michael Ramsey, Archbishop of Canterbury, following the precedent set by one of his predecessors who had dedicated the old building in 1880. The opening ceremony was performed by Her Royal Highness in 1967. As the headmistress, Miss E. B. J. Cameron, has written, the new school 'is lovely, and is an exciting place'. It is spacious, splendidly proportioned and modern in the best sense of the word. Seniors and juniors are housed in separate buildings: the senior school, specially designed on the principle of subject centres, radiates from the sixth-form 'suite' with its own library, common room and pantry.

Croydon High School represents the summit of the Trust's building activities to date. It is the largest of all the schools, but those less favoured architecturally and those in crowded districts are also full to capacity showing, as one headmistress remarked, that amenities weigh less with parents than the academic standards, atmosphere and spirit of a school.

9. Sheffield High School; student teachers in training, about 1900.

10. Miss Florence Gadesden, Headmistress of Blackheath High School, 1886–1919, with some of her staff who became headmistresses of Trust and other schools, at the Conference of the Association of Head Mistresses in 1919: *Back Row* (*left to right*): Miss Lewis (Wimbledon), Miss Whyte (Kettering), Miss Hopkirk (Ashby-de-la-Zouch), Miss Sanders (Sydenham), Miss Weeks (Richmond), Miss Martin (Wakefield), Miss Morant (Kentish Town), Miss Frood (Dudley), Miss Stafford (Walsall), Miss Vivian (Roundhay, Leeds). *Second Row*: Miss Haig Brown (Oxford), Miss Sheldon (Sydenham), Miss Gadesden, Miss Major (Putney). *on Ground*: Miss Lowe

11. *Above*: Sheffield High School; Science lesson, about 1900. *Below*: Sydenham High School; work in one of the laboratories, 1970.

12. *Above*: Birkenhead High School; the Kindergarten, early 1900s. *Below*: Kensington High School (Junior School); the Kindergarten, 1970.

13. *Above*: Blackheath High School; original Assembly Hall. *Below*: Birkenhead High School; Assembly Hall, 1970.

14. *Above*: Bath High School. *Below*: Norwich High School.

15. *Above*: Brighton & Hove High School. *Below*: Croydon High School.

16. *Above*: Kensington High School; sixth form study groups, about 1900. *Centre*: Oxford High School; sixth formers, 1970. *Below*: Notting Hill & Ealing High School; a corner of the Library and Sixth Form block, 1970.

Chapter 18
The Trust and the Future

For twenty years following the Education Act of 1944 the direct grant schools flourished. Successive H.M. Inspectors who visited Trust schools commented most favourably on the high intellectual standing and vitality, the development of sixth forms and the steady rise in the number of university scholarships and exhibitions, the change in methods which brought the teaching of the younger children into line with modern thought. They felt that the success of the schools owed much to the freedom which a wise and sensible Council allowed the headmistresses, and also to the fact that a large proportion of the girls came from homes with a tradition of learning. In spite of the selective entry to the senior school there was still to be found in some Trust schools a higher proportion of academically limited girls than in the maintained grammar schools, so that the Trust schools had not altogether lost their multilateral character.

To the proposed reorganization of State education on comprehensive lines outlined in Circular 10/65 the approach of the local authorities varied considerably. They were required to submit their schemes by July 1966: meanwhile, some were in favour of making an immediate change and some were prepared to spread the change over a lengthy period while others were hesitant and resistant. Headmistresses of direct grant schools were anxious about their own educational position: in some cases L.E.A.s proposed to send them unselected children, in others they suggested a transfer at thirteen instead of eleven.

In June 1965 the Secretary of State, the Rt. Hon. Anthony Crosland, received a deputation led by Lord James of Rusholme, formerly High Master of Manchester Grammar School and a Vice-President of the Trust. In reply to a question about the future, Mr Crosland indicated that the educational system was still in an evolutionary stage and that it was hoped that the direct grant schools would be able to evolve within that system.

The real problem, as the Council and headmistresses discussed it

N

at their annual conference the same year, was that the comprehensive principle to which the Government were committed was incompatible with the selective entry essential for the efficient functioning of the schools, which were equipped to provide predominantly academic courses leading, for the majority of the pupils, to some form of continuing education. The schools had not the buildings, equipment or staff to cover a full cross-section of abilities or aptitudes.

The Council proceeded to explore various ways in which the conditions of entry might be modified to meet local circumstances, such as widening the range of ability, altering the age of entry, accepting direct entry to the sixth form or to any special courses available in the schools. By and large, however, the problem remained unresolved.

In 1965 it was learnt that the Government were not, as had been expected, in the process of setting up an educational trust to incorporate the public schools within the national system, but intended instead to undertake a survey of the schools. An approach was immediately made to the Secretary of State asking for the direct grant schools to be included in the survey. As a result the Public Schools Commission was subsequently instructed to advise 'on the most effective methods by which direct grant grammar schools in England and Wales and the grant-aided schools in Scotland can participate in the movement towards comprehensive reorganization, and to review the principle of Central Government Grant to these Schools'.

In 1967 the Council of the Trust were informed that they would be invited to give evidence before the Commission. One of its members was Dame Kitty Anderson who had been appointed Chairman of the Council of the Trust in 1965. In 1967 she resigned from the Public Schools Commission, for she wished to be closely associated with the presentation of the evidence on behalf of the Trust and the other girls' direct grant schools.

During 1968 members of the Commission and their Chairman, Professor David Donnison, visited several Trust schools. In September of the same year the position of the Girls' Public Day School Trust in the changing educational scene was the theme of a conference between the Council and the headmistresses. It was agreed at this conference that the fundamental aim of the Trust was to continue to provide grammar schools leading directly to higher education.

In December the Council submitted their evidence to the Commission. In defence of their position as grammar schools with a

194

selective entry they argued that they had fulfilled their obligations under the direct grant system. They had opened the schools to all girls who could profit from a grammar school education – to free-placers and fee-payers alike – regardless of parental means, preference always being given to girls who by reason of ability and aptitude were most likely to benefit. Within the framework of the state system and their responsibility to the Department of Education and Science they had preserved the variety of the schools, so that whilst all had a good academic standard some, by virtue of the areas they served, were more academic than others which catered for a wider ability range. They had continued to administer the schools as economically as possible, through an independent Council and local Governing Bodies with L.E.A. representation, giving the maximum amount of freedom to headmistresses to run their schools and develop the courses they considered the most appropriate. 'Experience over the years', they declared, 'has confirmed us in our belief that the direct grant system is a bridge between the maintained and independent sectors of education. It is a happy combination of control and independence. In February 1966, in a debate in the House of Lords, Lord James said of the direct grant system: "The direct grant school is an example of that reconciliation of academic freedom with public accountability that is at once an example and a stimulus to those of us who experience it." We endorse this view. It is because we believed that the system was both imaginative and far-sighted, with its central and local links, and enabled a school to make its contribution through a partnership, whose terms embrace responsibilities and freedoms, that we made this choice for the Trust schools in 1945.'

The Council's evidence was supplemented by evidence from the Board of the Friends of the Girls' Public Day School Trust, based on contributions from teachers, past and present, past pupils, and relatives of those still present. While the schools, they said, deemed it necessary to maintain certain standards of intellectual attainment and aptitude in their entrants in order to enable them in due course to qualify for entrance to professional and academic careers, 'their aim is not to have only one kind of pupil or "cream" other schools in the neighbourhood. They do not insist, indeed have never insisted, on a strict priority of ability in the admission of children, whether holding fee-paying or holding local authorities' places.' It would be impossible – even if thought desirable – for the Trust schools as a whole 'to provide the width of curriculum to be found in a comprehensive school, since even the largest have little more than a thousand pupils (including the junior school). It is an

advantage to have in any district schools of somewhat smaller size
than comprehensive schools and many local authorities have indeed
found it so.' There were some girls who were lost in a very large
community and headmistresses, who always wished to know every
one of their pupils, could achieve this aim in a school of several
hundred but not in one of several thousand. 'For many girls and
their parents this personal link with the Head of the School is
greatly valued and can make a vital contribution to a child's
development.' The policy of the Council had given the schools 'an
individual character' and had 'attracted to them, both as Heads and
members of staff, women endowed with enterprise and the character
to give their schools a special quality. We do not claim that these
characteristics are peculiar to Trust schools, but we believe that
there are no schools in which they are more clearly evident. Our
history and conditions of working make it easier to maintain
standards in what may be called a way of life. . . .'

Any one visiting a number of Trust schools today will discover
that they have not become mere forcing-houses for the universities.
Each school, while it retains something of the old traditions, has
maintained its own identity, its respect for individuality, and the
special flavour of the community it serves. Thus South Hampstead
High School, for example, educates, among others, the daughters
of actors, artists and musicians. Oxford High School, home of
intellectuals, also has a boarding-house and so draws its pupils
from all over the world, as do Bath and Brighton, the two other
schools with boarding-houses. The smallest of the schools –
Streatham Hill and Clapham – has perhaps the richest and most
varied social background of them all: it numbers among its pupils
Poles, Greek Cypriots, East and West Africans, Indians and
Pakistanis, and Jewesses – Orthodox, Reform and Liberal. It has
been the work of successive headmistresses, as varied in character
and personality as their schools, to weld the disparate elements into
a cohesive whole without sacrificing the interests of the majority or
lowering the educational standard. During the past few years they
have introduced some of the reforms which have been pressed by the
much publicized Schools Action Union: the establishment of school
councils, for instance, collective sixth-form responsibility in place of
the old prefectorial system, a modification of the rules, and permission for the older girls to wear their own clothes instead of
school uniform. Headmistresses are constantly in touch with one
another, with their local Governing Bodies, and with the Trust at
the centre: this interdependence has always been part of their
strength and vitality.

196

In the spring of 1970 their future looked very dark. The Donnison Report, published on March 24th, recommended that the direct grant schools should be incorporated in schemes for comprehensive education as soon as possible. The Commissioners put forward alternative schemes: under the first a school grants committee would administer a form of nationally aided status for the schools, thus preserving their links with the central government; under the second the schools would be maintained by education authorities. Under neither scheme would the schools be allowed to charge fees. They would therefore have the choice of accepting one or other of the schemes or else of opting for independent status. For some schools there was a more drastic solution. As the Report pointed out: 'We hope that all schools will wish to play a part in reorganization, but we recognize that some may be unable to find a place in comprehensive systems. They may be too small or lack space or other resources for expansion. . . . If they cannot choose independence, or do not wish to do so, a few direct grant schools may have to close.'

At a press conference held in London the same day the direct grant schools – including the schools of the Trust – emphasized that they welcomed neither scheme. Both removed two essential freedoms: the principle of fee-paying which was closely linked with a school's control of its own finance, and the right to select pupils. It was, however, pointed out that the schools were prepared to consider adjustment in the light of local circumstances, in terms of age of entry and method of choice.

On June 3rd the Council of the Trust issued a statement expressing their disappointment with the Donnison proposals and their possible effect, if implemented, on the opportunities open to girls. They reaffirmed their intention to carry on the work of the Trust to provide and administer, as an autonomous body, schools which encouraged girls to develop their academic gifts within the framework of a good general education and to go forward to the many fields of higher education now open to women. Their statement concluded: 'The Council have on several occasions, notably in their evidence to the Public Schools Commission, made clear the various ways in which their schools could co-operate within a comprehensive system of education, but they do not consider that the proposals of the Donnison Report would enable their schools to make their maximum educational contribution or to retain their essential freedoms. If, therefore, the recommendations of the Report were put into effect without modification, the Council would with very great reluctance, choose independence. Nevertheless they earnestly

197

hope that discussions will continue . . . and that a way may still be found to enable direct grant schools to continue their work in partnership with both national and local authorities.'

A fortnight later the General Election returned a Conservative Government, and there was an immediate and dramatic change in educational policy. The Secretary of State for Education and Science, Mrs Margaret Thatcher, herself a former grammar school girl, announced the withdrawal of the controversial Circular 10/65 and its replacement by Circular 10/70. The Government's aim, stated the Circular, 'is to ensure that all pupils shall have full opportunities for secondary education suitable to their needs and abilities. The Government, however, believe it is wrong to impose a uniform pattern of secondary education on local education authorities by legislation or other means . . .' Authorities would now be freer to determine the shape of secondary provision in their areas, but Mrs Thatcher would 'expect education considerations in general, local needs and wishes in particular, and the wise use of resources, to be the main principles determining the local pattern'. L.E.A.s whose reorganization plans had been approved by the former Government could either go ahead or else inform the Department of Education and Science that they wished to modify them. Those whose plans were still under consideration could withdraw them if they wished. Whatever course individual L.E.A.s adopted, Mrs Thatcher urged that any proposed changes should be discussed with teachers, and that full opportunities should be given to parents to express their views before a decision was reached.

During the subsequent debate on the Queen's Speech in the House of Commons on July 7th the former Secretary of State, Mr Short, who moved an Opposition amendment regretting the Conservative policy for the organization of secondary education, attacked the Circular on the ground that it would reinforce the old system of eleven-plus segregation and thus perpetuate a system which was 'educationally indefensible, socially unjust, and economically wasteful'. In her reply Mrs Thatcher declared that the Government accepted the view that the age of eleven was too early to make a final decision about a child's future but, she said, 'I believe it is possible – Mr Short does not – to have a mixed system of comprehensive and grammar schools alongside. . . . I believe . . . that there is still a place for special selective schools of excellence.'

At the conclusion of the debate, in the first division of the new Parliament, the Government gained a majority of forty-six, a figure higher than its overall paper majority.

Under the present dispensation the position of the direct grant schools will, of course, vary. The Labour-controlled Inner London Education Authority, for example, reaffirmed an earlier decision not to take up places at direct grant and independent schools from September 1971, a decision which would affect five of the London schools of the Trust – Blackheath, Putney, South Hampstead, Streatham Hill and Clapham, and Sydenham.

Elsewhere the position is fluid, although it seems clear that many direct grant schools will have earned a reprieve. The Girls' Public Day School Trust has always been convinced – as Mrs Thatcher is convinced – that there is a place for the direct grant schools side by side with the comprehensive schools. The Chairman, Dame Kitty Anderson, has underlined the importance of maintaining, rather than severing, the links between the maintained and independent sectors of education, of keeping variety within the State system and of making use of all the facilities which exist and are working well. The direct grant schools, she has said, 'have a contribution to make and therefore a duty to survive'. At the moment their future looks brighter than it has done for some considerable time, and the schools of the Trust can look forward with confidence to the celebration of their hundredth birthday.

References

CHAPTER 1

1. *On the Education of Women*: a paper read by Mrs William Grey at a meeting of the Society of Arts, May 31, 1871.
2. *Thoughts on Self-Culture Addressed to Women* by Maria G. Grey and her sister, Emily Shirreff (Simpkin Marshall, 1850; new edition, 1872), preface.
3. *On the Special Requirements for Improving the Education of Girls*: a paper read at the Social Science Congress, Leeds, 1871.
4. *The Amberley Papers*, edited by Bertrand and Patricia Russell (Hogarth Press, 1937), Vol. I, p. 18.
5. *The Autobiography of Bertrand Russell, 1872–1914* (Allen & Unwin, 1967), pp. 33–4.
6. *The Ladies of Alderley*, edited by Nancy Mitford (Chapman & Hall 1938).
7. *ibid.*
8. *ibid.*
9. *ibid.*
10. *ibid.*
11. *ibid.*
12. *ibid.*
13. *The Stanleys of Alderley*, edited by Nancy Mitford (Hamish Hamilton, reissued 1968).
14. *Frances Mary Buss* by Annie E. Ridley (Longmans Green, 1895), p. 19.

CHAPTER 2

1. *Thoughts on Self-Culture*, preface.
2. *ibid*, p. 2.
3. *ibid*, pp. 9–10.
4. *ibid*, p. 19.
5. *ibid*, p. 41.
6. *ibid*, pp. 221–2.
7. *ibid*, p. 233.
8. *ibid*, pp. 36–7.
9. *Intellectual Education and its Influence on the Character and Happiness of Women* by Emily Shirreff (John W. Parker & Son, 1858), pp. 179–83.
10. *Reports Issued by the Schools' Inquiry Commission on the Education of*

Girls, reprinted with extracts from the Evidence and a Preface by D. Beale, pp. 2–3.

11. *Emily Davies and Girton College* by Barbara Stephen (Constable, 1937), pp. 110–11.
12. *Frances Mary Buss*, p. 261.
13. *Emily Davies and Girton College*, pp. 227–8.
14. *ibid*, pp. 233–4.
15. *That Infidel Place*, a Short History of Girton College, 1869–1969, by M. C. Bradbrook (Chatto & Windus, 1969), p. 50.
16. *Emily Davies and Girton College*, pp. 233–4.
17. *ibid*, p. 269.
18. *The Amberley Papers*, Vol. I, pp. 16–18.
19. *The Autobiography of Bertrand Russell*, p. 32.
20. *The Amberley Papers*, Vol. I, pp. 16–18.
21. Obituary of Emily Shirreff, *The Educational Review*, May 1897.

CHAPTER 3

1. *The Story of my Life* by Augustus Hare (George Allen, 1896), Vol. IV, p. 473.
2. *Frances Mary Buss*, p. 19.
3. Published by the London National Society for Women's Suffrage, 1870.
4. *Dearest Mama*, edited by Roger Fulford (Evans Brothers, 1968).
5. *Victoria R.I.* by Elizabeth Longford (Weidenfeld & Nicolson, 1964; Pan edition, 1966), p. 244.
6. 'The Women's Educational Movement' by Mrs William Grey, a chapter in Mrs Stanton's *Woman Question in Europe* (1833, proof copy only), pp. 48–50, 61.
7. *ibid.*
8. *ibid.*
9. *ibid.*

CHAPTER 6

1. *The Englishwoman's Review*, No. XLVII, March 15, 1877.
2. Public Record Office, ED 12/145.
3. *Contemporary Review*: Women and the Universities.

CHAPTER 7

1. *The Woman Question*, p. 53.
2. *Frances Mary Buss*, pp. 278–9.

3. *Last Words to Girls on Life in School and after School* by Mrs William Grey (Rivingtons, 1889), Introduction, VII.
4. *ibid*, pp. 218–19.

CHAPTER 8

1. North London Collegiate School archives.
2. *Secondary Education of Girls during the Past Fifty Years*: National Educational Association Fiftieth Anniversary Volume, 1857–1906.
3. *Hope Deferred: Girls' Education in English History* by Josephine Kamm (Methuen, 1965), p. 227.
4. Public Record Office ED 12/145.
5. *ibid*.
6. *Boring – Never* by Margaret E. Popham c.b.e. (Johnson, 1968), p. 18.
7. Public Record Office ED 24/388.
8. *The Jubilee Book of the Girls' Public Day School Trust*, 1873–1923, by Laurie Magnus (Cambridge University Press) pp. 29–30.

CHAPTER 9

1. Public Record Office ED 24/388.

CHAPTER 10

1. Public Record Office ED 12/392.

CHAPTER 11

1. Public Record Office ED 12/388.

CHAPTER 12

1. *A River Full of Stars* by Elizabeth Hamilton (André Deutsch, 1956), pp. 87–90.
2. Public Record Office ED 12/394.
3. *The Jubilee Book of the Girls' Public Day School Trust*, 1873–1923, pp. 25, 43–4, 178.

CHAPTER 13

1. Public Record Office ED 12/394.

2. *ibid*, ED 12/393.
3. *ibid*, ED 12/394.

CHAPTER 14

1. Public Record Office ED 12/395.
2. *The Jubilee Book of the Girls' Public Day School Trust*, p. 68.

Appendix I

Patrons, Presidents and Officers of the G.P.D.S.T.

Patrons:
>H.R.H. PRINCESS LOUISE, Marchioness of Lorne (later Duchess
>of Argyll), 1872–1939
>H.R.H. THE DUCHESS OF GLOUCESTER, 1940–

Presidents:
>1872 The Earl of Airlie
>1881 The Lord Aberdare G.C.B.
>1896 The Earl Spencer K.G.
>1908 The Earl (later Marquess) of Crewe K.G.
>1947 Dame Lucy Sutherland D.B.E., M.A., D.LITT., F.B.A.

Vice-Presidents, 1970:
>The Lord Conesford M.A., Q.C.
>The Lady Alethea Eliot
>Mrs V. H. Galbraith M.A., PH.D.
>Miss D. M. Hammonds C.B.E.
>The Lord James of Rusholme M.A., D.PHIL, LL.D
>The Hon. Mrs John Mulholland D.C.V.O.
>Sir Arthur Norrington M.A., J.P.

Chairmen of Council:
>1872 Mr Joseph Payne F.C.P. and others
>1873 Mr C. S. Roundell M.P.
>1877 Mr W. H. Stone
>1896 Mr (later Sir William) Bousfield
>1910 The Rev. Prebendary the Hon. J. S. Northcote F.K.C.
>1920 Mr M. Llewelyn Davies
>1929 Mr Laurie Magnus M.A.
>1933 Professor Alfred Hughes M.A.
>1938 Mr H. J. Simmonds C.B., C.B.E., B.A.
>1944 Mr F. B. Stead C.B.E., M.A.
>1948 Mr (later Sir William) Cash M.A., F.C.A.

1964 Mr H. F. Collins C.M.G., DOC. de l'U., M.A.
1965 Dame Kitty Anderson D.B.E., B.A., PH.D., F.C.P.,
       LL.D., Hull, D.UNIV., York

Council, 1872–3:
    The Earl of Airlie
    The Rev. W. Arthur
    Mrs Baden-Powell
    Mr William Barber
    Mr George C. T. Bartley
    The Rev. G. C. Bell
    The Lady Frederick Cavendish
    Mr H. W. Eve
    Captain Douglas Galton C.B.
    Mrs William Grey
    Miss Mary Gurney
    Sir Walter James, Bt
    Sir James Kay-Shuttleworth, Bt
    The Marquess of Lorne
    Mr Joseph Payne F.C.P.
    Mr C. S. Roundell M.P.
    Miss Emily Shirreff
    The Dowager Lady Stanley of Alderley

Council, 1970:
    Dame Kitty Anderson D.B.E., B.A., PH.D., F.C.P., LL.D., Hull,
       D.UNIV., York (Chairman)
    Sir Alec Cairncross K.C.M.G., F.B.A., M.A., PH.D.
    Lady Cairns M.A.
    Mrs D. M. Edwards B.A.
    Mrs J. H. Galbraith M.A.
    Mrs M. Good
    Mrs C. G. Hardie M.A., PH.D.
    Professor W. K. Hayman M.A., SC.D., F.R.S., HON. A.R.C.S.
    Mr Leighton L. Irwin M.A., LL.B., J.P.
    Lady Johnston M.A., B.C.L., J.P.
    Mr S. Lane F.C.A.
    Mr E. R. Lawrence M.A.
    Miss A. R. Murray M.A., B.SC., D.PHIL., J.P.
    Mrs E. H. Sondheimer M.A., PH.D.
    Mr R. C. Steele O.B.E., M.A.
    Miss P. N. Wilshere M.A.
    Mrs S. Woodcock M.A. (Deputy Chairman)

Secretaries:

1872	Rev. S. F. Hiron LL.D., D.C.L.
1874	Mr A. McDowall B.SC., B.A.
1910	Mr A. H. H. Maclean O.B.E., Barrister-at-law
1939	Mr A. C. Lightfoot M.C., A.A.C.C.A.
1952	Mr W. L. Lister A.C.C.A.

Appendix II

The G.P.D.S.T. High Schools and their Headmistresses

BATH
Opened 1875 Miss S. Wood
1882 Miss H. Weld (Mrs Griffiths)
1886 Miss F. K. Firth (*and Weymouth*)
1895 Miss K. M. Heale
1898 Miss E. A. A. Shekleton
1907 Miss E. Nicol
1919 Miss R. M. Fletcher
1926 Miss E. M. Cull
1942 Miss G. S. Blackburn
1969 Miss D. J. Chapman

BIRKENHEAD
Opened 1901 Miss B. E. Anderson
1903 Miss K. M. Baines
1914 Miss F. H. Johnston
1915 Miss C. Spurling
1917 Miss E. M. L. Lees (*and Sutton*)
1923 Miss J. M. H. McCaig (*and Notting Hill & Ealing*)
1930 Miss H. N. Stephen
1952 Miss P. Winter
1964 Miss I. Hindmarsh
1971 Miss F. Kellett

BLACKHEATH
Opened 1880 Miss S. Allen-Olney
1886 Miss F. Gadesden
1919 Miss M. Gale (*and Ipswich; Oxford*)
1931 Miss A. K. Lewis (*and Brighton & Hove*)
1945 Miss J. S. A. Macaulay
1956 Miss S. M. Wheatley (Mrs Stoker)
1962 Miss F. M. Abraham (*and Belvedere, Liverpool*)

BRIGHTON & HOVE (originally BRIGHTON)
Opened 1876 Miss E. E. M. Creak
     1883 Mrs A. L. Luxton (*and Nottingham*)
     1899 Miss R. Mayhew (Mrs Head)
     1904 Miss M. Phillimore (*and York*)
     1907 Miss A. C. P. Lunn (*and Sheffield*)
     1917 Miss A. S. Barratt (*and Clapham; East Liverpool*)
     1921 Miss A. K. Lewis (*and Blackheath*)
     1931 Miss I. M. Oakden (*and Notting Hill & Bayswater*)
     1934 Miss G. Farquhar (Mrs Woodcock)
     1936 Miss K. Lockley (*and Putney*)
     1950 Miss I. Ashcroft
     1969 Miss J. P. Turner

BROMLEY
Opened 1883 Miss M. L. Heppel
     1908 Miss M. A. Hodge
     1924 Miss K. D. B. Littlewood (*and Wimbledon*)
     1940 Miss E. K. East (*and Tunbridge Wells*)
     1949 Miss M. Leale (*and Newcastle*)
     1963 Miss M. Hardwick
     1971 Miss P. M. F. Reid

CROYDON
Opened 1874 Miss D. Neligan
     1901 Miss E. M. Leahy (*and Oxford; Dover*)
     1925 Miss E. Ransford (*and Ipswich*)
     1939 Miss M. F. Adams O.B.E., LL.D.
     1960 Miss E. B. J. Cameron

IPSWICH
Opened 1878 Miss S. E. Youngman
     1899 Miss B. Kennett
     1909 Miss M. Gale (*and Blackheath; Oxford*)
     1919 Miss E. Ransford (*and Croydon*)
     1925 Miss C. N. Williams
     1936 Miss L. E. Neal
     1960 Miss B. Strong
     1966 Mrs N. Small (Mrs Middlemas)
     1971 Miss P. Hayworth

KENSINGTON (originally CHELSEA, re-named 1880;
Upper School closed 1948)
Opened 1873 Miss M. E. Porter

1875 Miss M. A. Woods
1876 Miss M. E. Bishop (*and Oxford*)
1879 Miss A. M. Hitchcock
1900 Miss E. Home
1931 Miss L. E. Charlesworth C.B.E. (*and Sutton*)
1939 Miss M. M. Burke (*and Wimbledon*)
1948 Miss M. L. Baker
1966 Mrs J. Bayldon

LIVERPOOL: BELVEDERE (originally LIVERPOOL)
Opened 1880 Mrs C. F. Bolton (*and Nottingham*)
1883 Miss S. M. Huckwell (*and Putney*)
1893 Miss E. Cannings (*and Shrewsbury*)
1903 Miss I. L. Rhys
1922 Miss M. C. Fraser
1932 Miss A. F. Cossey (*and Portsmouth*)
1935 Mrs J. E. Hobson
1955 Miss F. M. Abraham (*and Blackheath*)
1962 Miss M. C. L. Ward

NEWCASTLE (CENTRAL)
Opened 1895 Miss M. Moberly (*and Gateshead; Tunbridge Wells*)
1911 Miss D. F. P. Hiley
1935 Miss W. A. Odell
1940 Miss M. Leale (*and Bromley*)
1949 Miss G. K. Belton
1962 Miss C. Russell

NORWICH
Opened 1875 Miss A. Benson (*and Oxford*)
1875 Miss L. B. Wills
1882 Miss M. A. Tapson (Mrs Help)
1884 Miss L. Gadesden (*and Newton Abbot*)
1907 Miss G. M. Wise (*and Shrewsbury*)
1928 Miss E. P. Jameson
1946 Miss P. R. Bodington (*and South Hampstead*)
1954 Miss D. F. Bartholomew

NOTTINGHAM
Opened 1875 Miss C. F. Bolton (*and Belvedere, Liverpool*)
1876 Miss E. M. Hastings (*and Wimbledon*)
1880 Mrs A. L. Luxton (*and Brighton & Hove*)
1883 Miss M. E. Skeel (*and Paddington & Maida Vale*)

O

1898 Miss C. C. Clark (*and York*)
1921 Miss W. D. Philipps
1936 Miss E. M. Merrifield (*and Notting Hill & Ealing*)
1950 Miss F. M. Milford
1967 Miss L. L. Lewenz

NOTTING HILL & EALING (originally NOTTING HILL & BAYSWATER; moved 1931)

Opened 1873 Miss H. M. Jones
1900 Miss E. Gavin (*and Shrewsbury; Wimbledon*)
1908 Miss A. T. Steele (*and Portsmouth*)
1910 Miss A. S. Paul (*and Clapham*)
1912 Miss M. M. Berryman
1924 Miss I. M. Oakden (*and Brighton & Hove*)
1930 Miss J. M. H. McCaig (*and Birkenhead*)
1950 Miss E. M. Merrifield (*and Nottingham*)
1960 Miss J. M. S. Hendry

OXFORD

Opened 1875 Miss A. Benson (*and Norwich*)
1879 Miss M. E. Bishop (*and Kensington*)
1887 Miss L. Soulsby
1898 Miss E. M. Leahy (*and Croydon; Dover*)
1902 Miss R. M. Haig Brown
1931 Miss M. Gale (*and Ipswich; Blackheath*)
1937 Miss V. E. Stack
1959 Miss M. E. A. Hancock (*and Sheffield*)
1966 Mrs M. Warnock

PORTSMOUTH

Opened 1882 Miss A. Ledger
1906 Miss A. T. Steele (*and Notting Hill & Bayswater*)
1908 Miss A. F. Cossey (*and Belvedere, Liverpool*)
1932 Miss G. E. Watt
1941 Miss E. M. Thorn
1968 Miss M. L. Clarke

PUTNEY (originally EAST PUTNEY)

Opened 1893 Miss S. M. Huckwell (*and Belvedere, Liverpool*)
1899 Miss E. H. Major
1911 Miss R. E. Hewetson
1920 Miss M. G. Beard
1930 Miss K. E. Chester

1950   Miss K. Lockley (*and Brighton & Hove*)
1963   Miss R. Smith

SHEFFIELD

Opened 1878   Miss M. A. Alger (*and Clapham Middle; Dulwich*)
1878   Mrs E. Woodhouse (*and Clapham*)
1898   Miss A. E. Escott (*and Clapham*)
1917   Miss A. C. P. Lunn (Mrs Doncaster)
(*and Brighton & Hove*)
1919   Miss M. C. Aitken
1926   Miss D. L. Walker (*and South Hampstead*)
1936   Miss M. E. Macaulay (*and Streatham Hill & Clapham*)
1947   Miss M. E. A. Hancock (*and Oxford*)
1959   Miss M. C. Lutz

SHREWSBURY

Opened 1885   Miss E. Cannings (*and Belvedere, Liverpool*)
1893   Miss E. Gavin (*and Notting Hill & Bayswater; Wimbledon*)
1900   Miss G. M. Wise (*and Norwich*)
1907   Miss D. Gale
1935   Miss G. I. Hudson
1957   Miss A. A. M. Wells
1963   Miss M. Crane

SOUTH HAMPSTEAD (originally ST JOHN'S WOOD)

Opened 1876   Miss R. Allen-Olney
1886   Miss M. S. Benton
1918   Miss D. L. Walker (*and Sheffield*)
1927   Miss M. L. Potter
1954   Miss P. R. Bodington (*and Norwich*)
1969   Mrs S. Wiltshire

STREATHAM HILL & CLAPHAM (originally BRIXTON HILL; re-named STREATHAM HILL & BRIXTON 1888; merged with Clapham 1938)

Opened 1887   Miss A. Tovey
1898   Miss R. Oldham
1923   Miss E. R. Gwatkin
1938   Miss M. Jarrett (*and Clapham*)
1947   Miss M. E. Macaulay (*and Sheffield*)
1963   Miss I. A. Wulff

SUTTON
Opened 1884   Miss M. C. Whyte (*and Highbury & Islington*)
     1890   Miss J. F. Duirs (*and Weymouth*)
     1903   Miss M. K. Bell
     1923   Miss E. M. L. Lees (*and Birkenhead*)
     1939   Miss L. E. Charlesworth C.B.E. (*and Kensington*)
     1959   Miss J. R. Glover

SYDENHAM
Opened 1887   Miss I. Thomas
     1901   Miss H. Sheldon (*and Dover*)
     1917   Miss A. F. E. Sanders (*and Tunbridge Wells*)
     1931   Dr M. S. Smith
     1942   Miss M. D. Yardley
     1966   Miss M. Hamilton

WIMBLEDON
Opened 1880   Miss E. M. Hastings (*and Nottingham*)
     1908   Miss E. Gavin (*and Shrewsbury; Notting Hill & Bayswater*)
     1918   Miss M. E. Lewis
     1940   Miss K. D. B. Littlewood (*and Bromley*)
     1949   Miss M. M. Burke (*and Kensington*)
     1962   Mrs A. A. Piper

SCHOOLS CLOSED, TRANSFERRED OR MERGED

CARLISLE
Opened 1884   Miss I. Bain
     1892   Miss A. Beevor
     1902   Miss S. Gardiner
     1909   School transferred to Cumberland County Council

CLAPHAM (Middle School)
Opened 1875   Miss M. A. Alger (*and Dulwich; Sheffield*)
     1877   Miss A. A. O'Connor (*and Clapham High*)
     1882   Miss M. H. Page
     1890   Miss A. H. Wheeler
     1898   Middle School merged with High School

CLAPHAM
Opened 1882   Miss A. A. O'Connor (*and Clapham Middle School*)

1898 Mrs E. Woodhouse (*and Sheffield*)
1913 Miss A. S. Paul (*and Notting Hill & Bayswater*)
1917 Miss A. E. Escott (*and Sheffield*)
1921 Miss A. S. Barratt (*and East Liverpool; Brighton & Hove*)
1934 Miss M. Jarrett (*and Streatham Hill*)
1938 School merged with Streatham Hill & Brixton

CLAPTON (originally HACKNEY)

Opened 1875 Miss M. Pearse
1892 Miss I. Cooper (*and Dulwich; Gateshead*)
1894 Miss E. A. Dawson
1899 School closed

DOVER

Opened 1888 Miss G. E. Frost
1895 Miss E. M. Leahy (*and Oxford; Croydon*)
1898 Miss H. Sheldon (*and Sydenham*)
1901 Miss L. C. Courtenay
1908 School closed

DULWICH

Opened 1878 Miss M. A. Alger (*and Clapham Middle; Sheffield*)
1894 Miss I. Cooper (*and Hackney & Clapton; Gateshead*)
1900 Miss L. Silcox (*and East Liverpool*)
1909 Miss C. W. Matthews
1909 Miss S. M. Furness
1913 School transferred to Church Schools' Company; closed 1938

GATESHEAD

Opened 1876 Miss J. P. Rowdon
1879 Miss I. Cooper (*and Dulwich; Hackney & Clapton*)
1891 Miss M. Moberly (*and Tunbridge Wells; Newcastle*)
1895 Miss M. Vickers
1899 Miss F. E. Tooke
1907 School merged with Newcastle (Central)

HIGHBURY & ISLINGTON

Opened 1878 Miss M. C. Whyte (*and Sutton*)
1883 Miss M. A. A. Minasi
1911 School closed

LIVERPOOL (EAST)
Opened 1891   Miss L. Silcox (*and Dulwich*)
1901   Miss A. Silcox
1909   Miss A. S. Barratt (*and Brighton & Hove; Clapham*)
1912   School closed

NEWTON ABBOT
Opened 1881   Miss L. Gadesden (*and Norwich*)
1884   Miss E. A. Ridley
1888   School transferred to Miss Ridley

PADDINGTON & MAIDA VALE (originally MAIDA VALE)
Opened 1878   Miss A. C. Andrews
1899   Miss M. E. Skeel (*and Nottingham*)
1907   Miss W. M. Slater
1912   School transferred to London County Council

SWANSEA
Opened 1888   Miss M. E. Vinter
1895   School closed

TUNBRIDGE WELLS
Opened 1883   Miss M. Moberly (*and Gateshead; Newcastle*)
1891   Miss E. M. Julian
1908   Miss A. F. E. Sanders (*and Sydenham*)
1917   Miss M. W. Byrne
1927   Miss E. K. East (*and Bromley*)
1945   School closed

WEYMOUTH
Opened 1880   Miss F. K. Firth (*and Bath*)
1886   Miss J. F. Duirs (*and Sutton*)
1890   Miss A. Blagrave
1894   School closed

YORK
Opened 1880   Miss E. K. W. Chambers
1889   Miss M. Ward
1891   Miss J. B. McLeod
1893   Miss C. C. Clark (*and Nottingham*)
1898   Miss M. Phillimore (*and Brighton & Hove*)
1904   Miss C. L. Primrose

1905   Miss E. B. Bower
1907   School transferred to Church Schools' Company;
       now York College for Girls

TRAINING OF TEACHERS

CLAPHAM TRAINING COLLEGE, opened 1900 (recognized by Board of Education 1903). Departments: Domestic Science (closed 1921); Art (closed 1938); Post-graduate (closed 1942); Kindergarten (Froebel). Moved to Streatham in 1938 and re-named CLAPHAM & STREATHAM HILL TRAINING COLLEGE. Transferred to London County Council 1949 and re-named PHILIPPA FAWCETT COLLEGE, in new buildings opened in 1953.

KENSINGTON MUSIC TRAINING DEPARTMENT, opened 1908, closed 1935.

The greater number of the other schools had smaller, recognized, Training Departments, Post-graduate, Kindergarten or Art, at one time or another from about 1903, the largest being at THE BELVEDERE SCHOOL, LIVERPOOL.

Appendix III

Distinguished Old Girls

The following list, which has been compiled by the Girls' Public Day School Trust, is a representative selection of past pupils eminent in varying fields at some time during the last hundred years.

EDUCATION AND SCHOLARSHIP

DAME DOROTHY BROCK D.B.E., M.A. CANTAB., LITT.D.   Bromley
    DUBLIN, LL.M. LOND.
    Headmistress of Mary Datchelor School.
    Member of many government committees.
    Freeman of the Clothworkers' Company and of
    the Metropolitan Borough of Camberwell.

ROSE BRUFORD   Bath
    Principal of the Rose Bruford Training College
    of Speech and Drama.

MURIEL ST CLARE BYRNE O.B.E., M.A. OXON.   Liverpool:
    Writer and authority on life in Elizabethan   Belvedere
    England.

LILIAN CHARLESWORTH C.B.E., B.A. LOND.   Clapham
    (And see pp. 169, 190).

HELEN DARBISHIRE C.B.E., HON. D.LITT. OXON.   Oxford
    Authority on Wordsworth and Milton.
    Principal of Somerville College, Oxford.

HENRIETTE DENT M.A. CANTAB. (And see p. 122.)   Sydenham

PHILIPPA FAWCETT MATHEMATICS HONS. CANTAB.   Clapham
    (And see pp. 109, 165.)

PROFESSOR UNA ELLIS FERMOR M.A., B.LITT. OXON.   South Hampstead
    Hildred Carlile Professor, London.
    Author of critical studies of drama.

BARBARA FLOWER B.A. OXON.   Croydon
    Classical scholar.
    First woman to gain the Craven Scholarship.

GEORGINA GALBRAITH (née COLE-BAKER) M.A.   Portsmouth
OXON., PH.D. MANCHESTER
Historian. (And see p. 122.)

CONSTANCE GARNETT (née BLACK) CLASSICAL   Brighton & Hove
TRIPOS CANTAB.
Translator of the Russian Classics.

WINIFRED GERIN (Mrs JOHN LOCK, née BOURNE)   Sydenham
F.R.S.L.
Authority on the Brontës.
Awarded Tait Black Memorial Prize and Heine-
man Prize by Royal Society of Literature.

ROSE GRAHAM C.B.E., M.A., D.LITT. OXON., F.S.A.,   Notting Hill
F.R.HIST.S.
Authority on English ecclesiastical history in the
Middle Ages.
One of the first two women elected a Fellow of
the Royal Society of Antiquaries.

PROFESSOR AGNES HEADLAM-MORLEY M.A., B.LITT.   Wimbledon
OXON.
Montague Burton Professor of International
Relations, Oxford.

KATHARINE ADA MCDOWALL (Mrs ARUNDEL   Notting Hill
ESDAILE).
Authority on English Monumental Sculpture.

DAME MARGARET MILES D.B.E., B.A. LOND.   Ipswich
Headmistress of Mayfield School, Putney.
Member of many educational committees.
Writer and speaker on the comprehensive school.

PROFESSOR EILEEN POWER M.A., D.LITT. CANTAB.,   Oxford
HON. D.LITT. MANCHESTER.
Professor of Economic History, London School
of Economics.
Authority on English Medieval and Tudor
History.

EMMA GURNEY SALTER CLASSICAL TRIPOS CANTAB.,   Notting Hill
M.A., D.LITT. DUBLIN.
Scholar, writer on medieval and renaissance
subjects.

PROFESSOR DOROTHY TARRANT PH.D. LOND., M.A.   Clapham
CANTAB.
First woman holder of a classical Professorship
in England and of Presidency of the Classical
Association and the Hellenic Society.

217

HELEN WODEHOUSE MORAL SCIENCES TRIPOS CANTAB.,   Notting Hill
    M.A., D.PHIL. BIRMINGHAM.
Professor of Education, Bristol University.
Mistress of Girton College, Cambridge.

PUBLIC AND INTERNATIONAL SERVICE

MONICA ALLANACH F.I.A.   Wimbledon
One of the first women Fellows, and the first
woman elected to the Council of the Institute of
Actuaries.

COUNTESS BUXTON (née MILDRED SMITH) C.B.E.   Kensington
Distinguished public service in England and   (Chelsea)
South Africa. (And see p. 57.)

DAME MAY CURWEN D.B.E., M.A. CANTAB., NANSEN   Birkenhead
    MEDAL AWARD, JUGOSLAV ORDER OF ST SAVA
Authority on welfare work, especially for women,
children and refugees.

SELINA FOX M.D., B.S. DURHAM   Wimbledon
First woman Governor and Medical Officer of a
Borstal institution.
Founded the Bermondsey Medical Mission,
1894.

MARY GLASGOW C.B.E., CHEVALIER L'ORDRE   Newcastle
    NATIONAL DU MÉRITE, B.A. OXON.
Secretary-General, Arts Council of Great Britain.

FREDA GWILLIAM C.B.E., M.A. CANTAB.   Notting Hill
First woman Educational Adviser to the Colonial
Office.
Consultant for UNESCO in the Pacific.

ROSE HEILBRON (Mrs BURSTEIN) Q.C., LL.M.   Liverpool:
    LIVERPOOL   Belvedere
Recorder of Burnley.
One of the first two women Q.C.s.

HILDA MARTINDALE C.B.E.   Brighton & Hove
Deputy Chief Home Office Inspector and
Director of Women's Establishments.

BERYL POWER B.A. CANTAB.   Oxford
Distinguished Civil Servant and adviser to
UNRRA on social welfare in China and Asia.

KATHARINE RAMSAY, DUCHESS OF ATHOLL D.B.E.,   Wimbledon
    HON. D.C.L. OXON AND DURHAM, LL.D. GLASGOW,
    MANCHESTER, LEEDS, MCGILL AND COLUMBIA,
    A.R.C.M., M.P. (And see p. 120.)

ELEANOR RATHBONE M.A., D.C.L. OXON., LL.D.   Kensington
    LIVERPOOL, M.P.   (Chelsea)
  Pioneer advocate of social reforms, including
  family allowances.

MAUDE ROYDEN (Mrs SHAW) C.H., MOD. HIST. HONS.   Liverpool:
    OXON., D.D. GLASGOW. HON LL.D. LIVERPOOL   Belvedere
  Speaker and writer on religion and ethics.

LADY SEEAR (NANCY SEEAR) HONS. HIST. TRIPOS,   Croydon
    CANTAB.
  President of the Liberal Party, since created Life
  Peer.

DAME MARY SMIETON D.B.E., M.A. OXON.   Wimbledon
  Permanent Secretary, Ministry of Education.
  U.K. representative, UNESCO Executive Board.

DAME NANCY SNAGGE (née SALMON) D.B.E.   Notting Hill
  Director of Women's Royal Air Force.
  A.D.C. to King George VI and Queen Elizabeth.

DAME MERIEL TALBOT D.B.E.   Kensington
  Distinguished public service, especially in rela-   (Chelsea)
  tionship to the Government Overseas Settlement
  Committee. (And see p. 57.)

FRANCESCA WILSON   Newcastle
  Social work among refugees, especially victims
  of war; writer on refugee problems.

JOAN WILSON HIST. TRIPOS, CANTAB.   Clapham
  Governor of the Women's Prison, Manchester,
  and of Women's Open Prison, Hill Hall, Epping.

DR ELIZABETH WISKEMANN M.A., D.LITT. OXON.   Notting Hill
  Montague Burton Professor of International
  Relations, Edinburgh. (And see p. 58.)

SCIENTISTS AND DOCTORS

JOSEPHINE BARNES M.A., D.M. OXON., F.R.C.P. LOND.,   Oxford
    F.R.C.S. ENG., F.R.C.O.G.
  Obstetrician and gynaecologist of English and
  European reputation.

DAME EDITH BROWN D.B.E., M.D. BRUSSELS, F.R.C.S.   Croydon
    EDINBURGH
  Founder of Ludhiana, first Christian Hospital
  in India.

DAME JANET CAMPBELL D.B.E., M.D., M.S. LOND., HON.D.HY. DURHAM, J.P. Senior medical officer for maternity and child welfare to the Ministry of Health. Chief woman medical adviser to the Board of Education.	Brighton & Hove
DAME HARRIETTE CHICK D.B.E., D.SC. LOND., HON. D.SC. MANCHESTER. Hon. Fellow of the Royal Society of Medicine. Authority on nutrition. (And see p. 77.)	Notting Hill
LOUISA MARTINDALE C.B.E., M.D., B.S. LOND., F.R.C.O.G., J.P. A pioneer in the treatment of cancer by radium.	Brighton & Hove
GLADYS SANDES (Mrs MAXWELL ALSTON) M.B., B.S., F.R.C.S., L.R.C.P. LOND. Fellow of the Royal Society of Medicine. Surgeon and gynaecologist.	Wimbledon
MARTHA WHITELEY O.B.E., D.SC., F.R.I.C. Co-inventor of tear gas used in the 1914–18 war.	Kensington (Chelsea)

WRITERS

ENID BLYTON Writer of children's books.	Ipswich
EDWARD CANDY (BARBARA NEVILLE, née BOODSON) B.S. LOND., D.C.H. Writer of detective stories and novels.	South Hampstead
E. H. CLEMENTS Novelist	Sutton
CLEMENCE DANE (WINIFRED ASHTON) C.B.E. Novelist, dramatist, artist.	Sydenham
MURIEL GRINDROD B.A. CANTAB. Editor, writer on Italy. Winner of the John Florio Prize for translation.	Ipswich and Bath
ELIZABETH HAMILTON M.A. LOND. Biographical writer.	Streatham Hill
ELIZABETH JENNINGS F.R.S.L. Poet.	Oxford
DAME ROSE MACAULAY D.B.E., HIST. HONS. OXON., HON. D.LITT. CANTAB. Traveller and author of novels, verse and essays.	Oxford
ESTHER MCCRACKEN Dramatist.	Newcastle

RHODA POWER   Oxford
    Writer and pioneer of broadcasting for children.

NAOMI ROYDE-SMITH   Clapham
    Novelist.

MARGERY SHARP B.A. LOND.   Streatham Hill
    Novelist and dramatist.

NANCY SPAIN   Newcastle
    Novelist and broadcaster.

G. B. STERN   Notting Hill
    Novelist.

ANGELA THIRKELL   Kensington
    Novelist.

JENNIFER WAYNE (Mrs C. R. HEWITT) B.A. OXON.   Blackheath
    Script-writer and producer, B.B.C.
    Writer of children's books.

PATRICIA WENTWORTH (née DORA ELLES – Mrs   Blackheath
    TURNBULL).
    Writer of mystery novels.

MRS ERIC WHELPTON (née BARBARA CROCKER).   Putney
    Writer and illustrator of travel books.

E. H. YOUNG   Newcastle and
    Novelist.   Sutton

ARCHITECTURE

JANE DREW (Mrs MAXWELL FRY) F.R.I.B.A., F.I.ARB.,   Croydon
    LL.D. HON. IBADAN.
    Architect of international reputation.
    Senior Architect to capital project of Chandigarh,
    Punjab, India.
    First woman President of the Architectural
    Association.

SCULPTORS

MARY TUTIN (Mrs GILLICK) O.B.E.   Nottingham

ASTRID ZYDOWER M.B.E.   Sheffield

MUSICIANS

ANTONIA BUTLER   Kensington
    Violoncellist.

ASTRA DESMOND (Lady NEAME) C.B.E., B.A. LOND.,   Notting Hill
    HON. R.A.M., MEDAL OF ST OLAF, NORWAY
  Contralto.
  President of the Incorporated Society of
  Musicians.

JACQUELINE DU PRÉ   Croydon
  Violoncellist.

ACTRESSES

ANN BELL	Birkenhead
DAME LILIAN BRAITHWAITE D.B.E.	Croydon and South Hampstead
GWEN FFRANGCON-DAVIES	South Hampstead
GLYNIS JOHNS	South Hampstead
MIRIAM KARLIN	South Hampstead
MARGARET LOCKWOOD	Sydenham
MARGARET RAWLINGS (Lady BARLOW)	Oxford
DAME MARGARET RUTHERFORD D.B.E., A.R.C.M., L.R.A.M. ELOC.	Wimbledon
MAGGIE SMITH C.B.E.	Oxford
JANE WENHAM	Sutton
GLADYS YOUNG O.B.E.	Newcastle and Sutton

SPORT

BETTY NUTHALL   Kensington
  Women's Singles Tennis Champion, Wimbledon.
DIANA FISHWICK (née CRITCHLEY)   Sydenham
  British Women's Golf Champion.

Apologies are offered by the G.P.D.S.T. to other eminent past pupils whose names do not appear in the above list, which of necessity could not be comprehensive.

Appendix IV

G.P.D.S.T. Headmistresses elected President of the Association of Head Mistresses

1897 HARRIET MORANT JONES, d. 1917
Notting Hill & Bayswater High School
1905 FLORENCE GADESDEN, d. 1934
Blackheath High School
1907 ELIZA WOODHOUSE, d. 1924
Clapham High School
1915 A. E. ESCOTT, d. 1921
Sheffield High School
1917 R. OLDHAM, d. 1933
Streatham Hill & Brixton High School
1919 E. H. MAJOR, d. 1951
King Edward H.S. Birmingham, formerly Putney High School, 1900–10
1935 E. R. GWATKIN, d. 1952
Streatham Hill & Clapham High School
1944 M. S. SMITH, d. 1952
King Edward H.S. Birmingham, formerly Sydenham High School, 1934–41
1946 M. F. ADAMS
Croydon High School
1948 L. E. CHARLESWORTH
Sutton High School
1966 P. R. BODINGTON
South Hampstead High School
1970 J. R. GLOVER
Sutton High School

Twelve out of thirty-seven from Trust Schools. At least four others were former Trust pupils.

Appendix V

The Friends of the G.P.D.S.T.

President:
Marion, Countess of Harewood

Chairmen:
1951   Mr (later Sir William) Cash M.A., F.C.A.
1964   Mr H. F. Collins C.M.G., DOC. de l'U., M.A.
1965   Miss L. E. Charlesworth C.B.E., B.A.
1971   Miss M. M. Burke B.A. (Acting Chairman)

Honorary Secretaries:
1951   Mrs Eric Whelpton
1953   Miss J. M. H. McCaig M.A.
1963   Miss M. M. Burke B.A.
1971   Miss P. R. Bodington M.A.

Honorary Treasurers:
1951   Miss A. K. Lewis M.A.
1962   Miss M. C. Allanach F.I.A.

Honorary Editors of the annual News Letter:
1951   Mrs Eric Whelpton
1954   Miss J. M. H. McCaig M.A.
1955   Miss M. L. Potter M.A.
1963   Miss V. E. Stack M.A.
1970   Miss M. D. Yardley M.A.

Index

P

225